THE CANADIAN BOY SCOUT

THE FIRST 1911 HANDBOOK FOR SCOUTS IN CANADA

BY **LORD ROBERT BADEN-POWELL**

ORIGINALLY PUBLISHED IN 1911

LEGACY EDITION

THE LIBRARY OF AMERICAN OUTDOORS CLASSICS
BOOK II

FEATURING
REMASTERED CLASSIC WORKS OF THE HIGHEST
QUALITY FROM **THE TIMELESS MASTERS AND
TEACHERS** OF CAMPING, OUTDOORS SKILLS,
WOODCRAFT, AND TRADITIONAL HANDCRAFTS

Doublebit Press
Eugene. OR

INTRODUCTION
To The Doublebit Press Legacy Edition

Lord Robert Baden-Powell's scouting movement grew quickly after its founding in 1908 in Great Britain. Between the founding of the Boy Scouts of America in 1910, the Camp Fire Girls in 1910, and other youth scouting programs like the Girl Guides and Rovers, scouting was an instant hit with kids at the start of the 1900s.

Youth from other countries also wanted to be scouts, too. Lord Baden-Powell, seeing the need for scouting in Canada, adapted a version of his manual *Scouting for Boys* to create a special unique version of a scout manual that would be used by scouts in Canada. This volume, *The Canadian Boy Scout*, represents the first manual dedicated to the youth of Canada who desired to be a scout, much like their American and British fellows.

The Canadian Boy Scout clearly uses some of BP's early versions of the popular *Scouting for Boys*, but includes a substantial amount of new material that is unique to Canada. Although Canada was still a part of the regular British Empire at the time (which is a fact that BP reminds his Canadian readers frequently), there is a good deal of Canada-specific material, such as wildlife, camping climate, plant life, history, and song. This unique content makes *The Canadian Boy Scout* a worthwhile volume for any outdoorsperson's or scout's library!

Also included in this volume is knowledge from BP and other outdoors masters from the era (e.g., Ernest Thompson Seton, Nessmuk). In this manual, scouts held in their hand the collective knowledge of thousands of combined years worth of outdoors expertise in camping, wilderness survival, cooking, woodcraft, nature lore, and outdoors travel. The Canadian wilderness is vast – Canadian Scouts would need an equally vast set of skills to master the landscape and camp with ease.

Enjoy your copy of *The Canadian Boy Scout* for its historical record of the times. Of course, take its advice with a grain of salt, as some content may be outdated such as medical advice and outdoors practices. However, most of the material is timeless! Perhaps you may even learn an old scout skill or two. Happy journeys!

About the Library of American Outdoors Classics

The old experts of the woods and mountains taught timeless principles and skills for decades. Through their books, the old experts offered rich descriptions of the outdoor world and encouraged learning through personal experiences in nature. Over the last 125 years, camping, outdoors recreation, and woods activities have substantially changed. Many things have gotten simpler as gear has improved, and life outside or on the trail now brings with it many of the same comforts enjoyed in town. In addition, some activities of the olden days are now no longer in vogue, or are even outright considered inappropriate or illegal, such as high-impact camping practices like chopping down live trees. However, despite many of the positive changes in outdoors methods that have occurred over the years, *there are many other skills and much knowledge that have been forgotten* from the golden era of American outdoors recreation.

By publishing the Library of American Outdoors Classics, it is our goal at Doublebit Press to do what we can to preserve and share the works from forgotten teachers that form the cornerstone of the history of the American outdoors. Through remastered reprint editions of timeless classics of outdoor recreation, perhaps we can regain some of this lost knowledge for future generations.

Because there were fewer options for finding outdoors gear in the early 1900's, experts in *"woodcraft"* skills (not to be confused with today's use of the word to mean woodworking or making things of wood) had to have a deep knowledge of the basic building blocks of outdoor living. This involved not only surviving in the outdoors, but to also have a comfortable and enjoyable time. As Nessmuk puts it in his book *Woodcraft,* "We do not go to the woods to rough it; we go to smooth it — we get it rough enough in town. But let us live the simple, natural life in the woods, and leave all frills behind." Nessmuk did not advocate for folks to go outside and have a terrible time. That would be contrary to the whole point of getting outside. Instead, he advocated for a "simpler" life by leaving some of the creature comforts of the city behind, but also entering the outdoors in a smart and practiced way that made the experience a much more satisfying vacation from home. The goal is to be comfortable so you can focus on having a good time outside and take in everything exposure to nature can offer. However, to be comfortable, one has to know the ins and outs of camping and outdoors life. Despite all the advances in campcraft and outdoors recreation, the old masters of the woods would all likely argue that this will only come from practicing the basics.

Because there was no market yet for specialty outdoors recreational gear (and thus, few outfitters), most outdoors gear came from military surplus piles or was custom made. As such, the old masters of woodcraft often made their own gear suited to their tastes. Through much experience in the woods and field, the great outdoors experts had to know why things worked the way they did by understanding the great web of cause and effect in nature. They had to learn from experience why certain gear worked better in different conditions or know how to solve problems off-the-cuff when things got hairy. They used the basic blocks of camping and outdoors knowledge to fine-tune their gear. They gained experience whenever they could and tried things different ways so they could gain mastery over the fundamentals and see challenges from many angles.

Today, much of the outdoor experience has been greatly simplified by neatly arranged campsites at public campgrounds and gear that has been meticulously improved and tested in both the lab and the field. Many modern conveniences are only a brief trek away, with many parks, campgrounds, and even forests having easy-access roads, convenience stores, and even cell phone signal. In some ways, it is much easier to camp and go outdoors today, and that is a good thing! We should not be miserable when we go outside — lovers of the outdoors know the essential restorative capability that the woods can have on the body, mind, and soul. Although things have gotten easier on us in the 21st Century when it comes to the outdoors, it certainly does not mean that we should forget the foundations of outdoors lore, though. All modern camping skills, outdoors equipment, and cool gizmos that make our lives easier are all founded on principles of the outdoors that the old masters knew well and taught to those who would listen.

Every woods master had their own curriculum or thought some things were more important than others. This includes the present author — certain things appear in this book that other masters leave out of theirs. The old masters also taught common things in slightly different ways or did things differently than others. That's what makes each of the experts different and worth reading. There's no universal way of doing something, especially now. Learning to go about something differently helps with mastery or learn a new skill altogether. Again, to use the metaphor from the above paragraphs, outdoors skills mastery consists of learning the basic building blocks of outdoors living, woods and nature lore, and the art of packing properly for trips. Each master goes about describing these building blocks differently or shows a different aspect of them.

Therefore, we have decided to publish this Legacy Edition in our Library of American Outdoors Classics series. This book is an important contribution to the early American recreational outdoors literature and has important historical and collector value toward preserving the American outdoors tradition. The knowledge it holds is an invaluable reference for practicing skills and hand craft methods. Its chapters thoroughly discuss some of the essential building blocks of knowledge that are fundamental but may have been forgotten as equipment gets fancier and technology gets smarter. In short, this book was chosen for Legacy Edition printing because much of the basic skills and knowledge it contains has been forgotten or put to the wayside in trade for more modern conveniences and methods.

Although the editors at Doublebit Press are thrilled to have comfortable experiences in the woods and love our high-tech and light-weight equipment, we are also realizing that the basic skills taught by the old masters are more essential than ever as our culture becomes more and more hooked on digital stuff. We don't want to risk forgetting the important steps, skills, or building blocks involved with thriving in the outdoors. The Legacy Edition series represents the essential contributions to the American outdoors tradition by the great experts of outdoors life and traditional hand crafting.

With technology playing a major role in everyday life, sometimes we need to take a step back in time to find those basic building blocks used for gaining mastery – the things that we have luckily not completely lost and has been recorded in books over the last two centuries. These skills aren't forgotten, they've just been shelved. *It's time to unshelve them once again and reclaim the lost knowledge of self-sufficiency.*

Based on this commitment to preserving our outdoors and handcraft heritage, we have taken great pride in publishing this book as a complete original work. We hope it is worthy of both study and collection by outdoors folk in the modern era of outdoors and traditional skills life.

Unlike many other photocopy reproductions of classic books that are common on the market, this Legacy Edition does not simply place poor photography of old texts on our pages and use error-prone optical scanning or computer-generated text. We want our work to speak for itself, and reflect the quality demanded by our customers who spend their hard-earned money. With this in mind, each Legacy Edition book that has been chosen for publication is carefully remastered from original print books, *with the Doublebit Legacy Edition printed and laid out in the exact way that it was presented at its original publication.* We provide a beautiful, memorable experience that is as true to the original text as best as possible, but with the aid of modern technology to make as beautiful a reading experience as possible for books that are typically over a century old.

Because of its age and because it is presented in its original form, the book may contain misspellings, inking errors, and other print blemishes that were common for the age. However, these are exactly the things that we feel give the book its character, which we preserved in this Legacy Edition. During digitization, we ensured that each illustration in the text was clean and sharp with the least amount of loss from being copied and digitized as possible. Full-page plate illustrations are presented as they were found, often including the extra blank page that was often behind a plate. For the covers, we use the original cover design to give the book its original feel. We are sure you'll appreciate the fine touches and attention to detail that your Legacy Edition has to offer.

For outdoors enthusiasts who demand the best from their equipment, this Doublebit Press Legacy Edition reprint was made with you in mind. Both important and minor details have equally both been accounted for by our publishing staff, down to the cover, font, layout, and images. It is the goal of Doublebit Legacy Edition series to preserve outdoors heritage, but also be cherished as collectible pieces, worthy of collection in any outdoorsperson's library and that can be passed to future generations.

Every book selected to be in this series offers unique views and instruction on important skills, advice, tips, tidbits, anecdotes, stories, and experiences that will enrichen the repertoire of any person who enjoys escaping the city and finding their way to the trails of the wilds. To learn the most basic building blocks of outdoors life leads to mastery of all its aspects.

Studying This Book

The pages within this book present an overwhelming amount of information, facts, and directions to memorize that are often outdated and at the least, out of practice by modern standards. That doesn't mean that these pages have nothing to teach! It's just going to likely be new stuff for many readers.

Our one suggestion is *don't try to memorize everything,* especially when you're thumbing through the book or even reading it cover-to-cover. Writings from the late 1800's to early 1900's can be dense and out of style for someone not used to reading these types of books. Instead, gain some basic familiarity with each topic by thumbing through the pages, looking at the illustrations, and seeing the section headers. Then, choose a few topics or skills for deeper study.

Before camping or other outdoors trips can even begin, some planning and reflection is useful, which may be best done in town before you go out to the field. First, it might be helpful to read through the book with plans in mind. The book can provide useful material for close study and reflection when in town before you head out to the field to practice.

Secondly, once you've come up with a practice plan, you will of course want to start doing tasks and skills in the field. Doublebit Legacy books and the Library of American Outdoors Classics represents many field skills to master that have long sense been out of practice, but hopefully not forgotten! These include making and trying different kinds of tents or shelters, cooking (including any fish and game caught by you in the field), making many types of fires, setting up camp to suit your personal needs, beating the bugs and elements, understanding the terrain and weather, making furniture, brushing up on your nature lore, emergency survival, and testing your personal outfit and tools.

Any of the old tutors of woodcraft will tell you in their classic books that you can only truly learn how to go camping and do woodcraft by *actually doing it*. Home study indeed does you well by using the many guidebooks that have been published over the previous 125 years. However, hundreds more lessons will become immediately available to you the moment you start with some of the old-style tasks. This old style of outdoorsing is indeed outdated in many ways, but the approach still has much to teach modern campers who have become accustomed to carved out campsites, cabin and RV camping, and high-tech equipment.

Before the days of outfitters, outdoors adventurers made their gear, which was tailored to their individual needs. Many experiments were done in the field to tweak their gear to get that ever-changing point of "perfect." Aside from experiencing wonderful lessons in history, getting outside and doing some of the activities this book will give you an appreciation for modern advances in outdoors and handcraft method and tools of the trade, as well as a deeper understanding of the foundations of outdoors and hand-craft life in the event that your gear fails you or you otherwise find yourself in situations where knowing the principles will get you unstuck fast.

If we were to tally up each of the individual tips in the Doublebit Library of American Outdoors Classics, they would easily number in the thousands. The old masters represent centuries of previous knowledge that have been all but lost to 21st Century, technology-driven folks. To this point, although experience and *actually doing stuff* are the best forms of learning, taking a mindful approach to study of these works also benefit your development as a competent outdoorsperson and handcrafter.

You may also find it invaluable to take these volumes with you on your camping or other outdoors trips. In addition to having reading material on a variety of topics in the field for down time, you'll also find a thousand things to try in these pages if you're bored. Although skills may be best studied when in the field through experience and reflection, you may also study woods skills at home as well. Gaining familiarity through reading, videos, and other media are a great start toward building your ability toward gaining mastery in the field.

So, without blabbering on further, we hope you enjoy your Doublebit Legacy Edition. May your trails be clear and your experiences be memorable!

- The Doublebit Press Editors

THE CANADIAN BOY SCOUT

THE BOY SCOUTS

PATRON
HIS MAJESTY KING GEORGE V.

THE CHIEF SCOUT
SIR ROBERT BADEN-POWELL.

CHIEF SCOUT FOR CANADA
His Excellency the Governor-General EARL GREY, G.C.M.G.

DOMINION COUNCIL

COMMISSIONERS
Chief Commissioner: COLONEL SHERWOOD, M.V.O., and assistant commissioners. Appointed by the Dominion Council to inspect, and to act as its local representatives.

PROVINCIAL COUNCILS
Composed of leading representative men in each Province, to father the Local Associations.

LOCAL ASSOCIATIONS
Composed of local representative men interested in work among boys and of Scoutmasters. To administer and develop the movement locally.
WITH LOCAL SECRETARY
to keep Register and to report to the Commissioner.

TROOPS
Under Scoutmasters. Containing three or more Patrols.

PATROLS
Under boy leaders. Containing six to eight Scouts.

SCOUTS
Including: Silver Wolves, Kings Scouts, All-round Scouts, 1st class, 2nd class Scouts, and Tenderfoots.

THE BOY SCOUT

THE

CANADIAN BOY SCOUT

A HANDBOOK FOR INSTRUCTION
IN GOOD CITIZENSHIP

BY

SIR ROBERT BADEN-POWELL
K.C.B., K.C.V.O., LL.D.

TORONTO
MORANG & CO., LIMITED
1911

PREFACE

SEEING that the Boy Scouts movement promises to spread so widely in Canada and that the training in the Old Country is carried out under such different conditions to those obtaining over here, I am venturing to reproduce the original book of " Scouting for Boys " altered and amended to suit the Canadian Scouts in their own land, and I sincerely hope that it may be found of use by Scoutmasters and Scouts in their endeavor to attain efficiency.

EXPLANATION OF SCOUTING

[See also Chapter X.]

N.B. — Sentences in italics throughout the book are addressed to Scoutmasters (Instructors).

By the term "scouting" is meant the work and attributes of backwoodsmen, explorers, and frontiersmen.

In giving the elements of these to boys we supply a system of games and practices which meets their desires and instincts, and is at the same time educative.

From the boys' point of view Scouting puts them into fraternity-gangs, which is their natural organization, whether for games, mischief, or loafing; it gives them a smart dress and equipments; it appeals to their imagination and romance; and it engages them in an active, open-air life.

From the parents' point of view it gives physical health and development; it teaches energy, resourcefulness, and handicrafts; it puts into the lad discipline, pluck, chivalry, and patriotism; in a word, it develops "character," which is more essential than anything else to a lad for making his way in life, and which is yet practically untaught in the schools.

The method of instruction in "Scouting" is that of creating in the boy the desire to learn for himself, and not by drilling knowledge into him.

From the national point of view our aim is solely to make the rising generation into good citizens. We avoid military training for reasons given in Chapter X, and we do not interfere with the religion of the boy.

Moreover, Scouting appeals to boys of every class, and can be carried out in towns just as well as in the country.

Experience now shows that by using this handbook any one can teach scouting to boys, even though he may have no previous knowledge of it himself. He should begin with small numbers, a patrol or two of eight boys. A great step is to have a head-quarters room, barn, or hut, and a camp in summer.

When a Scoutmaster has not sufficient knowledge in any one subject he can generally get a friend who is an expert to come and give his troop the required instruction.

Funds must be earned by the Scouts themselves, by their work, not by begging. Various ways of making money are given in the book.

Scouting is applicable to existing organizations, such as Boys' Brigades, Clubs, Schools, Training-ships, etc.

R. S. S. B.-P.

Toronto, January, 1911.

NOTE. — *All applications for affiliation, equipment, etc., and all inquiries should be directed to the Secretary,*

CAPT. R. J. BIRDWHISTLE,

Castle Building,
Ottawa.

CONTENTS

CHAPTER V

WOODCRAFT, OR KNOWLEDGE OF ANIMALS AND NATURE

CHAPTER VI

ENDURANCE FOR SCOUTS, OR HOW TO BE STRONG

CHAPTER VII

CHIVALRY OF THE KNIGHTS

CHAPTER VIII

SAVING LIFE, OR HO   TO DEAL WITH ACCIDENTS

CHAPTER IX

PATRIOTISM, OR OUR DUTIES AS CITIZENS

CHAPTER X

SCOUTS CAMP,
BROWNSEA ISLAND
POOLE.

To every Canadian boy

In the South African War I had in my force an officer who was a first rate all-round Scout, who could follow a track, hide, watch and report an enemy, and was as brave and hardy as anyone could wish. But he had one failing — he could not obey orders.

One day we were lying in ambush to surprise a force of Boers who were coming along. My orders were that everybody was to lie low and not to stir out of our hiding-place

But this young Scott thought he
knew best what was wanted and
slipped away from the column to do
a bit of scouting on his own.
Shortly afterwards shots were heard.
He had met a Boer Scout; they had
fired at each other; the Boer was killed
and our Scout mortally wounded.
Other Boer Scouts hearing the shots
came up & finding a British Scout
there guessed that more of us must
be in the neighbourhood, so they
searched the country more carefully
and thus discovered our ambush
in time to warn their main body.

No, I have no use for a fellow who cannot obey orders, even though he may be a good Scout in other ways.

From what I have seen of you Canadian boys I have a great admiration for you. You are already good Scouts in the woods but to be perfectly reliable you must also be sure that you are disciplined and can obey orders, however distasteful they may be, without any hesitation — and cheerily.

Canada can be a very big nation in a few years if each one of you determines to do his bit in making it so. A nation is not made merely by its territory or wealth, it is made by its men. If they are men of grit and energy who work together like a football Team, each in his place "playing the game" in obedience to the rules and to the orders of the captain, they will win, they will make it a great nation. If they only loaf through the game, each in his own way, it is not likely that the country will succeed against others.

So — play up, Canadian lads! 'Play the game'. Sink your own personal comfort, think of your Country, and work hard, each one of you, to be an allround good Scout who can be relied upon in a tight corner to stick it out and obey orders.

Your friend
Robert Baden Powell.

To EVERY CANADIAN BOY:—

In the South African war I had in my force an officer who was a first-rate all-round Scout, who could follow a track, hide, watch and report an enemy, and was as brave and hardy as any one could wish. But he had one failing — he could not obey orders.

One day we were lying in ambush to surprise a force of Boers who were coming along. My orders were that everybody was to lie low and not to stir out of our hiding-places. But this young Scout thought he knew best what was wanted as I slipped away from the column to do a bit of Scouting on his own. Shortly afterwards shots were heard. He had met a Boer Scout; they had fired at each other; the Boer was killed and our Scout mortally wounded. Other Boer Scouts hearing the shots came up and finding a British Scout there guessed that more of us must be in the neighborhood, so they searched the country more carefully and thus discovered our ambush in time to warn their main body. No, I have no use for a fellow who cannot obey orders, even though he may be a good Scout in other ways.

From what I have seen of you Canadian boys I have a great admiration for you. You are already good Scouts in the woods, but to be perfectly reliable you must also be sure that you are disciplined and can obey orders, however distasteful they may be, without any hesitation — and cheerily.

Canada can be a very big nation in a few years if each one of you determines to do his bit in making it so. A nation is not made merely by its territory or wealth, it is made by its men. If they are men of grit and energy who work together like a football team, each in his place and " playing the game " in obedience to the rules and to the orders of the captain, they will win, they will make it a great nation. If they only loaf through the game, each in his own way, it is not likely that this country will succeed against others.

So — play up, Canadian lads! " Play the game." Sink your own personal comfort, think for your Country, and work hard, each one of you, to be an all-round good Scout who can be relied upon in a tight corner to stick it out and obey orders.

Your friend,

ROBERT BADEN-POWELL.

CHAPTER I

SCOUTCRAFT

NOTES TO INSTRUCTORS

Instruction in scouting should be given as far as possible through practices, games, and competitions.

Games should be organized mainly as team matches, where the patrol forms the team, and every boy is playing, none merely looking on.

Strict obedience to the rules to be at all times insisted on as instruction in discipline.

The rules given in the book as to games may be altered by scoutmasters where necessary to suit local conditions.

The ideas given here are merely offered as suggestions, upon which it is hoped that instructors will develop further games, competitions, and displays.

Several of the games given here are founded on those in Mr. Thompson Seton's "Birchbark Roll of the Woodcraft Indians," called "Spearing the Sturgeon" (Whale Hunt), "Quick Sight" (Spotty Face), "Spot the Rabbit," "Bang the Bear," "Hostile Spy" (Stop Thief), etc.

A number of non-scouting games are quoted from the book "Social — to Save."

The following is a suggestion for the distribution of the work for the first week. It is merely a suggestion and in no sense binding.

Remember that the boy, on joining, wants to begin "Scouting" right away; so don't dull his keenness, as is so often done, by too much preliminary explanation at first. Meet his wants by games and scouting practices, and instil elementary details bit by bit afterwards as you go along.

N.B. — The foregoing paragraph was in the former editions of this book, but it was in some cases ignored by scoutmasters, with the result that their training was a failure.

FIRST EVENING

INDOORS

Address the boys on "Scoutcraft," giving a summary of the whole scheme, as in this chapter, with demonstrations or lantern slides, etc.

Form patrols, and give shoulder knots.

FOLLOWING DAY

Practical work, outdoors if possible, as follows: —

Alternatives according to whether in town or country, indoors or out.

MORNING

Parade, hoist Union Jack and salute it.

Scouting game: e.g., "Scout Meets Scout" (see page 52).

Practise salutes, secret signs, patrol calls, scouts' chorus, etc.

Practise drawing scout signs on ground or walls with stick or chalk (to be rubbed out afterwards).

Tie knots.

Make ration bags, leather buttons, etc.

Parade. Prayers or Church Parade (if Sunday).

Physical Exercises (see pages 196–201).

Drill (see pages 214–216).

Self-measurement by each scout of span, cubit, finger joint, stride, etc. (see page 100).

Send out scouts independently or in pairs to do a "good turn," to return and report how they have done it (see page 15).

March out the patrol to see the neighborhood.

Make them note direction of starting by compass, wind, and sun (see pages 67–71).

Notice and question them on details seen, explain "land marks," etc. (see page 133).

Practise scout's pace (see page 215).

Judge distances (see page 101).

AFTERNOON

Play an extended scouting game (see "Games," page 52).
Or indoors if wet — "Ju-Jitsu," "Scouts' War Dance," boxing, scouts' chorus and rally, etc.

EVENING

Camp Fire Yarns from this book or from books recommended (see page 11).
Or rehearse a scout play,   hold debate, Kim's game, etc.
Patrols to continue practice in these throughout the week in their own time or under the scoutmaster, with final games or exercises on the following Saturday afternoon.
If more evenings than one are available in the week, one of the subjects might be taken in turn more fully each evening, and rehearsals carried out of a display such as "Pocahontas" (see "Scouting Games," price 1/–).

CAMP FIRE YARN. No. 1

SCOUTS' WORK

Peace Scouts — "Kim" — Mafeking

Peace Scouts

I SUPPOSE every Canadian boy wishes to help his country and the great Empire to which he belongs in some way or other.

There is a way by which he can do so easily and that is by becoming a scout.

A scout, as you know, is generally a soldier who is chosen for his cleverness and pluck to go out in front of an army in war to find out where the enemy are, and report to the commander all about them.

But, besides war scouts, there are also peace scouts, *i.e.*, men who in peace time carry out work which requires the same kind of abilities. These are the frontiersmen of all parts of the Empire. The "trappers" of North America, the hunters of Central Africa, the British pioneers, explorers, and missionaries over Asia and all the wild parts of the world, the bushmen and drovers of Australia, the constabulary of South Africa, and your own Royal North-West Mounted Police — all are peace scouts, real *men* in every sense of the word, and thoroughly up in scoutcraft, *i.e.*, they understand living out on the prairies and in the forests, can find their way anywhere, and are able to read meaning from the smallest signs and foot-tracks; they know how to look after their health when far away from any doctors, are strong and plucky, are ready to face any danger, and are always keen to help each other. They are accustomed to take their lives in their hands, and to fling them down without hesitation if they can help their country by doing so.

They give up everything, their personal comforts and desires, in order to get their work done. They do not do all this for their own amusement, but because it is their duty to their King, fellow-countrymen, or employers.

The history of the Empire has been made by British adventurers and explorers, the scouts of the nation, for hundreds of years past up to the present time.

The Knights of King Arthur, Richard Cœur de Lion, and the Crusaders carried British chivalry into distant parts of the earth.

Raleigh, Drake, and Captain John Smith, soldiers and sailors of Queen Elizabeth's time, faced unknown dangers of strange seas, as well as the known dangers of powerful enemies, to take and hold new lands for the expansion of England.

Captain Cook in Australia, Lord Clive in India, opened up new countries. Speke, Baker, and Livingstone pushed their way through the savage deserts and forests of Africa; Davis, Franklin, and Ross braved the ice and snows of the Arctic regions.

In the present time, Selous, the great hunter, and Lieutenant Boyd Alexander, who recently crossed Africa, are peace scouts.

These are just a few names out of many hundreds of the scouts of the nation who have from all times down to the present spread the good name and power of Great Britain in all parts of the world.

And there have been women scouts of the nation, too: such as Grace Darling, who risked her life to save a shipwrecked crew; Florence Nightingale, who nursed sick soldiers in the Crimean War; Miss Kingsley, the African explorer; Lady Lugard, in Africa and Alaska; and many devoted lady missionaries and nurses in all parts of the Empire. These have shown that girls as well as boys may well learn scouting while they are young, and so be able to do useful work in the world as they grow older.

It is a grand life, but it cannot suddenly be taken up by any man who thinks he would like it, unless he has prepared himself for it beforehand.

Those who succeed best are those who learned scouting while they were still boys.

Scouting also comes in very useful in any kind of life you like to take up, whether it is soldiering or even business life in a city. Sir William Crookes says it is even valuable for a man who goes in for science, finding out little things about air, and light, and so on. And Sir Lauder Brunton points out how necessary it is for a doctor or a surgeon.

So I am going to show you how you can learn scoutcraft for yourself and can put it into practice at home.

It is very easy to learn and very interesting when you get into it. You ca 'est learn by joining the "Boy Scouts."

" Kim "

A GOOD example of what a boy scout can do is to be found in Rudyard Kipling's story of "Kim."

"Kim," or, to give him his full name, Kimball O'Hara, was the son of a sergeant of an Irish regiment in India. His father and mother died while he was a child, and he had been left to the care of an aunt who lived in a humble way in India.

His playmates were all natives, so he got to talk their language and to know their ways better than any European. He became great friends with an old wandering priest who was tramping about India, and with whom he travelled all over the north part of that country. At last, one day he chanced to meet his father's old regiment on the line of march, and in visiting the camp he was arrested on suspicion of being a thief. His birth certificate and other papers were found on him, and the regiment, seeing that he had belonged to them, took charge of him, and started to educate him. But whenever he could get away for holidays, he dressed himself in Indian clothes and went again among the natives as one of them.

After a time he became acquainted with a Mr. Lurgan, a dealer in old jewellery and curiosities, who, owing to his knowledge from dealing with natives, was a member of the Government Intelligence Department.

This man, finding that Kim had such special knowledge of native habits and customs, saw that he would make a useful agent for government intelligence work, that is, a kind of detective among the natives. But, first of all, before employing him, he put him to one or two tests to see whether he was sufficiently brave and strong-minded.

As a trial of his strong-mindedness he attempted to mesmerize him, that is to say, he tried to make Kim's thoughts obey what was in his own mind. It is possible for strong-minded men to do this with those of weaker mind. The way he attempted it was by throwing down a jug of water so that it smashed to pieces; he then laid his fingers on the boy's neck, and wished him to imagine the jug mended itself again. But do what he would to make his thought reach the boy's brain, he failed; Kim saw the jug was broken, and would not believe it was mended, although at one time he nearly obeyed him, for he saw a kind of vision of the jug being mended, but it faded away again.

Most boys would have let their mind and eyes wander, and would not have been able to keep them on the one subject, and would as a consequence have easily become mesmerized.

Lurgan, finding him strong-minded and quick at learning, then gave him lessons at noticing small details and remembering them, which is a most important point in the training of a scout; it is a thing that he should learn and be practising every hour of the day wherever he may be. Lurgan began it with Kim by showing him a tray full of precious stones of different kinds; he let him look at it for a minute, and then covered it with a cloth, and asked him to state how many stones and what sort were there. At first he found he could remember only a few, and could not describe them very accurately, but with a little practice he soon got to remember them all quite well. And so, also, with many other kinds of articles which were shown to him in the same way.

Then Kim travelled about the country a great deal with a fine old Afghan horse-dealer to whom he was much attached, who was also an agent of the Intelligence Department. On one occasion Kim was able to do him a good turn by carrying an important message for him secretly; and another time he saved his life by overhearing some natives planning to murder him when he came along. By pretending to be asleep and then having a nightmare which caused him to remove from his position, Kim got away from the neighborhood of the would-be murderers, and was able to give warning to his friend in good time.

At last he was made a member of the Secret Service, and was given a secret sign — namely, a badge to wear round his neck and a certain sentence to say, which, if said in a peculiar way, meant he was one of the service. Scouts generally have secret signs by which they can communicate with each other.

The members of the Intelligence Service are very numerous in India, and do not know each other by sight, so they have to have a secret sign by which they will recognize each other among other people who may be their enemies.

Once, when travelling in the train, Kim met another member whom he did not know. This was a native, who when he got into the carriage was evidently in a great state of alarm, and was rather badly cut about the head and arms. He explained to the other passengers that he had met with an accident from a cart while he was driving to the station, but Kim, like a good scout, noticed that the cuts were sharp and not grazes such as you would get by falling from a cart, and so did not believe him. While the man was tying up a bandage over his head, Kim noticed that he was wearing a locket like his own, so Kim let his own be seen. Directly the man saw it he brought into conversation some of the secret words, and Kim answered with the proper ones in reply. So then the stranger got into a corner with Kim and explained to him that he was carrying out some secret service work, and had been found out and hunted by some of the enemies of the government, who had nearly killed him. They probably knew he was in the train, and would therefore telegraph down the line to their friends that he was coming. He wished to get his message to a certain police officer without being caught by the enemy, but he could not tell how to do it if they were already warned of his coming. Kim thereupon hit upon the idea of disguising him.

In India there are a number of holy beggars who go about the country. They wear next to no clothing and smear themselves with ashes, and paint certain marks on their faces; they are considered very holy, and people always help them with food and money. So Kim made a mixture of flour and wood ashes, which he took from the bowl of a native pipe, and he undressed his friend and smeared these all over him, and finally, with the aid of a little paint-box which he carried he painted the proper marks on the man's forehead. He smeared the man's wounds with flour and ashes, partly so as to heal them, and also so that they did not show; and he brushed his hair down to look wild and shaggy like that of a beggar, and covered it with dust, so that the man's own mother would not have known him. Soon afterwards they arrived at a big station where on the platform they found the police officer to whom the report was to be made. The imitation beggar pushed up against him and was abused by the officer in English; the beggar replied with a string of native abuse into which he introduced the secret words. The police officer, although he had pretended not to know Hindustani, understood it quite well, and at once recognized from the secret words that this beggar was an agent; and so he pretended to arrest him and marched him off to the police-station where he could talk to him quietly. It was thus done without any one on the platform knowing that they were in league with each other, or that this native beggar was the escaped intelligence agent.

Finally, Kim became acquainted with another agent of the department — an educated native, or Babu as they are called in India — and was able to give him great assistance in capturing two Russian officers who were acting as spies against the British on the north-west frontier of India.

[*Note. — Point out on map respective positions of British and Russians.*]

The Babu pretended to the Russians that he was the manager for a local native prince who did not like the English, and travelled with them for some time as representative of this prince. In this way he came to know where they kept their secret papers in their baggage. At last he raised trouble between them and a holy priest, whom they struck; this caused great excitement among the natives, who rushed off with the baggage and were lost in the darkness. Kim, who was among the natives, opened the luggage and found the secret papers, which he took out and carried to headquarters.

These and other adventures of Kim are well worth reading, because they show what valuable work a boy scout can do for his country if he is sufficiently trained and sufficiently intelligent.

Mafeking Boy Scouts

WE had an example of how useful boy scouts can be on active service, when a corps of boys was formed in the defence of Mafeking during the Boer war, 1899–1900.

Mafeking, you may remember, was quite a small, ordinary country town out on the open plains of South Africa.

Nobody ever thought of its being attacked by an enemy any more than you would expect your own town or village to be attacked — the thing was so improbable.

But it just shows you how you must be prepared for what is *possible*, not only what is *probable* in war; and so, too, you ought to be prepared in Canada against being attacked by enemies; for though it may not be probable, it is quite as possible as it was at Mafeking; and every boy in Canada should be just as ready as those boys were in Mafeking to take his share in its defence.

Well, when we found we were to be attacked at Mafeking, we told off our garrison to the points that they were to protect — some 700 trained men, police, and volunteers. And then we armed the townsmen, of whom there were some 300. Some of them were old frontiersmen, and quite equal to the occasion; but

LORD EDWARD CECIL AND BOY SCOUTS IN MAFEKING

many of them, young mechanics, clerks, and others, had never even seen a rifle before, and had never learned to drill or to shoot, and so they were hopelessly at sea at first. It is not much fun to have to face an enemy who means to kill you, when you have never learned to handle a rifle.

Every boy should learn to shoot and to obey orders, else he is of very little use when war breaks out, and until he learns to handle his rifle, and shoot accurately, he is apt to be more of a hindrance than a help.

Altogether, then, we had only about a thousand men all told to defend the place, which contained 600 white women and children and about 7000 natives, and was about five miles around.

Every man was of value, and as their numbers gradually grew less, owing to men being killed and wounded, the duties of fighting and keeping watch at night were harder for the rest. It was then that Lord Edward Cecil, the chief staff-officer, got together the boys in the place and made them into a cadet corps, put them in uniform, and drilled them; and a smart and useful lot they were. We had till then used a large number of men for carrying orders and messages and keeping look-out, and acting as orderlies, and so on. These duties were now handed over to the boy cadets, and the men were released to go and strengthen the firing line.

And the cadets, under their sergeant-major, a boy named Goodyear, did good work, and well deserved the medals which they got at the end of the war. Many of them rode bicycles, and we were thus able to establish a post by which people could send letters to their friends in the different forts, or about the town, without going out under fire themselves; and for these letters we made postage stamps which had on them a picture of a cadet bicycle orderly.

I said to one of these boys on one occasion, when he came in through rather a heavy fire, " You will get hit one of these days riding about like that when shells are flying." And he replied, " I pedal so quick, sir, they'd never catch me." These boys didn't seem to mind the bullets one bit; they were always ready to carry out orders, though it meant risk to their life every time.

Would any of you do that? If an enemy were firing down this street, and I were to tell one of you to take a message across to a house on the other side, would you do it? I am sure you would. But probably you wouldn't much like doing it.

But you should prepare yourself for it beforehand. It's just like taking a header into cold water; a boy who is accustomed to bathing thinks nothing of it, as he has practised it over and over again; but ask a boy to do it who has never practised it, and he will probably back out.

So, too, with a boy who has been accustomed to obey orders at once, whether there is risk about it or not; the moment you order him to do a thing on active service, no matter how great the danger is to him, he does it, while another boy who has never cared to obey would likely object, and would then be despised as a coward, even by his former friends.

But you need not wait for war in order to be useful as a scout. As a peace scout there is plenty for you to do any day, wherever you may be.

BOOKS TO READ

The following books, which may be had from a Public Library or from friends, may be found useful in connection with Chapter I: —

"Rob the Ranger," by Herbert Strang. Price 6s. (Published by Hodder and Stoughton.) Describes the exciting adventures of boy scouts in Canada in the early days, including tracking and backwoods life.

Also,

"Kidnapped," by R. L. Stevenson. Price 8d.

"Kim," by Rudyard Kipling. Price 6s.

"Siege of Mafeking," by Major F. Baillie. Price 6s.

"Two Little Savages," by Ernest Thompson Seton. Price 6s. nett.

"Parents and Children," by Miss Charlotte Mason. Price 3s. 6d. nett.

"The Romance of Every Day," by L. Quiller Couch. Gives inspiring instances of heroism in everyday life. Price 5s.

"Heroes of Pioneering," by Edgar Sanderson. Price 5s.

CAMP FIRE YARN. NO. 2

SUMMARY OF SCOUTS' COURSE OF INSTRUCTION

To become a boy scout you should

1. Apply to a local secretary. A list of these is published periodically in the *Headquarters Gazette.*

2. Join, with the written permission of your parent, a patrol or troop raised by any man in your neighborhood.

3. Join one of the other organizations for boys who use the boy scout scheme as part of their instruction. Patrols should, if possible, be all about the same age. One boy is then chosen as Patrol Leader to command the patrol, and he selects another boy to be the Corporal or second in command. Several patrols together can form a " Troop," under an officer called a " Scoutmaster."

After one month's training as a " tenderfoot " you all take the scout's promise, that is, you promise, *on your honor*, three things, namely: —

1. To do your duty to God and the King.
2. To help other people at all times.
3. To obey the scout law.

You learn the scout sign of the scouts (see page 41), and also the call of your patrol (see pages 44 and 45).

Every patrol is named after some animal, and each scout in it has to be able to make the cry of that animal in order to communicate with his comrades, especially at night. Thus you may be "the Wolves," "the Curlews," "the Eagles," or "the Rats," if you like. But don't be a "Monkey Patrol," that is, a patrol that plays games, but has no discipline and wins no badges. No scout may ever use the call of another patrol. The scout law binds you to be loyal, kind, obedient, and cheerful. Most of your work then consists in playing scouting games and practices by which you gain experience as scouts. When you have learned sufficient to pass the tests, you can win the badge of either a first-class or second-class scout.

That of the first-class scout consists of a brass arrow-head with the motto on it " BE PREPARED."

That of the second-class scout is merely the motto without the arrow-head.

The meaning of the motto is that a scout must prepare himself by previous thinking out and practising how to act in any accident or emergency, so that he is never taken by surprise; he knows exactly what to do when anything unexpected happens.

The following subjects are what you have to know about to pass the test as a scout : —

WOODCRAFT means knowing all about animals, which is gained by following up their foot-tracks and creeping up to them so that you can watch them in their natural state, and learn the different kinds of animals and their various habits. You shoot them only if in need of food; but no scout wilfully kills an animal for the mere sake of killing, unless it is a harmful creature.

By continually watching animals in their natural state, one gets to like them too well to shoot them.

The whole sport of hunting animals lies in the woodcraft of stalking them, not in the killing.

Woodcraft includes, besides being able to see the tracks and other small signs, the power to read their meaning, such as, at what pace the animal was going, whether he was frightened, or unsuspicious, and so on. It enables the hunter also to find his way in the forest or desert; it teaches him which are the best wild fruits, roots, etc., for his own food, or which are favorite food for animals, and, therefore, likely to attract them.

In the same way, in scouting in civilized countries you read the tracks of men, horses, bicycles, etc., and find out from these that has been going on; noticing by small signs, such as birds suddenly starting up, that some one is moving near, though you cannot see them.

By noticing little things on the ground you will often find lost articles, which you can then restore to their owners.

By noticing details of harness, and so on, you can often save a horse from the pain of an ill-fitting strap or bit.

By noticing the behavior or dress of people, and putting this and that together, you can sometimes see that they are up to no good and can thus prevent a crime, or you can often tell when they are in distress and need help or sympathy — and you can then do what is one of the chief duties of a scout, namely, help those in distress in any possible way that you can.

Remember that it is a disgrace to a scout if, when he is with other people, they see anything, big or little, near or far, high or low, that he has not already seen for himself.

CAMPAIGNING. — Scouts must, of course, be accustomed to living in the open; they have to know how to put up tents or huts for themselves; how to lay and light a fire; how to kill, cut up, and cook their food; how to tie logs together to make bridges and rafts; how to find their way by night, as well as by day, in a strange country, and so on.

But very few boys learn or practise these things when they are living in civilized places, because they have comfortable houses and beds to sleep in, their food is prepared and cooked for them, and when they want to know the way " they ask a policeman."

Well, when those boys go out on the prairie, or try to go scouting, they find themselves helpless duffers.

Take the captain of your football or baseball team and put him out in the woods alongside a boy-trapper, and see which can look after himself. He is only a tenderfoot, and would be the object of continual fun until he got some scoutcraft into him.

And scoutcraft, mind you, comes in useful in any line of life that you like to take up. Football, baseball, and lacrosse are of very little use — though they are good games to play, and come in useful to a certain extent in training a boy's eye, nerve, and temper. But they are not to be compared with scouting, which teaches a boy to be a man.

*[Make each boy lay a fire in his own way and light it. After
failures, show them the right way (i.e., delicate use of dry
chips and shavings, and sticks in a pyramid), and make
them do it again. Also teach them how to tie knots. See
Chapter III.]*

CHIVALRY. — In the old days the knights were the scouts of
Britain, and their rules were very much the same as the scout
law which we have now; and very much like what the Japanese
have, too. We are of the same blood as they, and we ought to
keep up their good name and follow in their steps.

They considered that their honor was the most sacred thing
to uphold; they would not do a dishonorable thing, such as
telling a lie or stealing; they would really rather die than do it.
They were always ready to fight and to be killed in upholding
their king, or their religion, or their honor. Thousands of
them went out to Palestine (the Holy Land) to maintain the
Christian religion against the Mohammedan Turks.

Each knight had a small following of a squire and some men-
at-arms, just as our patrol leader has his corporal and four or
five scouts.

The knight's patrol used to stick to him through thick and
thin, and all carried out the same idea as their leader, namely: —

Their honor was sacred.

They were loyal to God and their king, and to their country.

They were particularly courteous and polite to all women
and children, and infirm people.

They were helpful to everybody.

They gave money and food where it was wanted, and saved
up their money in order to do so.

They taught themselves the use of arms in order to protect
their religion and their country against enemies.

They kept themselves strong and healthy and active in
order to be able to do these things well.

You scouts cannot do better than follow the example of your
forefathers, the knights, who made the tiny British nation into
one of the best and greatest that the world has ever known.

One great point about them was that every day they had to
do a good turn to somebody, and that is one of our rules. When
you get up in the morning, remember that you have got to do a

good turn for some one during the day, tie a knot in your handkerchief or necktie, and leave the tail of your necktie out-side your waistcoat to remind your-self of it; and when you go to bed at night think whom you did the good turn to.

If you should ever find that you had forgotten to do it, you must do two good turns the next day in-stead. Remember that by your scout's oath you are on your honor to do it.

A good turn need only be a very small one; if it is only to put a cent into a poor box, or to help an old woman to cross the street, or to make room on a seat for some one, or to give water to a thirsty horse, or to remove a bit of banana skin off the pavement where it is likely

A BOY SCOUT'S NECKTIE

to throw people down, it is a good turn.   But one must be done every day, and it counts as a good turn only when you do not accept any reward in return.

[Make each scout tie knot in his necktie to remind him to do a good turn next day.]

SAVING LIFE.— You have all heard of the Victoria Cross — the little bronze cross given by Queen Victoria to soldiers who specially distinguish themselves in action under the fire of the enemy.

But there is the companion medal to it, and that is the Albert Medal for those who are not soldiers, and who distinguish them-selves in saving life in peace time.   And there is the Stanhope Medal for civilian gallantry, and the Edward Medal for gallantry in mines, the Royal Humane Society's medals, and Mr. Carnegie's Heroes' Fund, as well as our Scout's Gallantry medals.

And I think the man who wins these medals, as he does in the sudden, appalling accidents which occur in big cities, mines, and factories, in every-day life, is no less a hero than the soldier who races into the thick of the fight to rescue a comrade amid all the excitement and glamour of the battle.

Since the scouts started two years ago, over one hundred have won medals for life-saving, and I hope that many more will do the same.

It is certain that very many of you will, at one time or another, get a chance oɩ it, if you are prepared to seize the opportunity. That is, you must be *prepared* for it; you should know what to do the moment an accident occurs — and do it then and ᴄhere.

It is not enough to read about it in a book and think that you know how to do it — but you must actually practise, and practise pretty often, the actual things to be done; such as how to cover your mouth and nose with a wet handkerchief to enable you to breathe in smoke, how to tear a sheet into strips and make a rope for escaping from fire, how to open a manhole to let air into a gassy sewer, how to lift and carry an insensible person, how to collar, save, and revive apparently drowned people, and so on.

When you have learnt all these things you will have confidence in yourself, so that when an accident happens and everybody is in a state of fluster, not knowing what to do, you will quietly step out and do the right thing.

Remember the case at the Hampstead Ponds a year or two ago, when a woman drowned herself in shallow water before a whole lot of men, who were too frightened to do anything but shout to her. It was a disgrace to our nation that there was not a real man amongst them. It would have been a grand opportunity for a boy scout, had there been one there, to go in and fetch her out. As it was, these cowards stood there clamoring and chattering on the bank — not one of them daring to go in because the others did not. And she was drowned before their eyes.

> [*Teach the scouts how to lift and carry an insensible man. Also how to drag an insensible man through smoke, gas, etc. Also how to cover nose and mouth with wet handkerchief. Divide them off into pairs, and let each in turn act as insensible patient to be rescued by his comrade.*]

ENDURANCE. — To carry out all the duties and work of a scout properly a boy has to be strong, healthy, and active. And he can make himself so if he takes a little care about it.

It means a lot of exercise, like playing games, running, walking, bicycling, and so on.

A scout has to sleep very much in the open, and a boy who is accustomed to sleep with his window shut will probably suffer, as many a tenderfoot has done, by catching cold and rheumatism when he first tries sleeping out. The thing is always to sleep with your windows open, summer and winter, and you will never catch cold. Personally I cannot sleep with my window shut or with blinds down, and when living in the country I always sleep outside the house, summer and winter alike. A soft bed and too many blankets make a boy dream bad dreams. which weaken him.

A short time spent at Swedish or ju-jitsu exercises every morning and evening is a grand thing for keeping you in good condition — not so much for making showy muscle as to work all your internal organs [*explain*], and to work up the circulation of the blood in every part of you.

A good rub down daily with a wet rough towel, even if you cannot get a bath, is what every real scout takes, and is of the utmost importance.

Scouts breathe through the nose, not through the mouth; in this way they don't get thirsty; they don't get out of breath so quickly; they don't suck into their insides all sorts of microbes or seeds of disease that are in the air; and they don't snore at night, and so give themselves away to an enemy.

" Deep breathing " exercises are of great value for developing the lungs, and for putting fresh air (oxygen) into the blood, provided that they are carried out in the open air, and are not overdone so as to injure the heart, etc. For deep breathing the breath must be taken in slowly and deeply through the nose, not through the mouth, till it opens out the ribs to the greatest extent, especially at the back; then, after a time, it should be slowly and steadily breathed out again without strain. But the best deep breathing, after all, is that which comes naturally from plenty of running exercise.

Alcohol is now shown to be quite useless as a health-giving drink, and it is mere poison when a man takes much of it. A man who is in the habit of drinking beer, wine, or spirits in strong doses every day is not the slightest use for scouting, and very little use for anything else.

Similarly a man who smokes much. The best war scouts don't smoke, because it weakens their eyesight; it sometimes makes them shaky and nervous; it spoils their noses for smelling (which is of great importance at night), and the glow of their pipe, or even the scent of tobacco carried on them at night, gives them away to watchful enemies. They are not such fools as to smoke. No boy ever began smoking because he liked it, but because he thought it made him look like a grown-up man. As a matter of fact it generally makes him look very foolish indeed.

[Show ju-jitsu or Swedish extension motions — one or two exercises only to begin with.   Also deep breathing.]

PATRIOTISM. — You are a Canadian, and you are a part of the great British Empire, one of the greatest empires that has ever existed in the world.

[Show on the map.]

From the little island of Great Britain have sprung Dominions and colonies all over the world, — Australia, New Zealand, South Africa, India, Canada, Newfoundland.

Almost every race, every kind of man, black, white, or yellow, in the world, furnishes subjects of King George V.

This vast Empire did not grow of itself out of nothing; it was made by your forefathers by dint of hard work and hard fighting, at the sacrifice of their lives — that is, by their hearty patriotism.

People say that we have no patriotism nowadays, and that therefore the British Empire will fall to pieces, as the great Roman Empire did, because its citizens became selfish and lazy, and cared only for amusements.   I am not so certain about that. I am sure that if you boys will keep the good of your country and your Empire in your eyes *above everything else* both will go on all right.

Therefore, in all that you do, remember to think of your country first; don't spend the whole of your time and money on games and at candy stores merely to amuse *yourself;* but think first how you can be of use in helping Canada and the Empire, and when you have done that you can justly and honestly sit down and enjoy yourself in your own way.   Perhaps you don't see how a mere small boy can be of use either to your own country or to the great British Empire; but by becoming a scout and carrying out the scout laws every boy can be of use.

" Country first, self second," should be your motto.   Probably, if you ask yourself truly, you will find you have at present got them just the other way about.

I hope, if it is so, that you will from this moment put yourself right and remain so always.   Patriot first, player second.   Don't be content, as the Romans were, and some people now are, to pay other people to play your football or to fight your battles for you.   Do something yourself to help in keeping the flag flying.

If you take up scouting in that spirit, you will be doing something; take it up, not merely because it amuses you, but because by doing so you will be fitting yourself to help your country. Then you will have in you the true spirit of patriotism, which every Canadian boy ought to have if he is worth his salt.

How to Fly the British Flag

RIGHT WAY UP

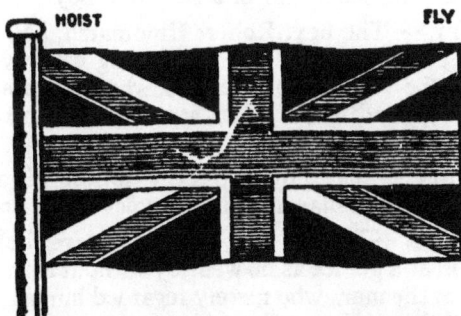

HOIST   FLY

UPSIDE DOWN

How not to Fly the British Flag

[*Show the Union Jack.   Explain its history and composition, and which is the right way of flying it.   See Chapter IX.*]

Headquarters Gazette is the official organ for scoutmasters, secretaries, etc., published monthly.   Price 2d.
The Scout, 1d. weekly, is the official paper for the boys.

The Elsdon Murder

[Note: The following story, which in the main is true, is a sample of a story that should be given by the instructor illustrating generally the duties of a boy scout.]

A BRUTAL murder took place many years ago in the North of England; and the murderer was caught, convicted, and hanged chiefly through the scoutcraft of a shepherd boy.

WOODCRAFT. — The boy, Robert Hindmarsh, had been up on the moor tending his sheep, and was finding his way home over a wild, out-of-the-way part of the hills, when he passed a tramp sitting on the ground with his legs stretched out in front of him eating some food.

OBSERVATION. — The boy in passing noticed his appearance, and especially the peculiar nails in the soles of his boots.

CONCEALMENT. — He did not stop and stare, but just took these things in at a glance as he went by without attracting much attention from the man, who merely regarded him as an ordinary boy not worth his notice.

DEDUCTION. — When he got near home, some five or six miles away, he came to a crowd round a cottage, where they had found the old woman (Margaret Crozier) who inhabited it lying murdered. All sorts of guesses were being hazarded as to who had done the deed, and suspicion seemed to centre on a small gang of three or four gypsies who were going about the country robbing and threatening death to any one who made any report of their misdeeds.

The boy heard all these things, but presently he saw some peculiar footprints in the little garden of the cottage; the nail-marks agreed with those he had seen in the boots of the man on the moor, and he naturally deduced from these that the man might have something to do with the murder.

CHIVALRY. — The fact that it was a helpless old woman who had been murdered made the boy's chivalrous feeling rise against the murderer, whoever he might be.

PLUCK AND SELF-DISCIPLINE, ALACRITY. — So, although he knew that the friends of the murderer might kill him for giving information, he cast his fears on one side and went at once and told the constable of the footmarks in the garden, and where he could find the man who had made them — if he went immediately.

HEALTH AND STRENGTH. --The man up on the moor had got so far from the scene of the murder, unseen (except by this one small boy), that he thought himself safe, and never thought of the boy being able to walk all the way to the scene of the murder

OBSERVING THE MURDERER'S BOOTS

and then to come back, as he did, with the police. So he took no precautions.

But the boy was a strong, healthy hill-boy, and did the journey rapidly and well, so that they found the man and captured him without difficulty.

The man was Willie Winter, a gypsy.

He was tried, found guilty, and hanged at Newcastle. His body was then brought and hung on a gibbet near the scene of the murder, as was the custom in those days, and the gibbet still stands to this day. Two of the gypsies who were his accomplices were caught with some of the stolen property, and were also executed at Newcastle.

KIND-HEARTEDNESS. — But when the boy saw the murderer's body hanging there on the gibbet he was overcome with misery at having caused the death of a fellow-creature.

SAVING LIFE. — However, the magistrate sent for him and complimented him on the great good he had done to his fellow-countrymen — probably saving some of their lives — by ridding the world of such a dangerous criminal.

DUTY. — He said: " You have done your duty, although it caused you personally some danger and much distress.   Still you must not mind that — it was your duty to the King to help the police in getting justice done, and duty must always be carried out regardless of how much it costs you, even if you have to give up your life."

EXAMPLE. — Thus the boy did every part of the duty of a boy scout without ever having been taught.

He exercised: —

>   Woodcraft.
>   Observation, without being noticed.
>   Deduction.
>   Chivalry.
>   Sense of duty.
>   Endurance.
>   Kind-heartedness.

He little thought that the act which he did entirely of his own accord would years afterwards be held up as an example to you other boys in teaching you to do your duty.   In the same way, you should remember your acts may be watched by others after you, and taken as an example, too.   So try to do your duty the right way on all occasions.

CAMP FIRE YARN. No. 3

BOY SCOUTS' ORGANIZATION

IT was not originally intended that boy scouts should form a corps separated from all others, but that boys belonging to any kind of existing organization, such as schools; football clubs, Boys' or Church Lads' Brigades, factories, district messengers, Telegraph Service, Cadet Corps, etc., etc., would *also* take up scouting in addition to their other work or play.

The spare moments of Sunday can be made more interesting and instructive through the quiet study of plants and animals, that is, of God's work in nature, and the practice of kindliness and " good turns " (see page 239 *re* Sunday work).

The following ranks only are recognized: —

Commissioner, appointed by the governing Council as its representative and inspector in a country or province.

District or Assistant Commissioner, similarly appointed to the charge of a district under a commissioner.

Scoutmaster, selected by District Association to have charge of a troop.

Assistant Scoutmaster.

Instructor, for any specific subject.

Chaplain is a minister of religion appointed to develop the religious training of a body of scouts.

A *Patrol Leader* is a scout appointed by a scoutmaster or by vote of the patrol to command a patrol for one year. A patrol consists of six or eight scouts. Any patrol leader who learns scouting from this book can train his boys to be scouts.

A *Corporal* is a scout selected by the patrol leader to be his assistant, and to take command of the patrol when he himself is away.

Silver Wolf, a Scout who has passed twenty-four tests for efficiency.

King's Scout is one qualified by efficiency badges to help in defence of the country.

All-Round Scout is one who has qualified in at least six efficiency tests.

A *Scout*, who must be between the ages of eleven and eighteen. A first-class scout is one who has passed certain tests to show that he is able to scout.

A *Second-Class Scout* is one who has passed certain easy tests in scouting.

A *Tenderfoot* is a boy who has joined the boy scouts, but has not yet passed his tests for second-class scout. In special cases boys of ten years old may become tenderfoots.

THE SCOUT'S PROMISE

Before he becomes a scout a boy must take the scout's promise thus: —

"*On my honor* I promise that I will do my best

"1. To do my duty to God and the King.
"2. To help other people at all times.
"3. To obey the scout law."

(For scout law, see page 50.)

THE TESTS

BOY SCOUTS' BADGE QUALIFICATIONS

Tenderfoot. — A boy on joining the boy scouts must be between the ages of eleven and eighteen and pass the following tests *before making the promise:* —

Know the scouts' laws and signs and salute.

Know the composition of the Union Jack and the right way to fly it (page 19)

Tie the following knots: reef, sheet bend, clove hitch, bowline, fisherman's, sheepshank.

He is then enrolled as a tenderfoot, and is entitled to wear the button-hole badge.

Second-Class Scout. – Before being awarded the second-class scout's badge a tenderfoot must

1. Have at least one month's service as a tenderfoot.
2. Have a knowledge of elementary first aid and bandaging. (See Scout Chart 16, excepting fracture of thigh.)
3. Know the semaphore or Morse sign for every letter in the alphabet.
4. Follow a track half a mile in twenty-five minutes; or, if in a town, describe satisfactorily the contents of one shop window out of four, observed for one minute each, or Kim's Game, to remember sixteen out of twenty-four well-assorted small articles after one minute's observation.
5. Go a mile in twelve minutes at " scout's pace." (twenty paces walking and twenty paces running alternately.)
6. Lay and light a wood fire in the open, using not more than two matches.
7. Cook a quarter of a pound of meat and two potatoes without cooking utensils other than the regulation billy.

8. Have at least ten cents in a savings bank.
9. Know the sixteen principal points of the compass.

First-Class Scout. — Before being awarded a first-class badge a second-class scout must

1. Swim fifty yards. (N.B. — This may be omitted where the doctor certifies that bathing is dangerous to the boy's health, in which case he must pass the test for Stalker's badge.)
2. Have twenty-five cents at least in the savings bank.
3. Send and receive a message either in semaphore or Morse, sixteen letters per minute.
4. Go on foot, or row a boat, alone or with another scout, to a point seven miles away and return again, or if conveyed by any vehicle (railways not allowed) or animal go a distance of fifteen miles and back. He must write a short report of the journey. It is preferable that he should take two days over the journey.
5. Describe the proper method of dealing with two of the following accidents (allotted by the examiners): Fire, drowning, runaway carriage, sewer gas, ice breaking, electric shock. Bandage an injured patient, or revive apparently drowned person. (See Scout Charts 10 and 16.)
6. Cook satisfactorily two out of the following dishes, as may be directed: porridge, bacon, hunter's stew; or skin and cook a rabbit, or pluck and cook a bird. Also, make a "damper" of half a pound of flour, or a "twist" baked on a thick stick.
7. Read a map correctly, and draw an intelligent, rough, sketch map. Point out a compass direction without the help of a compass.
8. Use an axe for felling or trimming light timber, or nine-inch scaffolding pole, or, as alternative, produce an article of carpentry or joinery, or metal work, made by himself satisfactorily.
9. Judge distance, area, size, numbers, height, and weight within 25 per cent. error.
10. Bring a tenderfoot trained by himself in the points required for a tenderfoot badge. (This may be postponed if recruits are not immediately desired, but must be carried out within three months of its being required or the badge given up.)

Service Mark. — For each year's service a six-point star may be worn above the cuff on the left arm.

King's Scout. — To be a King's scout a boy must be a first-class scout and pathfinder, and pass three of the following efficiency tests: —

Ambulance,	Marksman,
Bugler,	Seaman,
Cyclist,	Signaller.

He then receives a crown as badge to wear on the left arm above his scout's badge; and will rank above a first-class scout.

All-round cords may be gained by any scout who passes any six of the tests for proficiency badges.

The "Silver Wolf" is awarded to a King's scout who gains twenty-four of the number of the proficiency badges.

The "Honorary Silver Wolf" is given in certain cases of exceptionally valuable work on behalf of the movement.

Senior Scouts. — Those who, having attained the age of eighteen, desire to remain in the movement. They take rank and duties as assistant to the assistant scoutmaster and should as a rule each have some definite responsible share in the routine work of the troop. They dress as patrol leaders without staves.

"Swastika," the Badge of Brotherhood. — Can be given by a scout of any rank (except a tenderfoot) to anybody who has done him or the movement a good turn. It is a token of thanks.

This badge entitles the holder to the assistance of any scout at any time. A scout on seeing a person wearing this badge will go up, salute, and ask if he can be of any service.

QUALIFICATIONS FOR PROFICIENCY BADGES

All scouts who wish to obtain these badges must pass the necessary tests before two qualified examiners, appointed by the committee, and must be, in the first instance, second-class scouts. They are worn on the right sleeve, except the King's scout badges.

Those badges marked with an asterisk must be passed for annually.

*Ambulance Badge. — A scout must know: —

The fireman's lift.
How to drag an insensible man with ropes.
How to improvise a stretcher.
How to fling a life-line.
The position of the main arteries.
How to stop bleeding from vein, artery, internal or external.
How to improvise splints and to diagnose and bind fractured limbs.
The Schäfer method of artificial respiration.
How to deal with choking, burning, poison, grit in eye, sprains, and bruises, as the examiners may require.
Generally the laws of health and sanitation as given in " The Canadian Boy Scout," including dangers of smoking, incontinence, want of ventilation, and lack of cleanliness.

Airman. — A scout must have a knowledge of the theory of aeroplanes, ball-balloons and dirigibles, and must have made a working model of an aeroplane or dirigible that will fly at least twenty-five yards. He must also have a knowledge of the engines used for aeroplanes and dirigibles.

Bee-farmer. — A scout must have a practical knowledge of swarming, hiving, hives, and general apiculture, including a knowledge of the use of artificial combs, etc.

Blacksmith. — A scout must be able to upset and weld a one-inch iron rod, make a horseshoe, know how to tire a wheel, use a sledgehammer and forge, shoe a horse correctly, and rough a shod horse.

Bugler. — A scout must be able to sound properly on the bugle the Scout's Rally and the following army calls: Alarm, Charge, Orderlies (ord. corpls.), Orders, Warning for Parade, Quarter Bugle, Fall in, Dismiss, Rations, 1st and 2nd Dinner calls (men's), Réveillé, Last Post, Lights Out.

Carpenter. — A scout must be able to shute and glue a 4 ft. straight joint, make a housing, tenon and mortice, and halved joint, grind and set a chisel and plane iron, make a 3 ft. by 1 ft. 6 in. by 1 ft. by 6 ft. dovetailed locked box, or a table or chair.

Clerk. — A scout must have the following qualifications: —
Good handwriting and hand printing.
Ability to use typewriting machine.
Ability to write a letter from memory on the subject given verbally five minutes previously.
Knowledge of simple bookkeeping.
OR AS ALTERNATIVE TO TYPEWRITING: —
Write in short hand from dictation at twenty words a minute as minimum.

Cook. — A scout must be able to light a fire and make a cookplace with a few bricks or logs; cook the following dishes: Irish stew, vegetables, omelet, rice pudding, or any dishes which the examiner may consider equivalent; make tea, coffee, or cocoa; mix dough and bake bread in oven; or a " damper " or " twist " (round stake) at a camp fire; carve properly, and hand plates and dishes correctly to people at table.

*Cyclist. — A scout must sign a certificate that he owns a bicycle in good working order, which he is willing to use in the King's service if called upon at any time in case of emergency. He must be able to ride his bicycle satisfactorily and repair punctures, etc. He must be able to read a map, and repeat correctly a verbal message. On ceasing to own a bicycle the scout must be required to hand back his badge.

Dairyman. — A scout must understand: —
Management of dairy cattle, be able to milk, make butter and cheese, understand sterilization of milk, safe use of preservatives, care of dairy utensils and appliances.

Electrician. — A scout must have a knowledge of the method of rescue and resuscitation of a person insensible from shock.

Be able to make a simple electro-magnet, elementary knowledge of action of simple battery cells, and the working of electric bells and telephone.

Understand and be able to remedy fused wire, and to repair broken electric connections.

Engineer. — A scout must have a general idea of the working of motor-cars and steam locomotives, marine, internal combustion, and electric engines.

He must also know the names of the principal parts and their functions; how to start, drive, feed, stop, and lubricate any one of them chosen by himself.

Farmer. — A scout must have a practical knowledge of ploughing, cultivating, drilling, hedging, and draining. He must also have a working knowledge of farm machinery, hay-making, reaping, leading, and stacking, and a general acquaintance with the routine seasonal work on a farm, including the care of cattle, horses, sheep, and pigs.

Fireman. — A scout must know how to give the alarm to inhabitants, police, etc.

How to enter burning buildings. How to prevent spread of fire. Use of hose, unrolling, joining up, hydrants, use of nozzle, etc.

The use of escape, ladders, and shutes; improvising ropes, jumping-sheets, etc.

The fireman's lift, how to drag patient, how to work in fumes, etc.

The use of fire extinguishers. How to rescue animals. How to save property, climb, and pass buckets. " Scrum " to keep back crowd.

Farrier (for First Aid to Animals). — A scout must have a general knowledge of the anatomy of domestic and farm animals and be able to describe treatment and symptoms of the following: —

Wounds, fractures, and sprains, exhaustion, choking, lameness.

He must understand shoeing and shoes, and must be able to give a drench for colic.

(*Barton's small veterinary book recommended, price 6d., from Headquarters.*)

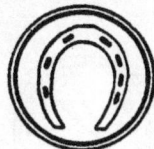

Gardener. — A scout must dig a piece of ground not less than 12 feet square.

Know the names of a dozen plants pointed out in an ordinary garden.

Understand what is meant by pruning, grafting, and manuring.

Plant and grow successfully six kinds of vegetables or flowers from seeds or cuttings.

Cut and make a walking stick, or cut grass with a scythe under supervision.

Handyman. — A scout must be able to paint a door or bath, whitewash a ceiling, repair gas-fittings, tap washers, sash lines, window and door fastenings, replace gas mantles and electric-light bulbs, hang pictures and curtains, repair blinds, fix curtain and portière rods, blind fixtures, lay carpets, mend clothing and upholstery, do small furniture and china repairs, and sharpen knives.

Horseman. — A scout must know how to ride at all paces, and to jump an ordinary fence on horseback.

How to saddle and bridle a horse correctly.

How to harness a horse correctly in single or double harness, and to drive.

How to water and feed, and to what amount.

How to groom his horse properly.

The evil of bearing and hame reins and ill-fitting saddlery. The principal causes and remedies of lameness.

Interpreter. — A scout must be able to carry on a simple conversation, write a simple letter on subject given by examiner, read and translate passage from a book or newspaper, in either Esperanto or any language that is not that of his own country.

Leather Worker. — A scout must have a knowledge of tanning and curing, and either

(a) Be able to sole and heel a pair of boots, sewn or nailed, and generally repair boots and shoes; or

(b) Be able to dress a saddle, repair traces, stirrup leathers, etc., and know the various parts of harness.

* Marksman.—A scout must pass the following tests for miniature rifle shooting from any position:—

N. R. A. Standard Target to be used. Twenty rounds to be fired at 15 or 25 yards. Highest possible, 100 points. A scout gaining 60 points or over to be classified as marksman.

Scoring: Bull's-eyes, 5 points; Inner, 4 points; Magpie, 3 points; Outer, 2 points.

Also:—

Judge distance on unknown ground: Five distances under 300 yards, five between 300 and 600 yards, with not more than an error of 25 per cent. on the average.

Master-at-arms.—A scout must attain proficiency in two out of the following subjects:—

Single-Stick, quarter-staff, fencing, boxing, jujitsu, and wrestling.

Missioner.—The qualifications are:—

A general elementary knowledge of sick-nursing; invalid cookery, sick-room attendance, bed-making, and ventilation.

Ability to help aged and infirm.

Musician.—A scout must be able to play a musical instrument correctly (other than triangle) and to read simple music. Or to play properly any kind of musical toy, such as a penny whistle, mouth-organ, etc., and sing a song.

* Pathfinder.—It is necessary to know every lane, by-path, and short cut for a distance of at least two miles in every direction around the local scouts' headquarters in the country, or for one mile if in a town, and to have a general knowledge of the district within a five-mile radius of his local headquarters, so as to be able to guide people at any time, by day or night.

To know the general direction of the principal neighboring towns for a distance of twenty-five miles, and

To be able to give strangers clear directions how to get to them.

To know, in the country, in the two-mile radius, generally, how many haystacks, strawstacks, wagons, horses, cattle, sheep, and pigs there are on the different neighboring farms; or, in a town, to know in a half-mile radius what livery stabling, flour and feed stores, forage merchants, bakers, butchers there are. In town or country, to know where are the police stations, hospitals, doctors, telegraph, telephone offices, fire engines, hydrants, blacksmiths, and job-masters, or factories where over a dozen horses are kept.

To know something of the history of the place, or of any old buildings, such as the church, or castle, etc.

As much as possible of the above information is to be entered by the scout on a large scale map.

Photographer. — A scout must have a knowledge of the theory and use of lenses, and the construction of cameras, action of developers. He must take, develop, and print twelve separate subjects, three interiors, three portraits, three landscapes, and three instantaneous " action " photos.

Pioneer. — A scout must

Have extra efficiency in pioneering in the following tests, or suitable equivalents: —

Fell a nine-inch tree or scaffolding pole neatly and quickly.

Tie eight kinds of knots quickly in the dark or blindfolded.

Lash spars properly together for scaffolding.

Build model bridge or derrick.

Make a camp kitchen.

Build a hut of one kind or another suitable for three occupants.

Piper. — A scout must be able

To play a march and a reel on the pipes.

To dance the sword-dance, and must wear kilt and Highland dress.

Plumber. — A scout must be able to make wiped and brazed joints, to cut and fix a window-pane, repair a burst pipe, mend a ball or faucet tap, and understand the ordinary hot and cold water system of a house.

Poultry Farmer. — A scout must have a good knowledge of incubators, foster-mothers, sanitary fowl-houses and coops and runs; also of rearing, feeding, killing, and dressing birds for market; also he must be able to pack birds and eggs for market.

Printer. — A scout must know the names of different types and paper sizes. Be able to compose by hand or machine, understand the use of hand or power printing machines.

He must also print a handbill set up by himself.

Seaman. — A scout must be able to

Tie eight knots rapidly in the dark or blindfolded.
Splice ropes.
Fling a rope coil.
Row and punt a boat single-handed, and punt with pole, or scull it over the stern. Steer a boat rowed by others. Bring the boat properly alongside and make it fast.
Box the compass.
Read a chart.
State direction by the stars and sun.
Swim fifty yards with trousers, socks, and shirt on.
Climb a rope or pole of fifteen feet, or, *as alternative*, dance the hornpipe correctly.
Sew and darn a shirt and trousers.
Understand the general working of steam and hydraulic winches, and have a knowledge of weather wisdom and knowledge of tides.

Signaller. — A scout must pass tests in both sending and receiving in semaphore and Morse signalling by flag. Not fewer than twenty-four letters per minute.

He must be able: to give and read signals by sound.

To make correct smoke and flame signals with fires.

To show the proper method of signalling with the staff (see page 87).

Stalker. — A scout must take a series of twenty photographs of wild animals or birds from life, and develop and print them.

Or alternatively —

He must make a collection of sixty species of wild flowers, ferns, or grasses, dried and mounted in a book and correctly named.

Or alternatively —

He must make colored drawings of twenty flowers, ferns, or grasses, or twelve sketches from life of animals and birds. Original sketches, as well as the finished pictures, to be submitted.

Or alternatively —

He must be able to name sixty different kinds of animals, insects, reptiles, or birds in a museum or zoölogical garden, or from unnamed colored plates, and give particulars of the lives, habits, appearance, and markings of twenty of them.

Star-Man. — A scout must have a general knowledge of the nature and movements of the stars.

He must be able to point out and name six principal constellations.

Find the north by means of other stars than the Pole Star in case of that star being obscured by clouds, etc., and tell the hour of the night by the stars or moon.

He must have a general knowledge of the positions and movements of the earth, sun, and moon, and of tides, eclipses, meteors, comets, sun-spots, planets.

Surveyor. — A scout must map correctly, from the country itself, the main features of half a mile of road, with 440 yards each side, to a scale of two feet to the mile, and afterwards redraw same map from memory.

Measure the heights of a tree, telegraph pole, and church steeple, describing method adopted.

Measure width of a river, and distance apart of two objects a known distance away and unapproachable.

Be able to measure a gradient.

Understand what is meant by H.E., V.I., R.F. Contours, conventional signs of ordnance survey and scales.

Swimming and Life Saving. — A scout must be able to dive and swim fifty yards with clothes on (shirt, trousers, socks, as minimum).

Able to fling and use life-line or life-buoy.

Able to demonstrate two ways of rescue of drowning person, and revival of apparently drowned.

MEDALS

These are worn on the right breast and are awarded as follows: —

Bronze Cross. Red Ribbon. — Highest possible award for gallantry. It can be won only where the claimant has shown special heroism, or has faced extraordinary risks in saving life.

Silver Cross. Blue Ribbon. — For gallantry with considerable risk to himself.

(Gilt) Medal of Merit. White Ribbon. — For a scout who does his duty exceptionally well though without grave risks to himself; or for twenty marks awarded by his scoutmaster for various specially good actions; or for specially good work on behalf of the Boy Scout movement. Full records of such deeds must be kept by the scoutmaster to accompany the claim.

Scroll of Honor: Is awarded for similar cases not quite deserving the medal.

These medals are only granted by the chief scout, or by the scout president in a Dominion or colony, on special recommendation from the local committee, who should send in a full account of the case.

All medals and badges are worn only as above when scouts are on duty or in camp. At other times they may be worn on the right breast of the waistcoat, underneath the jacket.

A small arrow-head badge may be worn at all times in the button-hole.

Scoutmasters may wear any badges for which they qualify.

It should be noted that the rules given in this book are gener-

ally intended to apply to units of boy scouts which do not belong to other existing organizations. Where scouting is taken up by any society, such, for instance, as the Boys' Brigade, that society takes up as much or as little as it likes of the training. Its own officers, properly qualified as scouts, will be considered to be scoutmasters without further recommendation, and the boys who take up scouting keep to the uniform of their corps, and do not wear Boy Scout uniform or badges unless their officers permit it.

If it is desired that such boys should wear scouts' uniform, the officers will be expected to work in conjunction with the local scout association; and if the officers wish for scoutmasters' warrants or the boys to wear the scouts' badges, life-saving medals, or badges of merit, they must pass the same tests as other scoutmasters or boy scouts.

DISTINCTION FOR BOY SCOUTS. — A boy scout when signing his name officially to any letter or document on scout business is entitled to put after his signature any distinctions which he may have gained, by drawing a small sketch of the badge.

Thus, if he is a first-class scout, who has passed in signalling and seamanship, he signs thus: —

James Harding ♣ ✗ ♣

Similarly, these signs may be shown after his name in official lists, etc.

If an " all-round " scout, he draws the Stafford knot; if a King's scout, the crown; if a " Wolf," the wolf.

HOW TO WEAR YOUR BADGES

A convenient way to wear the badges is to have a gauntlet-sleeve that will slip on over the shirt-sleeve and have the badges on it.

The " King's Scout " Badge is worn on the left arm above the First-class Badge, and the four badges which were won to qualify for the King's Badge are also worn, two on either side of the First-class Badge. All other Proficiency Badges are worn on the right arm.

Prize medals are never worn by scouts.

BADGES OF RANK, ETC.

A Corporal. — Wears a single white bar or chevron above elbow on left arm.

A Patrol Leader. — Wears a white metal fleur-de-lis and scroll with motto (like a First-class Badge) in front of hat, and white metal button-hole badge.

Assistant Scoutmaster. — Wears special hat badge on the side of hat, with red plume and miniature white metal fleur-de-lis button-hole badge or tie-pin, with scarlet shoulder-knot.

Scoutmaster. — Wears special hat badge on side of hat, with green plume and miniature bronze button-hole, or tie-pin fleur-de-lis, with shoulder-knot.

Commissioner. — Wears hat badge, with purple plume. Green enamel and gold miniature button-hole tie-pin badge, with " C " superposed.

Headquarters Staff. — Have green enamel and gold circular badge worded " Boy Scouts' Headquarters Staff " round rim, usual rank badges, and red, white, and blue shoulder-knots when in uniform.

DECORATIONS AUTHORIZED BY THE COUNCIL TO BE WORN ON SCOUT UNIFORM

1. All King's Medals, War Medals, and decorations.
2. The Scout Badges, Cords, and Medals.
3. St. John's or St. Andrew's Ambulance Badges.
4. Royal Humane Society's Medals.

REGULATIONS AS TO UNIFORMS

SCOUT UNIFORM

Hat. — Khaki color, flat brim, strap round crown, and chin-strap.

Neckerchief. — Of the color of the troop. The neckerchief is worn loosely knotted at the throat and also at the ends till the day's good turn is done.

Shirt. — Blue, khaki, green, or gray, two patch pockets (buttoned), shoulder-straps, or a jersey or sweater of the same color, if preferred.

Shorts. — Blue or khaki.

Belt. — Brown leather. Swivels, coat straps, pouch, and axe optional. Buckles, etc., should be of dull metal. Official design of belt is obtainable at headquarters.

Stockings. — Dark color or khaki, colored tops optional, green garters with tabs showing on outside of leg. Stockings are worn turned down below the knee.

Shoes or boots. — Brown or black.

Staff. — Marked in feet and inches.

Haversacks. — Worn as a knapsack.

Shoulder-knot. — Six inches, colors as for patrols to be worn by every scout.

Whistle and knife. — On lanyards.

Great coats. — Official pattern, obtainable at headquarters.
Nothing but the foregoing should be worn visibly. All extras to be carried in haversack. A scout's clothing should be of flannel or wool, as much as possible; cotton next the skin should be avoided, as it does not absorb the perspiration, and is likely to give a chill.

SCOUTMASTER'S UNIFORM

Those scoutmasters who are entitled to wear military uniforms should preferably not wear this dress when scouting with or drilling boy scouts. Miniature war medals or their ribbons may be worn on scout uniform.

UNIFORM FOR CAMP, GAMES, ETC.

Hat. — Flat brimmed (khaki), with the appropriate badge on left side.

Shirt. — Flannel, with colored collar and green tie, or the colored neckerchief may be worn. If needed, a white sweater may be worn over the shirt.

Shoulder-knot. — White on left shoulder.

Belts, Shorts, Stockings, and Shoes. — As for scouts.

UNIFORM FOR DRILLS AND PARADES

Scout hat, shirt (with collar and green tie), belt, as above, knicker breeches, stockings, puttees, or leather gaiters, walking-stick, whistle, and lanyard.

A coat may be worn, preferably khaki color or gray or brown, of " Norfolk " pattern; military tunics and equipments are out of place.

ASSISTANT SCOUTMASTERS

The uniforms should be the same as scoutmasters', except that the shoulder-knot is scarlet. The button-hole badge is white metal.

COMMISSIONER'S UNIFORM

(*If desired*)

Hat. — As for scoutmasters. Badge with purple plume at side.

Tie. — Green necktie (scouts' color).

Coat. — Norfolk jacket pattern.
Color — khaki.
Roll collar.
Leather buttons.
The coat is worn open at the neck, with the commissioner's small badge on the left top button-hole.

Belt. — Official pattern as for scoutmasters.

Breeches. — Bedford cord or to match the coat.

Gaiters, Boots, and Gloves of brown leather.

Overcoat. — Like Burberry's " Slip on," or khaki cape.

Hats, Belts, and Badges of the same quality as scoutmasters' may be obtained from headquarters.

In place of above, a plain Norfolk suit (gray, brown or khaki), with stockings, gaiters, or puttees, may be worn, with scout hat, appropriate badges, green tie, red, white, and blue shoulder-knot.

INVESTITURE OF SCOUTS

Ceremonial for a tenderfoot to be invested as a scout.

The troop is formed in a horseshoe formation, with scout-master and assistant scoutmaster in the gap.

The tenderfoot with his patrol leader stands just inside the circle, opposite to the scoutmaster. The assistant scoutmaster holds the staff and hat of the tenderfoot. When ordered to come forward by the scoutmaster, the patrol leader brings the tenderfoot to the centre. The scoutmaster then asks: "Do you know what your honor is?"

The tenderfoot replies: "Yes. It means that I can be trusted to be truthful and honest." (Or words to that effect.)

Scoutmaster: "Can I trust you, on your honor,

"1. To be loyal to God and the King?
"2. To do good turns to other people?
"3. To keep the scout law?"

Tenderfoot then makes the half salute, and so do the whole troop whilst he says:—

"I promise, on my honor,

"1. To be loyal to God and the King.
"2. To try and do good turns daily to other people.
"3. To obey the scout law."

Scoutmaster: "I trust you, on your honor, to keep this promise. You are now one of the great brotherhood of scouts."

The assistant scoutmaster then puts on his hat and gives him his staff.

The scoutmaster shakes hands with him.

The new scout faces about and salutes the troop.

The troop present staves.

The scoutmaster gives the word: "To your patrol, quick march."

The troop shoulder staves, and the new scout and his patrol leader march back to their patrol.

When taking this promise the scout will stand holding his right hand raised level with his shoulder, palm to the front, thumb resting on the nail of the little finger, and the other three fingers upright, pointing upwards:—

This is the scout's salute and secret sign.

When the hand is raised shoulder high it is called "The Half Salute."

When raised to the forehead it is the "Full Salute."

SCOUT'S SALUTE AND SECRET SIGN

The three fingers held up (like the three points of the scout's badge) remind him of his three promises in the scout's promise.

1. Honor God and the King.
2. Help others.
3. Obey the scout law.

When a scout meets another for the first time in the day, whether he is a comrade or a stranger, he salutes with the secret sign in the half salute.

He always salutes an officer — that is, a patrol leader, or a scoutmaster, or any commissioned officer of His Majesty's forces, army and navy — with the full salute.

Also the hoisting of the Union Jack, the colors of a regiment, the playing of " God Save the King," and any funeral.

A scout who has the " Silver Wolf " honor is entitled to make the sign with the first finger and thumb opened out, the remaining fingers clenched, thumb upwards. This is a sign with the Indians of America.

A man told me the other day that " he was an Englishman, and just as good as anybody else, and he was blowed if ever he would raise a finger to salute his so-called ' betters '; he wasn't going to be a slave and kow-tow to them, not he! " and so on. That is a churlish spirit, which is very common among boys who have not been brought up as scouts.

I didn't argue with him, but I might have told him that he had got hold of the wrong idea about saluting.

A salute is merely a sign between men of standing. It is a privilege to be able to salute any one.

In the old days the freemen of England all were allowed to carry weapons, and when they met each other each would hold up his right hand to show that he had no weapon in it, and that they met as friends. So, also, when an armed man met a defence-less person or a lady.

Slaves or serfs were not allowed to carry weapons, and so had to slink past the freemen without making any sign.

Nowadays people do not carry weapons; but those who would have been entitled to do so, such as knights, esquires, and men-at-arms, that is, those living on their own property or earning their own living, still go through the form of saluting each

other by holding up their hand to their cap, or even taking it off.

" Wasters " are not entitled to salute, and so should slink by, as they generally do, without taking notice of the freemen or wage-earners.

To salute merely shows that you are the right sort of a boy and mean well to the others; there is nothing slavish about it.

If a stranger makes the scout's sign to you, you should acknowledge it at once by making the sign back to him, and then shake hands with the LEFT HAND.   If he then shows his scout's badge, or proves that he is a scout, you must treat him as a brother-scout, and help him in any way you can.

SCOUTS' WAR SONGS

1. *The Scouts' Chorus*.

To be shouted on the march, or as applause at games, meetings, etc.   Must be sung exactly in time.

Leader: Een gonyâma — gonyâma.

Chorus: Invooboo.
Yah bô!   Yah bô!
Invooboo.

The meaning is —

Leader: " He is a lion ! "

Chorus: " Yes! he is better than that; he is a hippo-potamus ! "

Een - gon - yâm - a   Gon - yâm - a;   In - voo - boo!

Ya - Boh!   Ya - Boh!   In - voo - boo. . . .

2. *The Scouts' Rally.*

To be shouted as a salute, or in a game, or at any time.

Leader: Be prepared!

Chorus: Zing-a-Zing!
Bom! Bom!

(Stamp or bang something at the " Bom! Bom! ")

CHORUS.

SOLO (*Leader*).

Be   pre - pared.   Zing - a - zing! Bom! Bom!

3. *The Scouts' Call.*

For scoutmaster to call together his troop by bugle; or for scout
to whistle to attract attention of another scout.

NOTE TO INSTRUCTORS

*Although the war dance and songs may seem at first sight to
be gibberish — especially to those who have never had much to do
with boys — yet there is a certain value underlying them as a
corrective of self-consciousness.*

*If you want, for instance, to get discipline among your boys
it means their constantly bottling up some energy that requires
an occasional vent or safety-valve. A war dance supplies such
vent, but still in a certain disciplined way.*

*Also it forms an attraction to wilder spirits who would never
join a band of quieter boys.*

*Mr. Tomlin, " the hooligan tamer," catches and gets his boys in
hand entirely by the force of energetic singing and action in chorus.*

*Most schools and colleges have their " Ra-ra-ra " choruses,
of which " Zing-a-zing: bom, bom " is a type.*

*The war dance or any kind of dance is of great value in giving
the boys exercise in a confined space, and also in developing their
activity and command of their feet, and in getting rid of awkward
self-consciousness.*

Patrol Signs

Each troop is named after the place to which it belongs. Each patrol in that troop is named after an animal or bird. Thus the 33rd London Troop may have five patrols which are respectively the Wolves, the Ravens, the Curlews, the Bulls, the Owls.

Each scout in a patrol has his regular number, his patrol leader being No. 1, the corporal No. 2, and the scouts have the consecutive numbers after these. Scouts usually work in pairs as comrades, Nos. 3 and 4 together, Nos. 5 and 6 together, and Nos. 7 and 8.

A white shoulder-knot is worn by officers and umpires at games.

Each scout in the patrol has to be able to make the call of his patrol-animal — thus every scout in the "Ravens" must be

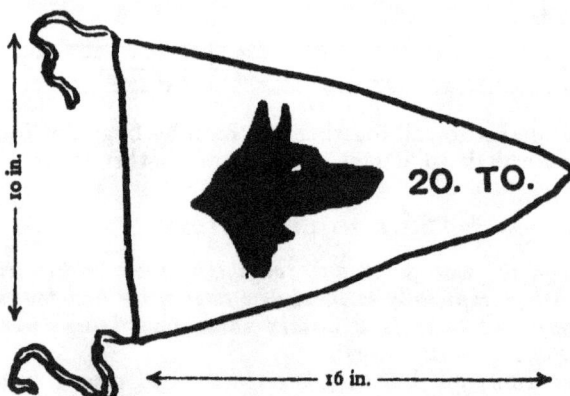

PATROL LEADER'S FLAG OF "THE WOLVES PATROL,"
20TH TORONTO TROOP.

able to imitate the croak of the raven. This is the sign by which scouts of a patrol can communicate with each other when hiding or at night. No scout is allowed to imitate the call of any patrol except his own. The patrol leader calls up the patrol at any time by sounding his whistle and uttering the call of the patrol.

Also, when a scout makes signs on the ground for others to read he also draws the head of the patrol animal. Thus, if he wants to show that a certain road should not be followed, he draws the sign across it, "Not to be followed," and adds the head of his patrol animal to show which patrol discovered that the road was no good, and his own number to the left of the head to show which scout discovered it, thus: —

Each patrol leader has a small white flag on his staff with the head of his patrol animal shown in red cloth stitched on to it on both sides. Thus the "Wolves" of the 20th Toronto Troop would have the flag shown above.

All these signs scouts must be able to draw according to the patrol to which they belong.

[*Practise with chalk on floors or walls, or with a stick on sand or mud.*]

Scout signs on the ground or wall, etc., close to the right-hand side of the road.

Road to be followed.

Letter hidden three paces from here in the direction of the arrow.

This path not to be followed.

"I have gone home."

(Signed) Patrol Leader of the Ravens, Fifteenth London Troop.

At night sticks with a wisp of grass round them or stones should be laid on the road in similar forms so that they can be felt with the hand.

[*Practise this.*]

INDIAN SIGNS AND BLAZES

From "The Boy Scouts of America" by Ernest Thompson Seton and Sir Robert Baden-Powell. Price 25 cents. Doubleday, Page & Company, New York.

INDIAN SIGNS AND BLAZES

Shaking a blanket, I want to talk to you.
Hold up a tree-branch, I want to make peace.
Hold up a weapon, means war; I am ready to fight.
Hold up a pole horizontally, with hands on it, I have found something.

This is good water.

Good water not far in this direction.

A long way to good water, go in direction of arrow.

Peace.

War or trouble about.

We camped here because one of us was sick.

Road to be followed.

Letter hidden three paces from here in the direction of the arrow.

This path not to be followed.

" I have gone home."

INDIAN SIGNS

Signs in Stones

This is the Trail   Turn to the Right   Turn to the Left   Important - Warning.

Signs in Twigs

This is the Trail   Turn to the Right   Turn to the Left   Important - Warning.

Signs in Grass

This is the Trail   Turn to the Right   Turn to the Left   Important - Warning.

Signs in Blazes

This is the Trail   Turn to the Right   Turn to the Left   Important - Warning.

Code for Smoke Signals

Camp is Here   I am lost. Help!   Good News   All come to Council

Some Special Blazes used by Hunters & Surveyors

A Trap to Right   A Trap to Left   Camp is to Right   Camp is to Left   Special   Adirondack Special   Surveyor's Line Here

MONGOOSE
Squeak —"Cheep"
BROWN AND ORANGE

HAWK
Cry —(same as Eagle)
—"Kreeee" PINK

WOLF
Howl — "How-oooo"
YELLOW AND BLACK

PEEWIT
Whistle —"Tewitt"
GREEN AND WHITE

HOUND
Bark —"Bawow-wow"
ORANGE

CAT
Cry —"Meeaow"
GRAY AND BROWN

JACKAL
Laughing Cry —"Wah-
wah-wah-wah-wah"
GRAY AND BLACK

RAVEN
Cry —"Kar-kar
BLACK

BUFFALO
Lowing — (same as Bull)
"Um-maouw"
RED AND WHITE

PEACOCK
Cry —"Bee-oik"
GREEN AND BLUE

BULL
Lowing —"Um-maouw"
RED

SEAL
Call —"Hark"
RED AND BLACK

OWL
Whistle —"Koot-koot-koot"
BLUE

TIGER
Purr —"Grrao"
VIOLET

LION
Call —"Eu-ugh"
YELLOW AND RED

KANGAROO
Call —"Coo-ee"
RED AND GRAY

HORSE
Whinney —"Hee-a-e-e"
BLACK AND WHITE

FOX
Bark — " Ha-ha "
YELLOW AND GREEN

BEAR
Growl — " Boorrr "
BROWN AND BLACK

STAG
Roar — " Baow "
VIOLET AND BLACK

STORK
Cry — " Korrr "
BLUE AND WHITE

PANTHER
Tongue in side of mouth —
" Keeook "
YELLOW

CURLEW
Whistle — " Curley "
GREEN

HYENA
Laughing Cry —
" Ooowah-oowah-wah "
YELLOW AND WHITE

RAM
Bleat — " Ba-a-a "
BROWN

WOOD PIGEON
Call — " Book-hooroo "
BLUE AND GRAY

EAGLE
Very Shrill Whistle — " Kreeee "
GREEN AND BLACK

HIPPO.
Hiss — " Brrussssh "
PINK AND BLACK

RATTLESNAKE
Rattle a pebble in a small
potted meat tin
PINK AND WHITE

WILD BOAR
Grunt — " Broof-broof "
GRAY AND PINK

BOBRA
Hiss — " Pssst "
ORANGE AND BLACK

CUCKOO
Call — " Cook-koo "
GRAY

OTTER
Cry — " Hoi-oi-oick "
BROWN AND WHITE

BEAVER
Slap made by clapping
hands
BLUE AND YELLOW

CAMP FIRE YARN. No. 4

Scout Law

Scouts, all the world over, have unwritten laws which bind them just as much as if they had been printed in black and white.

They come down to us from old times.

The Japanese have their Bushido, or laws of the old Samurai warriors, just as we have chivalry or rules of the knights of the Middle Ages. The Indians in America have their laws of honor; the Zulus, the natives of India, the European nations, — all have their ancient codes.

The following are the rules which apply to boy scouts, and which you swear to obey when you take your oath as a scout, so it is as well that you should know all about them.

The scouts' motto is:—

Be Prepared,

which means you are always to be in a state of readiness in mind and body to do your DUTY.

Be Prepared in mind by having disciplined yourself to be obedient to every order, and also by having thought out before-hand any accident or situation that might occur, so that you *know* the right thing to do at the right moment, and are willing to do it.

Be Prepared in body by making yourself strong and active and *able* to do the right thing at the right moment, and do it.

The Scout Law

1. A Scout's Honor is to be Trusted.

    If a scout says " On my honor it is so," that means that it *is* so, just as if he had taken a most solemn oath.

    Similarly, if a scout officer says to a scout, " I trust you on your honor to do this," the scout is bound to carry out the order to the very best of his ability, and to let nothing interfere with his doing so.

    If a scout were to break his honor by telling a lie, or by not carrying out an order exactly, when trusted on his honor to do so, he may be directed to hand over his scout badge, and never to wear it again. He may also be directed to cease to be a scout.

2. A SCOUT IS LOYAL to the King, and to his officers, and to his parents, his country, and his employers. He must stick to them through thick and thin against any one who is their enemy or who even talks badly of them.

3. A SCOUT'S DUTY IS TO BE USEFUL AND TO HELP OTHERS. And he is to do his duty before anything else, even though he gives up his own pleasure, or comfort, or safety to do it. When in difficulty to know which of two things to do, he must ask himself, " Which is my duty? " that is, " Which is best for other people? " — and do that one. He must BE PREPARED at any time to save life, or to help injured persons. And *he must try his best to do a good turn* to somebody every day.

4. A SCOUT IS A FRIEND TO ALL, AND A BROTHER TO EVERY OTHER SCOUT, NO MATTER TO WHAT SOCIAL CLASS THE OTHER BELONGS.

   Thus, if a scout meets another scout, even though a stranger to him, he must speak to him, and help him in any way that he can, either to carry out the duty he is then doing, or by giving him food, or, as far as possible, anything that he may be in want of. A scout must never be a SNOB. A snob is one who looks down upon another because he is poorer, or who is poor and resents another because he is rich. A scout accepts the other man as he finds him, and makes the best of him.

   " Kim," the boy scout, was called by the Indians " Little friend of all the world," and that is the name that every scout should earn for himself.

5. A SCOUT IS COURTEOUS: That is, he is polite to all — but especially to women and children, and old people and invalids, cripples, etc. And he must not take any reward for being helpful or courteous.

6. A SCOUT IS A FRIEND TO ANIMALS. He should save them, as far as possible, from pain, and should not kill any animal unnecessarily, for it is one of God's creatures. Killing an animal for food is allowable.

7. A SCOUT OBEYS ORDERS — of his parents, patrol leader, or scoutmaster without question.

   Even if he gets an order he does not like he must do as soldiers and sailors do, he must carry it out all the same *because it is his duty;* and after he has done it he can come and state any reasons against it; but he must carry out the order at once. That is discipline.

8. A Scout Smiles and Whistles under all circumstances. When he gets an order he should obey it cheerily and readily, not in a slow, hang-dog sort of way.

Scouts never grouse at hardships, nor whine at each other, nor swear when put out.

When you just miss a train, or some one treads on your favorite corn — not that a scout ought to have such things as corns — or under any annoying circumstances, you should force yourself to smile at once, and then whistle a tune, and you will be all right. (N.B. — Since this rule first appeared in print a great many scouts, old and young, have written to me saying how useful it has been to them.)

A scout goes about with a smile on and whistling. It cheers him and cheers other people, especially in time of danger, for he keeps it up then all the same.

The punishment for swearing or using bad language is for each offence a mug of cold water to be poured down the offender's sleeve by the other scouts. It was the punishment invented by the old British scout, Captain John Smith, three hundred years ago.

9. A Scout is Thrifty, that is, he saves every cent he can, and puts it into the bank, so that he may have money to keep himself when out of work, and thus not make himself a burden to others; or that he may have money to give away to others when they need it.

SCOUT GAMES

Scout Meets Scout

IN TOWN OR COUNTRY

Single scouts, or complete patrols or pairs of scouts, to be taken out about two miles apart, and made to work towards each other, either alongside a road, or by giving each side a landmark to work to, such as a steep hill or big tree, which is directly behind the other party, and will thus insure their coming together. The patrol which first sees the other wins. This is signified by the patrol leader holding up his patrol flag for the umpire to see, and sounding his whistle. A patrol need not keep together, but that patrol wins which first holds out its flag, so it is well for the scouts to be in touch with their patrol leaders by signal, voice, or message.

Scouts may employ any ruse they like, such as climbing into

trees, hiding in carts, etc., but they must not dress up in disguise unless specially permitted.

This game may also be practised at night.

Despatch Runners

A scout is sent out to take note of some well-known spot, say, the post-office in a neighboring town or district. He will there get the note stamped with the postmark of the office and return. The rest of the scouts are posted by their leader to prevent him getting there by watching all the roads and likely paths by which he can come, but none may be nearer to the post-office than two hundred yards. The despatch runner is allowed to use any disguise and any method of travelling that he can hit upon.

In the country the game may similarly be played, the scout being directed to go to a certain house or other specified spot.

Kim's Game

Place about twenty or thirty small articles on a tray, or on the table or floor, such as two or three different kinds of buttons, pencils, corks, rags, nuts, stones, knives, string, photographs — anything you can find — and cover them over with a cloth or coat.

Make a list of these, and make a column opposite the list for each boy's replies. Like this:

List	Jones	Brown	Smith	Atkins	Green	Long
Walnut . . .						
Button . . .						
Black button .						
Red rag						
Yellow rag . .						
Black rag . .						
Knife . . .						
Red pencil . .						
Black Pencil .						
Cork						
String knot . .						
Plain string .						
Blue bead . .						

Then uncover the articles for one minute by your watch, or while you count sixty at the rate of "quick march." Then cover them over again.

Take each boy separately and let him whisper to you each of the articles that he can remember, and mark it off on your scoring sheet.

The boy who remembers the greatest number wins the game.

Morgan's Game

(Played by the 21st Dublin Co. Boys' Brigade.)

Scouts are ordered to run to a certain hoarding where an umpire is already posted to time them. They are each allowed to look at this for one minute, and then to run back to headquarters and report to the instructor all that was on the hoarding in the way of advertisements.

Debates, Trials, Etc.

A good exercise for a winter's evening in the clubroom is to hold a debate on any subject of topical interest, the instructor acting as chairman. He will see that there is a speaker on one side prepared beforehand to introduce and support one view of the subject, and that there is another speaker prepared to expound another view. After hearing them, he will call on the others present, in turn, to express their views. And in the end he takes the votes for and against the motion.

At first boys will be very shy of speaking unless the subject selected by the instructor is one which really interests them and takes them out of themselves.

After a debate or two they get greater confidence and are able to express themselves coherently and also pick up the proper procedure for public meetings, such as seconding the motion, moving amendments, obeying chairman's ruling, voting, according votes of thanks to chair, etc.

In place of a debate a mock trial may be of interest as a change.

For instance, the story of the murder given on page 20 might form the subject of trial.

The instructor would appoint himself to act the judge, and detail boys to the following parts: —

Prisoner . . William Winter.
Witness . . Boy, Robert Hindmarsh.
    ,, . . Police Constable.
    ,, . . Villager.
    ,, . . Old woman (friend of the murdered woman).
Counsel for prisoner.
    ,,   ,, prosecution.
Foreman and jury (if there are enough scouts).

Follow, as nearly as possible, the procedure of a court of law
Let each make up his own evidence, speeches, or cross examination according to his own notions and imagination, the evidence
to be made up on the lines of the story, but in greater detail
Do not necessarily find the prisoner guilty unless the prosecution
prove their case to the jury.

In your summing up bring out the fact of the boy (Hindmarsh)
having carried out each part of the duty of a scout, in order to
bring home its lesson to the boys.

Unprepared Plays

Give the plot of a short, simple play, and assign to each player
his part, with an outline of what he has to do and say.

And then let them act it, making up the required conversation
as they go along.

This develops the power of imagination and expression on
points kept in the mind, and is a valuable means of education.

It is well before starting to act a play in this way to be a little
less ambitious, and to make two or three players merely carry
out a conversation on a given topic leading up to a given point,
using their own words and imagination in doing so.

Scouts' War Dance

Scouts form up in one line with leader in front, each holding
his staff in the right hand, and his left on the next man's shoulder.

Leader sings the Eengonyama song. Scouts sing chorus, and
advance to their front a few steps at a time, stamping in unison
on the long notes.

At the second time of singing they step backwards.

At the third, they turn to the left, still holding each other's
shoulders, and move round in a large circle, repeating the chorus
until they have completed the circle.

They then form into a wide circle, into the centre of which one steps forwards and carries out a war dance, representing how he tracked and fought with one of his enemies. He goes through the whole fight in dumb show, until he finally kills his foe; the scouts, meantime, still singing the Eengonyama chorus and dancing on their own ground. So soon as he finishes the fight, the leader starts the " Be Prepared " chorus, which they repeat three times in honor of the scout who has just danced.

Then they re-commence the Eengonyama chorus, and another scout steps into the ring, and describes in dumb show how he stalked and killed a wild buffalo. While he does the creeping up and stalking the animal, the scouts all crouch and sing their chorus very softly, and as he gets more into the light with the beast, they simultaneously spring up and dance and shout the chorus loudly. When he has slain the beast, the leader again gives the " Be Prepared" chorus in his honor, which is repeated three times, the scouts banging their staffs on the ground at the same time as they stamp " Bom ! bom ! "

At the end of the third repetition, " Bom ! bom ! " is repeated the second time.

The circle then close together, turn to their left again, grasping shoulders with the left hand, and move off, singing the Eengonyama chorus, or, if it is not desired to move away, they break up after the final " Bom ! bom ! "

The Eengonyama song should be sung in a spirited way, and not droned out dismally like a dirge.

FOR WINTER IN THE COUNTRY

Arctic Expedition

Each patrol makes a bob-sleigh with ropes, harness, for two of their number to pull (or for dogs if they have them, and can train them to the work). Two scouts go a mile or so ahead, the remainder with the sleigh follow, finding the way by means of the spoor, and by such signs as the leading scouts may draw in the snow. All other drawings seen on the way are to be examined, noted, and their meaning read. The sleigh carries rations and cooking-pots, etc.

Build snow huts. These must be made narrow, according to the length of sticks available for forming the roof, which can be made with brushwood, and covered with snow.

Snow Fort

The snow fort may be built by one patrol according to their own ideas of fortification, with loop-holes, etc., for looking out. When finished it will be attacked by hostile patrols, using snowballs as ammunition. Every scout struck by a snowball is counted dead. The attackers should, as a rule, number at least twice the strength of the defenders.

Siberian Man Hunt

One scout as fugitive runs away across the snow in any direction he may please, until he finds a good hiding-place, and there conceals himself. The remainder, after giving him twenty minutes' start or more, proceed to follow him by his tracks. As they approach his hiding-place, he shoots at them with snowballs, and every one that is struck must fall out dead. The fugitive must be struck three times before he is counted dead.

In Towns

Scouts can be very useful in snowy weather by working as a patrol under their leader in clearing away the snow from pavements, houses, etc. This they may either do as a " good turn," or accept money to be devoted to their funds.

CHAPTER II

CAMPAIGNING

CAMP FIRE YARN. No. 5

LIFE IN THE OPEN

On the Veldt — Exploration — Boat Cruising — Weather Wisdom — Mountaineering — Patrolling — Night Work — Finding the North.

THE native boys of the Zulu and Swazi tribes in South Africa learn to be scouts before they are allowed to be considered men, and they do it in this way: When a boy is about fifteen or sixteen he is taken by the men of his village, stripped of all clothes, and painted white from head to foot, and he is given a shield and one assegai or small spear, and he is turned out of the village and told that he will be killed if any one catches him while he is still painted white. So the boy has to go off into the jungle and mountains and hide himself from other men until the white paint wears off, and this generally takes about a month; so that all this time he has to look after himself and stalk game with his one assegai, and kill it and cut it up; he has to light his fire by means of rubbing sticks together, in order to cook his meat; he has to make the skin of the animal into a covering for himself; and he has to know what kind of wild roots, berries, and leaves are good for food as vegetables. If he is not able to do these things he dies of starvation, or is killed by wild animals. If he succeeds in keeping himself alive, and is able to find his way back to his village, he returns when the white paint has worn off, and is then received with great rejoicings by his friends and relations, and is allowed to become a soldier of the tribe, since he has shown that he is able to look after himself.

And in South America the boys of the Yaghan tribe — down

in the cold, rainy regions of Patagonia— wear no clothes, and before they are allowed to consider themselves men they have to undergo a test of pluck, which consists in the boy driving a spear deep into his thigh and smiling all the time in spite of the pain.

It is a cruel test, but it shows that these savages understand how necessary it is that boys should be trained to manliness and not be allowed to drift into being poor-spirited wasters who can only look on at men's work.

The ancient British boys used to have the same kind of training before they were allowed to be considered men, and the training which we are now doing as scouts is intended to fill that want as far as possible. If every boy works hard at this course and really learns all that we try to teach him, he will, at the end of it, have some claim to call himself a scout and a man, and will find, if ever he goes on service, that he will have no difficulty in looking after himself and in being really useful to his country.

There is an old Canadian scout and trapper, now over eighty years of age, still living, and, what is more, still working at his trade of trapping. His name is Bill Hamilton. In a book which he lately wrote, called " My Sixty Years in the Plains," he describes the dangers of that adventurous line of life. The chief danger was that of falling into the hands of the Indians. " To be taken prisoner was to experience a death not at all to be desired. A slow fire is merciful beside other cruelties practised by the Indians. I have often been asked why we exposed ourselves to such danger. My answer has always been that there is a charm in the open-air life of a scout from which one cannot free himself after he has once come under its spell. Give me the man who has been raised among the great things of nature; he cultivates truth, independence, and self-reliance; he has generous impulses; he is true to his friends, and true to the flag of his country."

I can fully endorse what this old scout has said, and, what is more, I find that those men who come from the farthest frontiers of the Empire—from what we should call a rude and savage life — are among the most generous and chivalrous of their race, especially towards women and weaker folk. They become " gentle men " by their contact with nature.

Mr. Roosevelt, the ex-President of the United States of America, also is one who believes in outdoor life. When returning from his hunting trip in East Africa he inspected some boy scouts in London, and expressed great admiration for them. He writes: —

" I believe in outdoor games, and I do not mind in the least that they are rough games, or that those who take part in them are occasionally injured. I have no sympathy with the over-wrought sentiment which would keep a young man in cotton-wool. The out-of-doors man must always prove the better in life's contest. When you play, play hard; and when you work, work hard. But do not let your play and your sport interfere with your study."

I knew an old Boer who, after the war, said that he could not live in the country with the British, because when they arrived in the country they were so " stom," as he called it — *i.e.*, so utterly stupid when living on the veldt, that they did not know how to look after themselves, to make themselves comfortable in camp, to kill their food or to cook it, and they were always losing their way on the veldt; he admitted that after six months or so the English soldiers got to learn how to manage for them-selves fairly well if they lived so long, but that they often died, and they generally died through blundering about at the business end of the mule.

The truth is that, being brought up in a civilized country like England, soldiers and others have no training whatever in looking after themselves out on the veldt, or in the backwoods, and the consequence is that when they go to a new country or on a campaign they are, for a long time, perfectly helpless, and go through a lot of hardship and trouble which would not occur had they learnt, while boys, how to look after themselves both in camp and when on patrol. They are just a lot of tenderfoots.

They have never had to light a fire or to cook their own food: that has always been done for them. At home, if they wanted water they merely had to turn on the tap, and had no idea of how to set about finding water in a desert place by looking at the grass, or bush, or by scratching at the sand till they began to find signs of dampness; and if they lost their way, or did not know the time, they merely had to "ask a policeman." They had always found houses to shelter them, and beds to lie in. They had never to manufacture these for themselves, nor to make their own boots or clothing. That is why a tenderfoot talks of " roughing it in camp " ; but living in camp for a scout who knows the game is by no means " roughing it." He knows how to make himself comfortable in a thousand small ways, and then, when he does come back to civilization, he enjoys it all the more for having seen a contrast; and even there he can do very much more for himself than the ordinary mortal, who has never really learned to provide for his own wants. The man who has had to turn his hand to many things, as the scout does in camp, finds that when he comes into civilization he is more easily able to obtain employment, because he is ready to turn his hand to whatever kind of work may turn up.

Exploration

A good form of scout work can be had by scouts going about either as patrols on an exploring expedition, or in pairs, like knight-errants of old, on a pilgrimage through the country to find people needing help and to help them. This can equally well be done with bicycles, or in the winter by skating along the rivers.

Scouts in carrying out such a tramp should never, if possible, sleep under a roof — that is to say, on fine nights they would sleep in the open wherever they may be; or, in bad weather, would get leave to occupy a hay loft or barn.

You should on all occasions take a map with you, and find your way by it, as far as possible, without having to ask the way of passers-by. You would, of course, have to do your daily good turn whenever opportunity presented itself, but besides that, you should do good turns to farmers and others who may allow you the use of their barns, and so on, as a return for their kindness.

As a rule you should have some object in your expedition; that is to say, if you are a patrol of town boys, you would go off with the idea of scouting some special spot, say a particular lake, creek, or mountain, battlefield or beach. Or you may be on your way to join one of the larger camps.

If, on the other hand, you are a patrol from the country, you can make your way up to Ottawa, or to a large city or town, with the idea of going to see its buildings, and its zoölogical gardens, circuses, museums, etc. And you should notice everything as you go along the roads, and remember, as far as possible, all your journey, so that you could give directions to anybody else who wanted to follow that road afterwards. And make a map. Explorers, of course, keep a log or journal, giving a short account of each day's journey, with sketches or photographs of any interesting things they see.

Boat Cruising

Instead of tramping or cycling, it is also an excellent practice for a patrol to take a boat and make a trip in that way through the country; but no one should be allowed in the boat who is not a good swimmer, because accidents are pretty sure to happen, and if all are swimmers it does not matter — in fact, it is rather a good experience than otherwise.

I once made such a cruise with two of my brothers. We took a small folding-up canvas boat, and went as far up the Thames as we could possibly get, till it became so narrow and small a stream that we were continually having to get out and pull our boat over fallen trees and stopped-up bits of river. Then we took the boat on the Avon, which rises near the source of the Thames, but flows to the westward, and here, again, we began where the river was very small, and gradually worked our way down until it developed into a big stream, and so through Bath and Bristol on to the Severn. Then across the Severn and up the Wve into Wales. We carried with us our tent, stores, and cooking apparatus, so that we were able to live out, independent of houses, the whole time. A rare enjoyable trip could not be imagined, and the expense was very small.

Mountaineering

A good deal of interesting mountaineering can be done if you know where to go, and it is grand sport, and brings into practice all your scoutcraft to enable you to find your way, and to make yourself comfortable in camp.

You are, of course, continually losing your direction, because, moving up and down in the deep gullies of the mountainside, you lose sight of the landmarks which usually guide you, so that you have to watch your direction by the sun and by your compass, and keep on estimating in what direction your proper line of travel lies.

Then, again, you are very liable to be caught in fogs and mists, which are at all times upsetting to the calculations even of men who know every inch of the country. I had such an experience in Scotland one year, when, in company with a Highlander who knew the ground, we got lost in the mist. But, supposing that he knew the way, I committed myself entirely to his guidance, and after going some distance I felt bound to remark to him that I noticed the wind had suddenly changed, for it had been blowing from our left when we started, and was now blowing hard on our right cheek. However, he seemed in no way nonplussed, and led on. Presently I remarked that the wind was blowing behind us, so that either the wind, or the mountain, or we ourselves were turning round. And eventually it proved as I suggested, that it was not the wind that had turned, or the mountain; it was ourselves who had wandered round in a complete circle, and were almost back at the point we started from within an hour.

The scouts working on a mountain ought to practise the art of roping themselves together, as mountaineers do on icy slopes to save themselves from falling into holes in the snow and slipping down precipices. When roped together in this way, supposing that one man falls, the weight of the others will save him from going down into the depths.

When roped together, each man has about 14 feet between himself and the next man. The rope is fastened round his waist by a loop or bowline, the knot being on his left side. Each man has to keep back of the man in front of him, so as to keep the rope tight all the time; then if one falls or slips the others lean away from him with all their weight, and hold him up till he regains his footing. A loop takes up about 4 ft. 6 in. of rope, and should be a " bowline " at the ends of the rope, and an "overhand knot " or a " middleman's loop " for central men on the rope.

Patrolling

Scouts generally go about scouting in pairs, or sometimes singly; if more go together, they are called a patrol. When they are patrolling, the scouts of a patrol hardly ever move close together; they are spread out so as to see more country, and so that if cut off or ambuscaded by an enemy, they will not all get caught, some will get away to give information. A patrol of six scouts

PATROL IN THE OPEN

working in open country would usually move in this sort of formation, in the shape of a kite, with the patrol leader in the centre; if going along a street or road the patrol would move in a similar way, the flank scouts keeping close to the hedges or walls. No. 2 scout is in front, Nos. 3 and 4 to the right and left, No. 5 to the rear, and No. 6 with the leader (No. 1) in the centre.

Patrols when going across open country where they are likely to be seen by enemies or animals should get over it as quickly as possible, *i.e.*, by moving at the scout's pace, walking and running alternately from one point of cover to another. As soon as they are hidden in cover they can rest and look round before making the next move. If as leading scout you get out of sight of your patrol, you should, in passing thick bushes, reeds, etc., break branches or stems of reeds and grass every few yards, making the heads point *forwards* to show your path, for in this way you can always find your way back again, or the patrol or any one coming after you can easily follow you up, and they can judge,

PATROL ON A ROAD OR STREET

from the freshness of the grass, pretty well how long ago it was you passed that way. It is always useful to " blaze " trees — that means take a chip out of the bark with your axe or knife, or chalk marks upon walls, or make marks in the sand, or lay stones, or show which way you have gone by the signs which I have given you.

When a troop is marching as a body along a road it is well to "divide the road." That is, for the scouts to move in a single file along each side of the road. In this way they don't suffer from dust; and they don't interfere with the traffic.

Night Work

Scouts must be able to find their way equally well by night as by day. In fact, military scouts in the army work mostly by night, in order to keep hidden, and lie up during the day.

But unless they practise it frequently, boys are very apt to lose themselves by night, distances seem greater, and landmarks are hard to see. Also you are apt to make more noise than by day, in walking along, by accidentally treading on dry sticks, kicking stones, etc.

If you are watching for an enemy at night, you have to trust much more to your ears than to your eyes, and also to your nose, for a scout who is well practised at smelling out things, and who has not damaged his sense of smell by smoking, can often smell an enemy a good distance away. I have done it many times myself, and found it of the greatest value.

When patrolling at night, scouts keep closer together than by day, and in very dark places, such as woods, etc., they should keep touch with each other by each catching hold of the end of the next scout's staff.

When working singly the scout's staff is most useful for feeling the way in the dark, and pushing aside dry branches, etc.

Scouts working apart from each other in the dark keep up communication by occasionally giving tne call of their patrol-animal. An enemy would thus not be made suspicious.

All scouts have to guide themselves very much by the stars at night.

Finding the Way

Among the Indian scouts in America the man who was good at finding his way in a strange country was termed a " Pathfinder," which was with them a name of great honor, because a scout who cannot find his way is of very little use.

Many a tenderfoot has got lost on the prairie or in the forest, and has never been seen again, through not having learned a little scouting, or what is called " eye for a country," when a boy. I have known many instances of it myself.

In one case a man got off a coach, which was driving through the bush in Matabeleland, for a few minutes, while the mules were being changed. He apparently walked off a few yards into the bush, and when the coach was ready to start they called for him in every direction, and searched for him, but were unable to find him; and at last, the coach, being unable to wait any longer, pursued its journey, leaving word for the lost man to be sought for. Full search was made for him; his tracks were followed as far as they could be, in the very difficult soil of that country, but he was not found for weeks afterwards, and then his dead body was discovered nearly fifteen miles away from where he started, and close to the road.

It oftens happens that when you are tramping along alone through the bush, or even in a town, you become careless in noticing what direction you are moving in; that is, you frequently change it to get round a fallen tree, or some rocks, or some other obstacle, and having passed it, you do not take up exactly the correct direction again, and a man's inclination somehow is to keep edging to his right, and the consequence is that when you think you are going straight, you are really not doing so at all; and unless you watch the sun, or your compass, or your landmarks, you are very apt to find yourself going round in a big circle after a short time.

In such a case a tenderfoot, when he suddenly finds himself out of his bearings, and lost alone in the desert or forest, at once loses his head and gets excited, and probably begins to run, when the right thing to do is to force himself to keep cool and give himself something useful to do — that is, to track his own spoor back again; or, if he fails, start getting firewood for making signal fires to direct those who are looking for him.

The main point is not to get lost in the first instance.

Every old scout on first turning out in the morning notices which way the wind.is blowing.

When you start out for a walk or on patrol, you should notice which direction, by the compass, you start in, and also notice which direction the wind is blowing, as that would be a great help to you in keeping your direction, especially if you have not got a compass, or if the sun is not shining.

Then you should notice all landmarks for finding your way, that is, in the country notice any hills or prominent towers, steeples, curious trees, rocks, gates, mounds, bridges, and so on; any points, in fact, by which you could find your way back again, or by which you could instruct any one to go the same line which you have gone. If you notice your landmarks going out, you can always find your way back by them, but you should take care occasionally to look back at them after passing them, so that you get to know their appearance for your return journey. The same holds good when you are in a town, or when you arrive in a new town by train; the moment you step out from the station notice where the sun is, or which way the smoke is blowing. Also notice your landmarks, which would be prominent buildings, churches, factory chimneys, names of streets and shops, etc., so that when you have gone down numerous streets you can turn round and find your way back again to the station without any difficulty. It is wonderfully easy when you have practised it a little, yet many people get lost when they have turned a few corners in a town which they do not know.

The way to find which way the wind is blowing if there is only very light air is to throw up little bits of dry grass, or to hold up a handful of light dust and let it fall, or to suck your thumb and wet it all round and let the wind blow on it, and the cold side of it will then tell you which way the wind is blowing.   When you are acting as scout to find the way for a party, you should move ahead of them and fix your whole attention on what you are doing, because you have to go by the very smallest signs, and if you get talking and thinking of other things you are very apt to miss them. Old scouts are generally very silent people, from having got into this habit of fixing their attention on the work in hand. Very often you see a tenderfoot, out for the first time, thinking that the leading scout looks lonely, go and walk or ride alongside of him and begin a conversation, until the scout shows him by his manner, or otherwise, that he does not particularly want him there. On steamers you sometimes see a notice, "Don't speak to the man at the wheel," and the same thing applies with a scout who is guiding a party. When acting as scout you must keep all your thoughts on the one subject, as Kim did when Lurgan tried to mesmerize him.

Weather Wisdom

WEATHER. — Every scout ought to be able to read signs of the weather, especially when going mountaineering or cruising, and to read a barometer.

He should remember the following points: —

Red at night, shepherd's delight (*i.e.*, fine day coming).
Red in morning is the shepherd's warning (*i.e.*, rain).
Yellow sunset means wind.
Pale yellow sunset means rain.
Dew and fog in early morning mean fine weather.
Clear distant view means rain coming or just past.
Red dawn means fine weather — so does low dawn.
High dawn is when sun rises over a bank of clouds; high above the horizon means wind.
Soft clouds, fine weather.
Hard-edged clouds, wind.
Rolled or jagged, strong wind.

> "When the wind's before the rain,
> Soon you may make sail again;
> When the rain's before the wind,
> Then your sheets and halyards mind."

Finding the North

Every sailor boy knows the points of the compass by heart, and so should a scout. I have talked a good deal about the north, and you will understand that it is a most important help to a scout in pathfinding to know the direction of the north.

If you have not a compass, the sun will tell you by day where the north is, and the moon and the stars by night.

At six o'clock in the morning the sun is due east, at nine o'clock he is south-east, at noon he is south, at three o'clock in the afternoon he is south-west, and at six o'clock he is due west. In winter he will have set long before six o'clock, but he will not have reached due west when he is set.

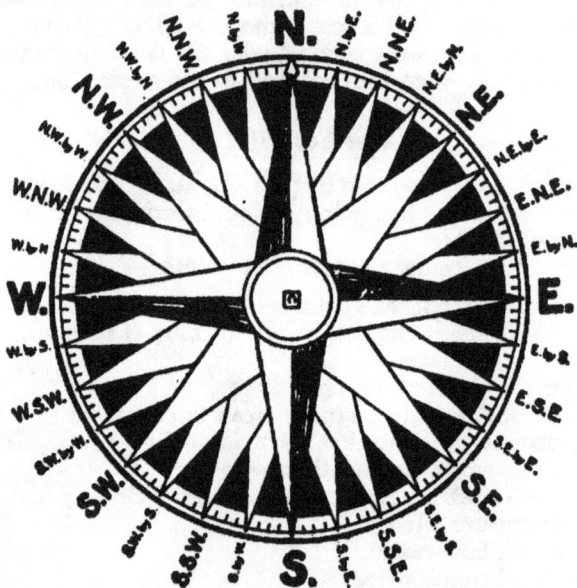

The Phœnicians who sailed round Africa in ancient times noticed that when they started the sun rose on their left-hand side — they were going south. Then they reported that they got to a strange country where the sun got up in the wrong quarter, namely, on their right hand. The truth was that they had gone round the Cape of Good Hope and were steering north again up the east side of Africa.

To find the south at any time of day by the sun — hold your watch flat, face upwards, so that the sun shines on it. Turn it round till the hour hand points at the sun. Then, without moving the watch, lay the edge of a piece of paper or a pencil across the face of the watch so that it rests on the centre of the dial and point out half-way between the figure XII and the hour hand. The line given by that pencil will be the true south and north line.

(*Instructor should make each boy find the south for himself with a watch.*)

THE STARS. — The stars appear to circle over us during the night, which is really due to our earth turning round under them.

There are various groups which have had names given to them because they seem to make some kind of pictures or " sky-signs " of men and animals.

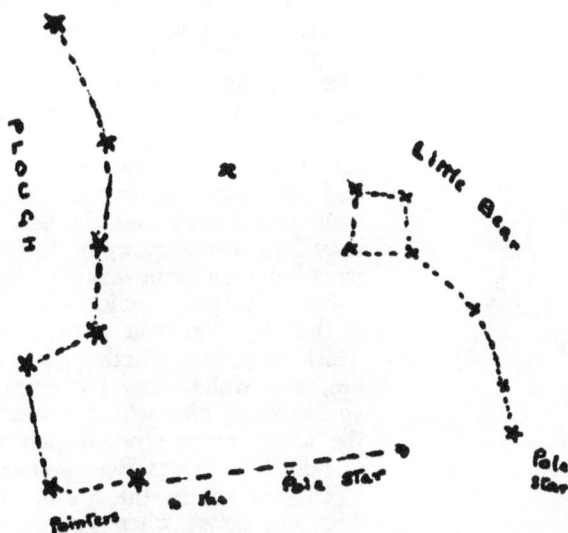

The " Dipper " is an easy one to find, being shaped something like a dipper. And it is the most useful one for a scout to know, because in the northern part of the world it shows him exactly where the north is. The Dipper is also called the " Great Bear," and the four stars in the curve make its tail. It is the only bear I know of that wears a long tail.

The two stars in the Dipper called the " Pointers " point out where the North or Pole Star is. All the stars and constellations move round, as I have said, during the night, but the Pole Star remains fixed in the north. There is also the " Little Bear," near the Great Bear, and the last star in his tail is the North or Pole Star.

The sky may be compared to an umbrella over you. The Pole Star is where the stick goes through the centre of it.

A real umbrella has been made with all the stars marked on it in their proper places. If you stand under it and twist it slowly round, you see exactly how the stars quietly go round, but the Pole Star remains steady in the middle.

Then another set of stars, or "constellation," as it is called, represents a man wearing a sword and belt, and is named "Orion." It is easily recognized by the three stars in line, which are the belt, and three smaller stars in another line, close by, which are the sword. Then two stars to right and left below the sword are his feet, while two more above the belt are his shoulders, and a group of three small stars between them make his head.

Now the great point about Orion is that by him you always can tell which way the North or Pole Star lies, and which way the south, and you can see him whether you are in the south or the north part of the world. The Great Bear you see only when you are in the north, and the Southern Cross when you are in the south.

If you draw a line, by holding up your staff against the sky, from the centre star of Orion's belt through the centre of his head, and carry that line on through two big stars till it comes to a third, that third one is the North or Pole Star.

ORION AND HIS SWORD ALWAYS POINT NORTH AND SOUTH

Roughly, Orion's sword — the three small stars — points north and south.

The Zulu scouts call Orion's belt and sword the "Ingolubu,"

or three pigs pursued by three dogs. The Masai in East Africa say that the three stars in Orion's belt are three bachelors being followed by three old maids. You see, scouts all know Orion, though under different names.

On the south side of the world, that is, in South Africa, South America, New Zealand, and Australia, the Dipper or Great Bear is not visible, but the Southern Cross is seen. The Southern Cross is a good guide as to where the exact south is, which, of course, tells a scout just as much as the Great Bear in the north pointing to the North Star.

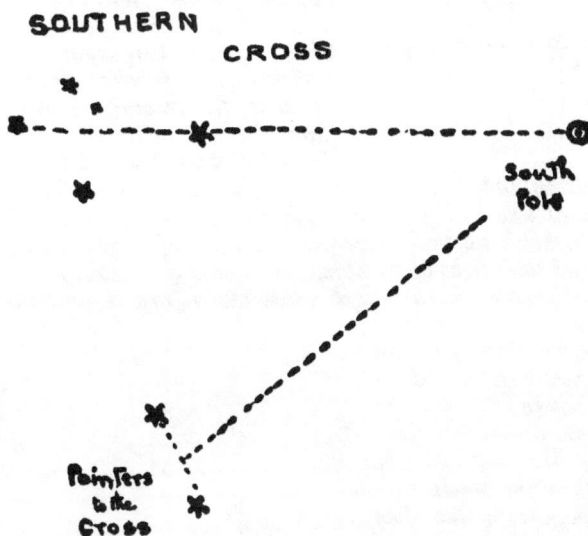

If you carry your eye along in the same direction, A, as the long stem of the cross for a distance of about one and a half times its length, this point will be about due south (see diagram). Or if you imagine a line between the two " Pointers " and another imaginary line B standing upright on this first line so long that it cuts the imaginary line A forming the continuation of the stem, the point where A and B cut each other will be the south.

HINTS TO INSTRUCTORS

Practices in Pathfinding

Teach the boys to recognize the Great Bear, and the Pole Star, and Orion; to judge time by the sun; find the south by the watch. Practise map-reading and finding the way by the map; and mark off roads by blazing, broken branches, and signs drawn on the ground.

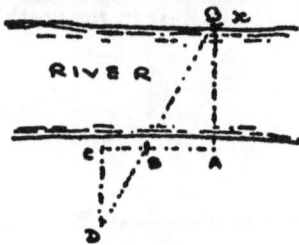

The way to estimate the distance across a river is to take an object x, *such as a tree or rock on the opposite bank; start off at right angles to it from* A, *and pace, say, ninety yards along your bank; on arriving at sixty yards, plant a stick or stone,* B; *on arriving at* C, *thirty yards beyond that, that is, ninety from the start, turn at right angles and walk inland, counting your paces until you bring the stick and the distant tree in line; the number of paces that you have taken from the bank* CD *will then give you the half distance across* AX.

To find the height of an object, such as a tree (AX), *or a house, pace a distance of, say, eight yards away from it, and there at* B *plant a stick, say, six feet high; then pace on until you arrive at a point where the top of the stick comes in line* C *with the top of the tree; then the whole distance* AC *from the foot is to* AX, *the height of the tree, the same as the distance* BC *from the stick is to the height of the*

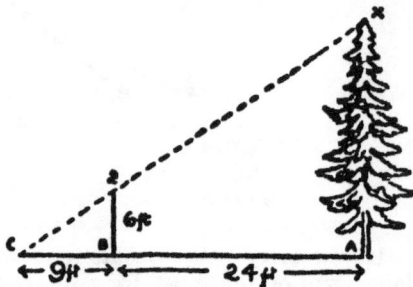

stick; that is, if the whole distance AC *is thirty-three feet, and the distance* BC *from the stick is nine (the stick being six feet high), the tree is twenty-two feet high.*

Games in Pathfinding

Instructor takes patrol in patrolling formation into a strange town or into an intricate piece of strange country, with a cycling map. He then gives instructions as to where he wants to go, makes each scout in turn lead the patrol, say for seven minutes if cycling, fifteen minutes if walking. This scout is to find the way entirely by the map, and points are given for ability in reading.

Mountain Scouting

This has been played by tourists' clubs in the Lake District of England, and is very similar to the "Spider and Fly" game. Three hares are sent out at daybreak to hide themselves about in the mountains; after breakfast a party of hounds go out to find them before a certain hour, say 4 p.m. If they find them, even with field glasses, it counts, provided that the finder can say definitely who it was he spotted. Certain limits of ground must be given, beyond which any one would be out of bounds, and therefore disqualified.

FIND THE NORTH. — Scouts are posted thirty yards apart, and each lays down his staff on the ground pointing to what he considers the exact north (or south), without using any instrument, and steps back three paces away from his staff. The umpire compares each stick with the compass; the one who guesses nearest wins. This is a useful game to play at night or on sunless days as well as sunny days.

HINTS TO INSTRUCTORS

Practices

Practise roping scouts together for mountain climbing. Practise (if boats available) coming alongside, making fast, sculling, punting, laying oars, coiling ropes, etc., and other details of boat management. Read barometer.

GAMES AND LIFE IN THE OPEN

Night Patrolling

Practise scouts to hear and see by night by posting some sentries, who must stand or walk about, armed with rifles and blank cartridges, or with whistles. Other scouts should be sent out as enemies to stalk and kill them. If a sentry hears a sound, he fires, calls, or whistles. Scouts must at once halt and lie still. The umpire comes to the sentry and asks which direction the sound came from, and if correct, the sentry wins. If the stalker can creep up within 15 yards of the sentry without being seen, he deposits some article, such as a handkerchief, on the ground at that point, and creeps away again. Then he makes a noise for the sentry to fire at, and when the umpire comes up, he can explain what he has done. This may also be practised by day, the sentries being blindfolded.

BOOKS TO READ

" Guide to the Umbrella Star Map," by D. MacEwan. Price 5s. nett. " The Umbrella Star Map." Price 12s. 6d. nett. An ordinary umbrella with all the stars in their proper places on the inside. This map can be correctly set for any day in the year and any hour, showing the approximate positions of the stars. ·(Kegan Paul & Co.)

" The Science Year Book," by Major Baden-Powell. Price 5s. (King, Sell & Olding, 27, Chancery Lane.)

" An Easy Guide to the Constellations," by the Rev. James Gall. Price 1s. (Gall. & Inglis.) Contains diagrams of the constellations.

" Astronomy for Boy Scouts," by T. W. Corbin. Price 1s. nett.

" Astronomy for Everybody," by Simon Newcomb. Price 7s. 6d. (Pitman.) Also books on astronomy by Professors Ball, Heath, Maunder, and Flammarion.

" Two Little Savages," by Ernest Thompson Seton. Price 6s. nett. (A. Constable & Co.)

" Mountaineering." Badminton Library. Price 6s. nett.

CAMP FIRE YARN. No. 6

SEA SCOUTING

Old Sea-dogs — Drake and Nelson — Lifeboatmen — Water-manship — Sea Games

Old Sea-dogs

In the days of Queen Elizabeth, some four hundred years ago, the sailors of Spain, of England, of Holland, and of Portugal were all making themselves famous for their daring voyages in small sailing ships across unknown oceans, by which they kept discovering new lands for their country in distant corners of the world.

There was one small cabin boy on a coasting brig in the

English Channel who used to long to become one of these discoverers, but when he looked at the practical side of the question, it seemed hopeless for a poor little chap like him ever to hope to rise in the world beyond his present hard life in the wretched little coaster, living on bad food and getting, as a rule, more kicks than halfpence.

But it shows you how the poorest boy can get on if he only puts his back into it. Young Drake — for that was his name — did get on, in spite of his difficulties; he worked hard at his duty, till his officers saw that he meant to get on and they promoted him, and in the end he became a captain of two small ships, one of seventy, the other of thirty tons; and with these he sailed to fight the Spaniards, who were at that time at war with England, away across the ocean in Central America. He not only fought them, but was successful in taking some of their ships and a great deal of valuable booty from their towns. On his return home he was promoted to command a larger expedition of five ships, the biggest of which, however, was only one hundred tons, and the smallest was fifteen tons. These were considered fine ships in those days, but were no bigger than the coasting schooners and fishing smacks of to-day.

[Show a map of the world.]

With these he sailed down the west coast of Africa, then across to Brazil and down the South American coast till he rounded the end of it through the dangerous and difficult Straits of Magellan into the Pacific. He coasted up the western side of America as far as California, and then struck across the ocean to India, and thence, via the Cape of Good Hope, to England. This voyage took him nearly three years to complete. His good ship, the *Golden Hind*, though much battered and wounded with war and weather, was received with much honor at Deptford. The Queen herself went on board, and while there she showed such pleasure at Drake's good work that she knighted him, using his own well-worn sword to make him Sir Francis Drake.

Soon after this King Philip of Spain began to prepare an enormous fleet, and though he told Queen Elizabeth that it was not intended to be used against England, Sir Francis Drake, who was now in command of a small fleet of English ships, maintained that it could be for no other purpose. And a secret letter was shortly afterwards intercepted, which proved that his suspicions were right. Drake went off with his fleet, and sailed up and down the Spanish coast, destroying their ships and stores wherever he could find them, and thus he hindered their preparations for war. In this way he sunk or burned some twelve thousand tons of shipping, which meant a great many ships in those days. He merely described it in his report as "singeing the Spanish King's beard."

In the end, in 1588, the great Spanish fleet — the *Armada* — was ready, and sailed against England. But there were a fine lot of English admirals and men awaiting it, for besides Lord Charles Howard of Effingham, the Lord High Admiral, there were Frobisher and Davis, Walter Raleigh and Francis Drake.

It is true they had only 67 ships with which to oppose the 130 of the Spaniards, but they sallied out and tackled them at once before the Spaniards were really ready for them and drove them into Dunkirk. Here the Spaniards felt secure, and would not come out till one night the English sent fire-ships in among them which forced them to put to sea. Then ensued a tremendous sea-fight in which Drake in the *Revenge* took the lead. The battle lasted all day, with guns roaring and ships foundering or exploding.

At length the Spaniards drew off northwards to the German Ocean, the only line of escape open to them. Round the north of Scotland and Ireland they went, damaged by shot and beset by a gale, so that in the end out of the magnificent fleet of 130 sail which had set out for the conquest of England, only 53 got back, with only about 9,000 out of the original 30,000 men.

"The pride of Spain was humbled to the dust, and England at once stepped into the highest rank among the nations of the world." [See "In Empire's Cause," by E. Protheroe.]

Nelson

Two hundred years after Drake came Nelson. He was the son of a clergyman in Norfolkshire, in England — a poor, sickly, little fellow, and was for a time in the Merchant Service. His first step to greatness was when the ship which he was in captured an enemy's ship, and the first lieutenant was ordered to take a boat and some men and go aboard the prize.

But owing to the heavy sea which was running, the officer gave up the attempt as too dangerous, whereupon Nelson, like a good scout, stepped forward and offered to go. He succeeded, and was thence marked as a good officer.

Every boy knows how, after a splendid career of fighting for

Britain, he at last won the great sea-battle of Trafalgar against the French and Spanish fleets, and fell mortally wounded in the hour of victory.

But his work and that of other great sea captains who served with him completed the supremacy of the British navy at sea begun by Drake and the sea-dogs of his time. The navies of our enemies were entirely swept from off the seas, and their merchant ships could carry on their trade only so long as their countries remained at peace with Great Britain.

And that supremacy has remained with Great Britain till to-day. But we have rivals who are continually growing stronger, and it will be the duty of many of our boys to become good seamen like their forefathers if we are going to keep up the power which they won for us.

Here in Canada we have to be prepared for our own defence, or to help our brother-Britons across the seas in time of war, so we are building up a Canadian navy. Make yourselves ready, scouts, to take your place in that navy, if needed, by learning your work as sea scouts now while you have the chance.

The sailor has a grand life of it, continually visiting strange and interesting lands, with a good ship to manœuvre through distant oceans, with plenty of contests with tides and winds. A free, open, and healthy life which breeds cheery handiness and pluck, such as make a sailor so deservedly loved by all — and all the time he is doing grand work for his country.

The Lifeboatmen

We are hearing a good deal of the heroes of every-day life, but there are perhaps no greater heroes, and no truer scouts than sailors of that kind who man the lifeboats all round the coasts of Great Britain. They have to BE PREPARED to turn out at any minute, when the dangerous storm is at its worst, to face danger in order to save others. Because they do it so often and so quietly we have come to look upon it almost as an every-day affair, to be expected, but it is none the less splendid of them and worthy of our admiration.

I hope that there are many boy scouts who, by taking up " sea scouting " and by learning boat management and seamanship, will be able to take their place in the service of their country as seamen on our battleships, or in our great merchant service, or as lifeboatmen upon our coasts.

A ship can be either a heaven or a hell; it depends entirely on the men in her. If they are surly, inclined to grouse, and untidy, they will be an unhappy ship's company. If they are, like scouts, cheerily determined to make the best of things, to give and take, and to keep their place tidy and clean, they will be a happy family and enjoy their life.

Watermanship

It is very necessary for a scout to be able to swim, for he never knows when he may have to cross a river, to swim for his life, or to plunge in to save some one from drowning. So those of you that cannot swim should make it your business to begin at once and learn; it is not very difficult.

Also, a scout should be able to manage a boat, to bring it properly alongside the ship or pier, that is, either by rowing it or steering it in a wide circle so that it comes up alongside with its head pointing the same way as the bow of the ship or towards the current. You should be able to row one oar in time with the rest of the boat's crew, or to scull a pair of oars, or to scull a boat by screwing a single oar over the stern. In rowing, the object of feathering, or turning the blade of the oar flat when it is out of the water, is to save it from catching the wind and thereby checking the pace of the boat. You should know how to throw a coil of rope so as to fling it on to another boat or wharf, or how to catch and make fast a rope thrown to you. Also you should know how to make a raft out of any materials that you can get hold of, such as planks, logs, barrels, sacks of straw, and so on, for often you may want to cross a river with your food and baggage where no boats are available, or you may be in a shipwreck where nobody can make a raft for saving himself. You should also know how to throw a lifebuoy to a drowning man. These things can be learned only by practice.

As a scout you must know how to fish, else you would find yourself very helpless, and perhaps starving, on a river which is full of food for you if only you were able to catch it.

SEA-SCOUTING PRACTICES. — Boat management: rowing or
sculling, single-handed and with others; steering; sailing;
swimming.

Knotting and splicing.

Build, repair, caulk, and paint a boat.

Principles of the engines and of steam or hydraulic winch,
etc. Knowledge of the different rigs of sailing vessels,
and of the different classes of men-of-war.

Cutting out and sewing sails and own clothes.

Signalling semaphore, flag.

Naval discipline.

Nautical songs, chanties, and hornpipe.

Climbing aloft.

Games

A Whale Hunt

The whale is made of a big log of wood with a roughly shaped
head and tail to represent a whale. Two boats will usually
carry out the whale hunt, each boat manned by one patrol — the
patrol leader acting as captain, the corporal as bowman or harpooner, the remainder of the patrol as oarsmen. Each boat
belongs to a different harbor, the two harbors being about a

A WHALE HUNT

mile apart. The umpire takes the whale and lets it loose about
half-way between the two harbors, and on a given signal the
two boats race out to see who can get to the whale first. The
harpooner who first arrives within range of the whale drives his
harpoon into it, and the boat promptly turns round and tows the
whale to its harbor. The second boat pursues, and when it
overtakes the other, also harpoons the whale, turns round, and

endeavors to tow the whale back to its harbor. In this way the two boats have a tug-of-war, and eventually the better boat tows the whale, and, possibly, the opposing boat, into its harbor. It will be found that discipline and strict silence and attention to the captain's orders are very strong points towards winning the game. It shows, above all things, the value of discipline. The game is similar to one described in E. Thompson Seton's " Birchbark of the Woodcraft Indians."

SEA–SCOUTING GAMES. — Exploration; whale hunt; shipwreck; cutting-out expedition; slavers; smugglers; shipwreck display. (See " Scouting Games," price 1s.)

BOOKS TO READ

" The Frontiersman's Pocket Book," by R. Pocock. Price 5s. nett. (J. Murray.) An excellent guide for all branches of scouting.

" The A B C of the Royal Navy." Price 1s. (Gale & Polden.)

" How Our Navy is Run," by A. S. Hurd. With preface by Lord Charles Beresford. Price 1s. nett. A popular account of life in the Navy.

" Hearts of Oak," by Gordon Stables. Price 6d. (J. F. Shaw & Co.)

" In Empire's Cause," by E. Protheroe. Price 3s. 6d. (Gay & Hancock.)

" The Cruise of the ' Cachelot,' " by Frank Bullen. Price 3s. 6d. (Smith, Elder & Co.)

HINTS TO INSTRUCTORS

Visit, if possible, a man-of-war, ocean liner, or dockyard.

CAMP FIRE YARN. No. 7

SIGNALS AND COMMANDS

Information by Signal — Hidden Despatches — Signal Fires — Words of Command — Whistle and Flag Signals

Information by Signal

SCOUTS have to be very clever at passing news secretly from one place to another, or signalling to each other, and if it should ever happen that an enemy got into Canada, the boy scouts would be of the greatest value if they have practised this art.

Before the siege of Mafeking commenced, I received a secret message from some unknown friend in the Transvaal, who sent me news of the Boers' plans against the place, and the numbers that they were getting together of men, horses, and guns. This news came to me by means of a very small letter which was rolled up in a little ball, the size of a pill, and put inside a tiny hole in a rough walking-stick, and plugged in there with wax. The stick was given to a native, who merely had orders to come into Mafeking and give me the stick as a present. Naturally, when he brought me this stick, and said it was from another white man, I guessed there must be something inside it, and soon found this very important letter.

Also I received another letter from a friend, which was written in Hindustani language, but in English writing, so that anybody reading it would be quite puzzled as to what language it was written in; but to me it was all as clear as daylight.

Then when we sent letters out from Mafeking we used to give them to natives, who were able to creep out between the Boer outposts, and once through the line of sentries, the Boers mistook them for their own natives, and took no further notice of them. They carried their letters in this way. The letters were all written on thin paper in small envelopes, and half a dozen letters or more would be crumpled up tightly into a little ball, and then rolled up into a piece of lead paper, such as tea is packed in. The native scout would carry a number of these little balls in his hand, and hanging round his neck loosely by strings. Then, if he saw he was in danger of being captured by a Boer, he would drop all his balls on the ground, where they looked exactly like so many stones, and he would notice landmarks from two or three points round about him, by which he would be able again to find the exact spot where the letters were lying; then he would walk boldly on until accosted by the Boer, who, if he searched him, would have found nothing suspicious about him. He would then wait about for perhaps a day or two until the coast was clear, and come back to the spot where the landmarks told him the letters were lying.

" Landmarks," you may remember, mean any objects — like trees, mounds, rocks, or other details — which do not move away, and act as sign-posts for a scout, who notices and remembers them.

Signalling

Captain John Smith was one of the first to make use of signals to express regular words, three hundred years ago.

He was then fighting on the side of the Austrians against the Turks. He thought it wicked for Christian men to fight against Christians if it could possibly be avoided, but he would help any Christian, although a foreigner, to fight against a heathen; so he joined the Austrians against the Turks.

He invented a system of showing lights at night with torches, which when held in certain positions with each other meant certain words.

Several officers in the Austrian forces practised these signals till they knew them.

On one occasion one of these officers was besieged by the Turks. John Smith brought a force to help him, and arrived on a hill near the town in the night. Here he made a number of torch signals, which were read by the officer inside, and they told him what to do when Smith attacked the enemy in the rear, and this enabled the garrison to break out successfully.

Signal Fires

Scouts of all countries use fires for signalling purposes — smoke fires by day and flame fires by night.

Smoke Signals. — Three big puffs in slow succession mean "Go on." A succession of small puffs mean " Rally, come here." A continued column of smoke means " Halt." Alternate small puffs and big ones mean " Danger."

To make a smoke fire light your fire in the ordinary way, and as soon as it is strong enough put on green leaves and grass, or damped hay, etc., to make it smoke.

Cover the fire with a damp blanket, and take off the blanket to let up a puff of smoke, and put it over the fire again. The size of puff depends on for how long you lift the blanket. For a short puff hold it up while you count two, and then replace the blanket while you count eight, then let up another puff while you count two, and so on.

For a long puff hold up the blanket for about six seconds.

Flare Signals. — Long or short flares mean at night the same as the above smoke signals by day.

You light a flare fire with dry sticks and brushwood, so as to make as bright a flame as possible.

Two scouts hold up a blanket in front of the fire, that is, between it and those to whom you are signalling, so that your friends do not see the flame till you want them to. Then you drop the blanket while you count two for a short flash, or six for a long one, hiding the fire while you count four between each flash.

In the American Civil War, Captain Clowry, a scout officer, wanted to give warning to a large force of his own army that the enemy were going to attack it unexpectedly during the night; but he could not get to his friends because there was a flooded river between them which he could not cross, and a storm of rain was going on.

What would you have done if you had been in his place?

A good idea struck him. He got hold of an old railway engine that was standing near him. He lit the fire and got up steam in her, and then started to blow the whistle with short and long blasts — what is called the Morse alphabet. Soon his friends heard and understood, and answered back with a bugle. And he then spelt out a message of warning to them, which they read and acted upon. And so their force of 20,000 men was saved from surprise.

Lieutenant Boyd-Alexander describes in his book, " From the Niger to the Nile," how a certain tribe of natives in Central Africa signal news to each other by means of beats on a drum. And I have known tribes in the forests of the west coast of Africa who do the same.

Every scout ought to learn the " dot and dash," or Morse method of signalling, because it comes in most useful whenever you want to send messages some distance by flag signalling, as in the army and navy, and it is also useful in getting you employment as a telegraphist. It is not difficult to learn if you set about it with a will. I found it most useful once during the Boer War. My column had been trying to get past a Boer force which was holding a pass in the mountains. Finding they were too strong for us, we gave it up late in the evening, and, leaving a lot of fires alight, as if we were in camp in front of them, we moved during the night by a rapid march right round the end of the mountain range, and by daylight next day we were exactly in rear of them without their knowing it. We then found a telegraph line, evidently leading from them to their headquarters some fifty miles farther off, so we sat down by the telegraph wire and attached our own little wire to it and read all the messages they were sending, and they gave us most valuable information. But we should not have been able to do that had it not been that some of our scouts could read the Morse code.

Then the semaphore signalling, which is done by waving your arms at different angles to each other, is most useful and quite easy to learn, and is known by every soldier and sailor in the

MORSE	SEMAPHORE	NUMERAL	MORSE	SEMAPHORE
A · —		1	N — ·	
B — · · ·		2	O — — —	
C — · — ·		3	P · — — ·	
D — · ·		4	Q — — · —	
E ·		5	R · — ·	
F · · — ·		6	S · · ·	
G — — ·		7	T —	
H · · · ·		8	U · · —	
I · ·		9	V · · · —	
J · — — —			W · — —	
K — · —		0	X — · · —	
L · — · ·			Y — · — —	
M — —			Z — — · ·	

service.   Here you have all the different letters, and the different angles at which you have to put your arms to represent those letters; and though it looks complicated in the picture, when you come to work it out you will find it is very simple.

For all letters from A to G one arm only is used, making a quarter of a circle for each letter in succession.   Then from H to

N (except J), the right arm stands at A, while the left moves round the circle again for the other letters. From O to S the right arm stands at B, and the left arm moves round as before. For T, U, Y, and the " annul," the right arm stands at C, the left moving to the next point of the circle successively.

The letters A to I also mean the figures 1 to 9 (K standing for o)—if you make the numerical sign to show that you are going to send numbers, followed by the alphabetical sign (J) when the figures are finished. They will be checked by being repeated back by the *receiving* station. Should figures be wrongly repeated by the *receiving* station, the *sending* station will send the " Erase or Annul " sign: (which is answered by the same signal), and then send the group of figures again.

MISCELLANEOUS SIGNALS

Signal	Meaning and Use
Both arms waving at letter J.	Calling up signal. Used after numerals.
K. Q.	Are you ready?
G.	Go on.
R. U.	Who are you?
M. Q.	Wait.
P. P.	"Private Palaver," not recorded.
V. E.	"Very End," finish of message.
R. D.	"Read," got message correct.
Z.	"Block Sign," sent before and after any special words or important names, to be written in BLOCK CAPITALS.
A. A. A.	"Full Stop."
S. S. S.	"Oblique Stroke," examples — c/o, i/c, b/i.
STOP.	Arms held out at letter R until answered, when repetition will be asked for.
C. I.	"Come in," finish work, come in to headquarters.

The sender must always face the station he is sending to. On a word failing to make sense, the *writer down* will say " No," when the *reader* will at once stop the sending station by raising both arms horizontally to their full extent (letter R). This demand for repetition the *sending station* will acknowledge by making " J." The signaller receiving the message will then send the last word he has read correctly, upon which the sender will continue the message from that word.

If you want to write a despatch that will puzzle most people to read, use the Morse or semaphore letters in place of the ordinary alphabet. It will be quite readable to any of your friends who understand signalling.

Also, if you want to use a secret language in your patrol, you should all set to work to learn Esperanto. It is not difficult, and is taught in a little book costing two cents. This language is being used in all countries, so tnat you would be able to get on with it abroad now.

Commands and Signals

Each patrol leader should provide himself with a whistle and a lanyard or cord for keeping it. The following commands and signals should be at your finger ends, so that you could teach them to your patrol, and know how to order it properly.

Words of Command

" Fall in " (in line).
" Alert " (stand up smartly).
" Easy " (stand at ease).
" Sit easy " (sit or lie down without leaving the ranks).
" Dismiss " (break off).
" Right " (or left); (each scout turns accordingly).
" Patrol right " (or left); (each patrol with its scouts in line wheels to that hand).
" Quick march " (walk smartly, stepping off on the left foot).
" Double " (run at smart pace, arms hanging loose).
" Scouts' pace " (walk twenty paces and jog twenty paces alternately).

Signals and Signs

When a scoutmaster wants to call his troop together he makes his bugler sound " The Scouts' Call."

Patrol leaders thereupon call together their patrols by sounding their whistles, followed by their patrol (animal) war cry. Then they double their patrol to the scoutmaster.

Whistle Signals are these:

1. One long blast means " Silence," " Alert," " Look out for my next signal."
2. A succession of long, slow blasts means, " Go out," " Get farther away," or " Advance," " Extend," " Scatter."

3. A succession of short, sharp blasts means " Rally," " Close in," " Come together," " Fall in."
4. A succession of short and long blasts alternately means " Alarm," " Look out," " Be ready," " Man your alarm posts."
5. Three short blasts followed by one long one from scout-master call up the patrol leaders — i.e., " Leaders come here ! "

Any whistle signal must be instantly obeyed at the double as fast as ever you can run — no matter what other job you may be doing at the time.

Hand signals — which can also be made by patrol leaders with their patrol flags when necessary.

Hand waved several times across the face from side to side, or flag waved horizontally from side to side opposite the face means " No," " Never mind," " As you were."

Hand or flag held high, and waved very slowly from side to side, at full extent of arm, or whistle a succession of slow blasts means " Extend," " Go farther out," " Scatter."

Hand or flag held high, and waved quickly from side to side at full extent of arm, or whistle a succession of short, quick blasts means " Close in," " Rally," " Come here."

Hand or flag pointing in any direction means " Go in that direction."

Clenched hand or flag jumped rapidly up and down several times means " Run."

Hand or flag held straight up over head means " Stop," " Halt."

When a leader is shouting an order or message to a scout who is some way off, the scout, if he hears what is being said, should hold up his hand level with his head all the time. If he cannot hear, he should stand still, making no sign. The leader will then repeat louder, or beckon to the scout to come in nearer.

The following signals are made by a scout with his staff when he is sent out to reconnoitre within sight of his patrol, and they have the following meanings: —

Staff held up horizontally, that is, flat with both hands above the head, means " A few enemy in sight."

The same, but with staff moved up and down slowly, means " A number of enemy in sight, a long way off."

The same, staff moved up and down rapidly, means " A number of enemy in sight, and close by."

The staff held straight up over the head means " No enemy in sight."

Practices in Signalling

Practise laying, lighting, and use of signal fires of smoke or flame.

Practise whistle and drill signals.

Teach semaphore and Morse codes; also Esperanto, if feasible.

Encourage competitive ingenuity in concealing despatches on the person.

HINTS TO INSTRUCTORS

In all games and competitions it should be arranged, as far as possible, that all the scouts should take part, because we do not want to have merely one or two brilliant performers and the others no use at all. All ought to get practice, and all ought to be pretty good. In competitions where there are enough entries to make heats, ties should be run off by losers instead of the usual system of by winners, and the game should be to find out which are the worst instead of which are the best. Good men will strive just as hard not to be worst as they would to gain a prize, and this form of competition gives the bad man most practice.

Despatch Running

A scout is given a despatch to take to the headquarters of a besieged town, which may be a real town (village, farm, or house), and he must return with a receipt for it. He must wear a colored rag, two feet long, pinned on to his shoulder. He must start at least four miles away from the town he is going to. Besiegers, who have to spot him, can place themselves where they like, but must not go nearer to the headquarters building than three hundred yards. (Best to give certain boundaries that they know or can recognize.) Any one found within that limit by the umpire will be ruled out as shot by the defenders at headquarters. The despatch runner can use any ruse he likes, except dressing up as a woman, but he must always wear the red rag on his shoulder. To catch him, the enemy must get the red rag from him. Ten hours may be allowed as the limit of time, by which the despatch runner should get his message to headquarters and get back again to the starting-point with the receipt. The enemy win three marks each if they spot him, and lose three marks if he succeeds. A similar game may be played in a city, but requires modifications to suit the local conditions.

On Trek. — Make a trek through Central Africa, each scout carrying his kit and food packed in a bundle on his head. Walk in single file, with scout 200 yards out in front, and find the way — he makes scout signs as to the road to follow; make bridge over stream or raft over lake; corduroy or faggots in boggy ground; leave signs and notes for any parties who may follow by day or night.

To teach your scouts individually ideas of time and distance, send each out in a different direction on some such order as this: "Go two miles to north-north-east. Write a report to show exactly where you are (with sketch map, if possible, to explain it). Bring in your report as quickly as possible."

Then test by ordnance maps or otherwise to see how far he was out of the distance and direction ordered.

Send out scouts in pairs, to compete each pair against the other. Each pair to be started by a different route to gain the same spot, finding the way by map, and to reach the goal without being seen by the others on the way.

This develops map-reading, eye for country, concealment, lookout, etc.

For judging time. Send out scouts in different directions, each with a slip of paper, to say how long he is to be away — say seven minutes for one, ten for another, and so on.

Note down his exact time of starting, and take it again on his return. Scouts must be put on their honor not to consult watches or clocks.

N.B. — Many of these games and practices may be carried out in town just as well as in the country.

Scouting Race. — Instructor stations three individuals or groups, each group differently clothed as far as possible, and carrying different articles (such as stick, bundle, paper, etc.) at distances from 300 to 1200 yards from starting-point. If there are other people about, these groups might be told to kneel on one knee, or take some such attitude to distinguish them from passers-by. He makes out a circular course of three points for the competitors to run, say about one quarter of a mile, with a few jumps if possible.

The competitors start and run to No. 1 point. Here the umpire tells them the compass-direction of the group they have to report on. Each competitor on seeing this group writes a report showing —

1. How many in the group.
2. How clothed or how distinguishable.

3. Position as regards any landmark near them.

4. Distance from his own position.

He then runs to the next point and repeats the same on another group, and so on; and finally he runs with his report to the winning-post.

Marks. — Full marks, 5 for each correct and complete description of a group — that is, an aggregate of 15 marks for the course. One mark deducted for every ten seconds later than the first boy handing in his report at the winning-post. Marks or half marks deducted for mistakes or omissions in reports.

Books. — "Signalling for Boy Scouts." (Brown & Sons, Glasgow.) "Scout Charts," No. 14, Morse Signalling Code, No. 15, Semaphore Signalling Code. (Published by the Editor of *The Scout.*)

"Esperanto." Price 1d. (Stead Publishing House, Kingsway, London, W.C.)

CHAPTER III

CAMP LIFE

CAMP FIRE YARN. No. 8

PIONEERING

Knot-tying — Hut-building — Felling Trees — Bridging —
Self-measurement — Judging Heights and Distances.

Knot-tying

PIONEERS are men who go ahead to open up a way in the jungles or elsewhere for those coming after them.

When I was on service on the west coast of Africa I had command of a large force of native scouts, and, like all scouts, we tried to make ourselves useful in every way to our main army, which was coming along behind us. So not only did we look out for the enemy and watch his moves, but we also did what we could to improve the road for our own army, since it was merely a narrow track through thick jungle and swamps. That is, we became pioneers as well as scouts. In the course of our march we built nearly two hundred bridges of timber over streams. But when I first set the scouts to do this most important work I found that, out of the thousand men, a great many did not know how to use an axe to cut down the trees, and, except one company of about sixty men, none knew how to make knots — even bad knots. So they were quite useless for building bridges, as this had to be done by tying poles together.

1. THE REEF KNOT, for tying two ropes together. Being a flat knot, it is much used in ambulance work. The best simple knot, as it will not slip and is easy to untie.

2. SHEET BEND for tying two rope-ends together. Make loop AB with one rope and pass rope-end C through and round whole loop and bend it under its own standing part.

3. HALF HITCH, made by passing rope-end round standing part and behind itself. If free end is turned back and forms a loop, the hitch can be easily loosened. A double half hitch is required to make a secure knot.

4. THE SHEEP SHANK, for shortening ropes. Gather up the amount to be shortened as in first illustration. Then with parts A and B make a half hitch round each of the bends, as in finished drawing.

5. THE BOWLINE, a loop that will not slip, to tie round a person being lowered from a building, etc. Form a loop, then in the standing part form a second and smaller loop. Through this pass the end of the large loop and behind the standing part and down through the small loop.

6. CLOVE HITCH, for fastening a rope to a pole. Either end will stand a strain without slipping, either lengthways or downwards.

7. FISHERMAN'S KNOT, used to tie two lines or ropes of different sizes together. A knot quickly made, and easy to undo, the ends being simply pulled apart.

8. MIDDLEMAN'S KNOT. Made in similar fashion to fisherman's knot. This loop will not slip when knots are drawn together, and can safely be used as a halter.

So every scout ought to be able to tie knots.

To tie a knot seems to be a simple thing, and yet there are right ways and wrong ways of doing it, and scouts ought to know the right way. Very often it may happen that lives depend on a knot being properly tied.

The right kind of knot to tie is one which you can be certain will hold under any amount of strain, and which you can always undo easily if you wish to.

A bad knot, which is called a "granny," is one which slips away when a hard pull comes on it, or which gets jammed so tight that you cannot untie it.

On page 92 are useful knots which every scout ought to know, and ought to use whenever he is tying string or rope, etc.

We had no rope with us in West Africa, so we used the strong creeping plants, and also used thin withes or long whippy sticks, which we made still more pliant or bendable by holding one end under foot and twisting the other round and round with our hands. The best wood for withes in England is willow or hazel. You see them used for binding faggots of wood together. You cannot tie all knots with them, as with rope, but they can generally make a timber hitch, or this withe knot.

Hut-building

To live comfortably in camp a scout must know how to make a bivouac shelter for the night, or a hut, if he is going to be for a long time in camp.

It all depends on the country and weather as to what sort of shelter you put up.

In making your roof — whether of branches of fir trees, or of grass or reeds, etc. — put them on as you would do tiles or slates, beginning at the bottom, so that the upper overlap the lower ones, and thus run off the rain without letting it through.

Notice which direction the wind generally blows from, and put the back of your shelter that way, with your fire in front of it.

The simplest shelter is to plant two forked sticks firmly in the ground, and rest a cross bar on them as ridge-pole. Then

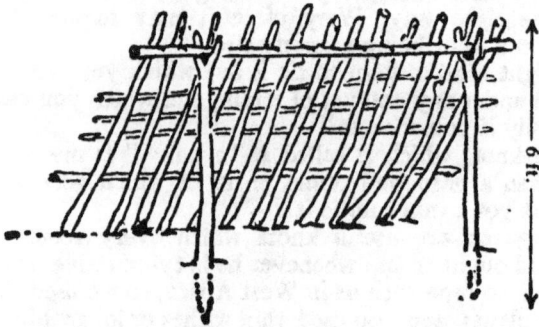

FRAMEWORK OF A BIVOUAC SHELTER

lean other poles against it, or a hurdle or branches, and thatch it with grass, etc.

Or another good way, and quicker, is to cut one pole only and lean it against a tree, binding its end there; then thatch it with branches or brushwood, etc.

Where you have no poles available you can do as the South African natives do — pile up a lot of brushwood, heather, etc.,

AN EASILY MADE HUT

into a small wall made in semicircle to keep out the cold wind, and make your fire in the open part.

If your tent or hut is too hot in the sun, put blankets or more straw, etc., over the top. The thicker the roof the cooler is the tent in summer. If it is too cold make the bottom of the walls thicker, or build a small wall of sods about a foot high round the foot of the wall outside. Never forget to dig a good drain all round your hut, so that if heavy rain comes in the night your floor will not get flooded from outside.

Zulus make their huts by planting in the ground a circle of long whippy sticks standing upright, then they bend the tops all down towards the centre and tie them together, then they weave more whippy sticks round in and out of the uprights horizontally, until they have made a kind of circular bird-cage; this they then cover with a straw mat or thatch, or with straw woven into the sticks. Sometimes a small hole is left at the top where all the sticks join, to act as a chimney.

The Indians make their " teepee " with several poles tied together in the form of a pyramid, and over these they pass a piece of canvas, which at a little distance looks like a bell tent.

Felling Trees

A scout must know how to use an axe or bill-hook for chopping down small trees and branches.

The way to cut down a tree is first to chop out a chunk of wood near the bottom of the stem on that side to which you want the tree to fall, then go round to the other side, and chop away on the opposite side of the stem a few inches above the first cut until the tree topples over. It is a matter of practice to become a woodcutter, but you have to be very careful at first lest in chopping you miss the tree, and chop your own leg.

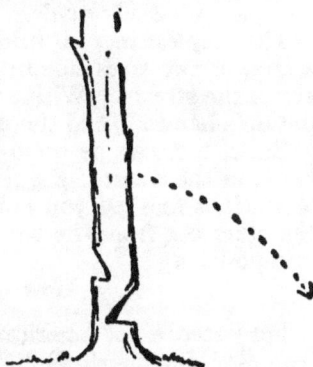

HOW TO FELL A TREE

How to Make Bridges

As I told you before, my scouts in Ashanti, when also acting as pioneers, had to build nearly two hundred bridges — and they had to make them out of any kind of material that they could find on the spot.

There are many ways of making bridges. In the British Army they are generally made of poles lashed together. In India, in the Himalaya Mountains, the natives make bridges out of three ropes stretched across the river and connected together every few yards by V-shaped sticks, so that one rope forms the footpath

ROPE BRIDGE

and the other two make the handrail on each side. They are jumpy kinds of bridges to walk across, but they take you over; and they are easily made.

The simplest way for bridging a narrow, deep stream is to fell a tree, or two trees side by side, on the bank, so that they fall across the stream. With an adze you then flatten the top side; put up a handrail, and there you have a very good bridge.

Rafts, too, can be used. You build your raft alongside the bank, in the water if the river is shallow; on the bank if deep. When it is finished you hold on to the down-stream end, push the other out from the bank, and let the stream carry it down into position.

How to Make a Tent

For "teepee," or American Indian tent, see Ernest Thompson Seton's "Birchbark Roll." Price 1s. nett. (A. Constable and Co.)

For light cyclists' tents, see "The Camper's Handbook," by J. H. Holding. Price 5s. nett.

"Boy Scouts" tent is made with canvas and scouts' staves. The three pictures on page 98 show the different stages.

To MAKE A LADDER WITH A POLE. — Tie firmly sticks, or tufts of twigs, or straw, arcoss the pole at intervals to form steps. A pole can be made by tying several scouts' staves together.

How to Make a Sleigh. — See " Camp Life," by Hamilton
Gibson. Price 5s. (Harper.)

N.B. — Before making a real article, whether tent, or boat, or
other thing, to scale, it is almost always best to make
a model on a small scale first — make an inch of
model represent a foot of the real thing.

Game. — *Food:* Name not less than twelve different
kinds of wild food, such as you would find in Canada,
supposing there were no supplies available from
butchers, bakers, or grocers. NB. — A pike and a trout
are not considered different *kinds* of food for this
competition.

Fire-lighting Race. — To collect material, lay,
and light a fire till the log given by umpire is alight.

How to Make a Rope. — Every scout takes off
his neckerchief, and knots the two ends firmly together.
Then link up all the loops thus made. This will
serve either as a rope or as a rope-ladder.

How to Make a Boat

From " Camp Life," by Hamilton Gibson. Price 5s. (Harper.)

Get two boards, A and B, 12 feet long, 20 inches wide, and
¾ inch thick. Cut them both as in Fig. 1. (See page 99.)

Nail a plank (C) between them at the centre to hold them in
position, and a second similar plank below it.

Cut solid block of wood (D) to form the stem or bow-piece,
and a stern board about 2 feet long, 10 inches deep.

Join the two bow ends of A and B by screwing them into the
block D.

Join the two stern ends by screwing them to each end of the
stern board, and strengthen by screwing stern seat (E) on to
both sides and stern-piece.

Turn the boat upside down, and screw on planks FF to form
the bottom. Caulk the seams between these by driving in tow
by means of a blunt chisel and mallet, and paint them with pitch,
if necessary, to make them water-tight. Mark where the seats
GG are to come, and nail pieces of plank to the sides of the
boat, reaching to a height of six inches from the floor, to act as
supports to the seats. Put the seats in resting on these chocks,
and screw them to the sides. Screw a pair of strong wooden
pins to each side of the boat (HH) to form rowlocks. Knock
out plank C, and your boat is ready.

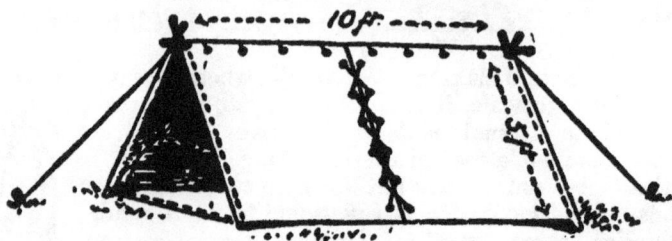

Frame of six Scouts' Staves, and an extra joint to lengthen ridge-pole.

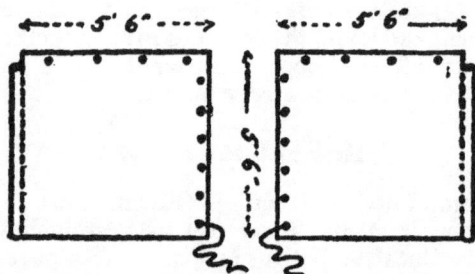

Six squares of canvas, 5 ft. 6 in. square, with eyelets and hemmed tube on one side. Each Scout carries one, and can pack his kit in it if necessary, or use it as a cape in rain.

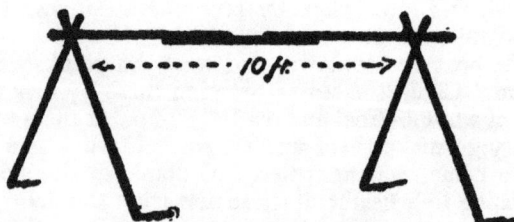

Boy Scouts' Tent for a Patrol. Four canvas squares make the tent. Two make the ground sheet.

HOW TO MAKE A TENT

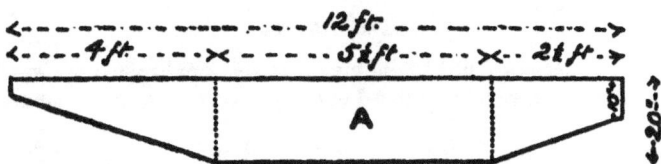

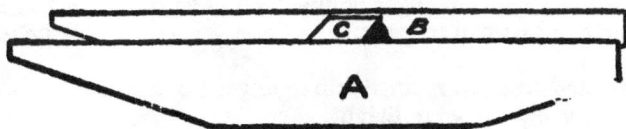

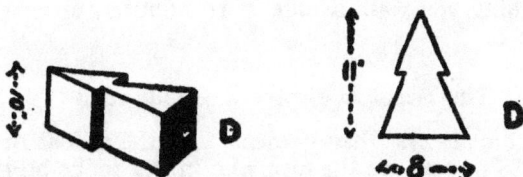

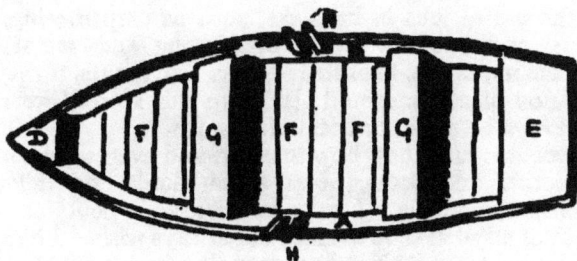

HOW TO MAKE A BOAT

See page 97.

Self-Measures

Every pioneer should know his exact personal measurement in the following details (of which I give the average man's measure):

Nail joint of forefinger, or breadth of thumb . .	1 inch
Span of thumb and forefinger	8 inches
Span of thumb and little finger or other finger .	9 inches
Wrist to elbow	10 inches
(This also gives you the length of your foot.)	
Elbow to tip of forefinger (called " cubit ") . .	17 inches
Middle of kneecap to ground	18 inches

Extended arms, from finger tip to finger tip, is called a fathom, and nearly equals your height.

Pulse beats about 75 times a minute: each beat is a little quicker than a second.

Pace: A pace is about 2½ feet; about 120 paces equal 100 yards. Fast walking paces are shorter than when going slowly.

Fast walking you walk a mile in 16 minutes, or nearly four miles an hour.

The Scout is always a Handy-man

Pioneers are always "handy-men." In the British Army the Regimental Pioneers are the men who in war make bridges and roadways for the troops to get along; they destroy the enemy's bridges and railways, so that he cannot get away; and they blow up his fortifications, so that the rest of the soldiers can rush in and capture the place, and so on. In peace time the pioneers do all the useful jobs in barracks, such as carpentering, doing plumbers' and painters' work, bricklaying and metal work, making chairs, tables, bookshelves, etc. So scouts, if they want to be handy pioneers, should also learn this kind of work; and it will always be useful to them afterwards.

Also, scouts must know how to mend and even to make themselves clothes and boots, because you don't find tailors and cobblers in the jungle. I have made myself boots as well as shoes out of all sorts of materials, but always wished I had, while a boy, learned to do a bit of boot-mending from a cobbler.

Judging Heights and Distances

Every scout must be able to judge distance from an inch up to a mile or more. You ought, first of all, to know exactly what is the span of your hand and the breadth of your thumb, and the length from your elbow to your wrist, and the length from one hand to the other with your arms stretched out to either side, and also the length of your feet; if you remember these accurately, they are a great help to you in measuring things. Also it is useful to cut notches on your staff, showing such measurements as one inch, six inches, one foot, and one yard. These you can measure off with a tape measure before you use your staff, and they may come in very useful.

Judging the distance of objects from you is gained only by practice, and judging the distance of a journey is generally estimated by seeing how long you have been travelling, and at what rate; that is to say, supposing you walk at the rate of four miles an hour, if you have been walking for an hour and a half, you know that you have done about six miles.

Distance can also be judged by sound; that is to say, if you see a gun fired in the distance, and you count the number of seconds between the flash and the sound of the explosion reaching you, you will be able to tell how far off you are from the gun.

Sound travels at the rate of 365 yards in a second; that is, as many yards as there are days in the year.

A scout must also be able to estimate heights, from a few inches up to three thousand feet or more; that is to say, he ought to be able to judge the height of a fence, the depth of a ditch, or the height of an embankment, of a house, tree, of a tower, or hill, or mountain. It is easy to do when once you have practised it for a few times, but it is very difficult to teach it by book.

You must also know how to estimate weights, from a letter of an ounce, or a fish, or a potato of one pound, or a sack of bran, or a cartload of coals; and also the probable weight of a man from his appearance — these, again, are only learned by practice, but as a scout you should take care to learn them for yourself.

Also you should be able to judge numbers; that is to say, you should be able to tell at a glance *about* how many people are in a group, or in a street car, or in a big crowd, how many sheep in a flock, how many marbles on a tray, and so on. These you can practise for yourself at all times in the street or field.

In the German Army instructions for judging distance are given as follows: —

At fifty yards, mouth and eyes of the enemy can be clearly seen.

At 100 yards eyes appear as dots; 200 yards buttons and details of uniform can still be seen; at 300 yards face can be seen; at 400 yards the movement of the legs can be seen; at 500 yards the color of the uniform can be seen.

For distances over these, think out for yourself which point is half-way to the object. Estimate how far this may be from you, and then double it to obtain the distance. Or another way is to estimate the farthest distance that the object can be away, and then the very nearest it could be, and strike a mean between the two.

Objects appear nearer than they really are: first, when the light is bright and shining on the object; secondly, when looking across water or snow, or looking uphill or down. Objects appear farther off when in the shade; across a valley; when the background is of the same color; when the observer is lying down or kneeling; when there is a heat haze over the ground.

JUDGING DISTANCE. — Take a patrol and station its members about in different directions and with different background, according to the color of their clothes; then take another patrol to judge distance of these points. Two competitors are sent in turn to three different points. At the first point they are merely given the compass bearing of the next one, which is some three hundred yards distant, and so on in succession. At each point each pair of scouts notices regarding the enemy: first, how many visible; second, how far off; third, what is their compass direction; fourth, how they are clothed. The best answers win, provided they are within the specified time. The time allowed should be one minute for observation at each station, and half a minute for each bit of running.

HINTS TO INSTRUCTORS

Start a carpentry class, or instruction in electricity, or plumbing, elementary engineering, etc.. with a view to teaching the boys handicrafts that may be of real use to them in their future life. If you do not know enough about it yourself, get a friend to come and demonstrate with models or instruments for a few evenings.

Get leave to take the scouts over a factory to study the engines, etc.

Teach the boys to chop firewood. If they learn to chop up old packing-cases, etc., and make the pieces into bundles for kindling wood, they can earn a good deal towards their funds.

Teach them to make wooden mechanical toys (from one or two cheap ones as models); thereby teaching them elementary mechanics and handiness with tools.

PRACTICE

Knot-tying should be practised against time, by knot-tying races between scouts in heats, the losers to pair off again for further heats till the slowest knot-tier is found. In this way (which should be used in other branches of instruction also) the worst performers get the most practice — and the emulation is just as great to avoid being the worst as it would be in striving to be the best, and win a prize.

Knot-tying races should also be carried out in the dark, the instructor turning out the light for a few seconds on naming the knot to be tied, or blindfolding the competitors.

Hurdle-making by planting a row of upright stakes and weaving in withes.

Make models of bridges with scouts' staves, cords, planks out of old packing-cases.

BOOKS TO READ

" The Frontiersman's Pocket Book," by R. Pocock (J. Murray).   Price 5s. nett.

" Manual of Military Engineering ": War Office Publication.

" Active Service Pocket Book," by Mr. Bertrand Stewart. Price 4s. nett.   (Clowes and Son.)

" Romance of Engineering and Mechanism."   Price 5s. each. (Seeley and Co.)

" How it Works," by Archibald Williams.

Showing how such things work as steam engines, motors, vacuum brakes, telephones, telegraph, etc.   Price 3s. 6d. (Nelson.)

" Wood Carving," by J. H. Garnett.   Price 1s.   (C. A. Pearson, Limited.)

" Metal Work, by George Day.   Price 1s.   (C. A. Pearson, Limited.)

" The Camper's Handbook," by T. H. Holding.   Price 5s. (Simpkin, Marshall, and Co.)

" Camping Out for Boy Scouts," by Victor Bridges.   With Introduction by Sir R. Baden-Powell.   Price 1s. nett.

" The Young Marooners," by F. Goulding.   Price 1s. 6d. (Nisbet.)   A story of resourcefulness in camp, including raft-building, shoe-making, first aid, etc.

"Carpentry and Cabinet-making," by W. M. Oakwood. Price 1s. (C. A. Pearson, Limited.)

"Model-making," by Cyril Hall. Price 1s. nett. Including steam-engine, turbine, electric motor, etc.

The "How Does it Work of Electricity," by T. W. Corbin. Price 1s. nett.

Further practical hints on campaigning and camping will be found in the "Boy Scouts of America," by Ernest Thompson Seton and Sir Robert Baden-Powell. Price 25 cents. (Doubleday, Page & Company, New York.)

CAMP FIRE YARN. No. 9

CAMPING

Comfort in Camp — Ground — Camp Equipment — Tidiness — Hints to Instructors — Camp Orders — Practices.

Comfort in Camp

SOME people talk of "roughing" it in camp. Those people are generally tenderfoots; an old backwoodsman doesn't rough it, he knows how to look after himself, and to make himself com-

RESOURCEFULNESS IN DOING A GOOD TURN

fortable by a hundred little dodges. For instance, if there are no tents he doesn't sit down to shiver and grouse, but at once sets to work to rig up a shelter or hut for himself. He chooses a good spot for it, where he is not likely to be flooded out if a storm of rain were to come on. Then he lights up a camp fire, and makes himself a comfortable mattress of ferns or straw. An old scout is full of resource, that is, he can find a way out of any difficulty or discomfort. He is full of devices, like the boy in this picture who had to rap on the door with the knocker which he could not reach. He showed resourcefulness.

Ground

In the first place you must think where you will have your camp, and what kind of camp it shall be.

The nearer you have it to your homes, the less will be the expense of travelling to and from camp.

The best place to my mind for a camp is in or close by a wood where you have leave to cut firewood and to build huts. So if you know of an owner in your neighborhood who is likely to give you leave to use a corner of his wood, there is your chance. Inside a wood is apt to be damp and to suffer from drip in wet weather, so you must be on the lookout for this. If you build good rain-proof huts, you need not have tents.

The seaside or lakeside also gives some good camp-grounds if you get a place where boats are available and bathing possible. Sometimes you can get the use of a boat-shed or the cabin of a disused vessel to live in. Don't forget that you will want good water and some firewood.

Or you can go to mountains, or river, and get leave to pitch your camp. But in choosing the site always think what it would be if the weather came on very rainy and windy, and get the driest and most sheltered place you can, and not too far away from your water supply.

Tramping Camps

Instead of a fixed camp, many scouts prefer a " tramping camp."

Of course, it is much better fun to go over new country; but to make a tramping camp enjoyable you need good weather.

In arranging your tramp, your first point will be to select the line of country you want to visit, and mark out from the map whereabouts you will halt for each night. You will find that about five miles a day is as much as you will want to do.

You would do well to make a baggage-barrow for carrying your tents, blankets, and waterproof sheets, etc. At the end of each day's march you would get leave from a farmer to pitch your camp in his field, or get the use of his barn to sleep in — especially if the weather be wet.

Boat Cruising

Another enjoyable way of camping is to take a boat and explore a river, camping out in the same way as in a tramping camp. But in this case every member of the patrol must be able to swim. It is often very convenient to make your tent inside the boat at night.

Tents

With so many different kinds of camps, it depends upon which kind you choose before you know what kind of tent you will want.

For a standing camp, from which you don't mean to move, bell tents are useful, or huts can be made. Bell tents can be hired in almost any town for a small sum per week, or you can buy a second-hand one in good condition. You could probably let it out on hire to other patrols when not using it yourself, and so get back your money on it.

Scouts' patrol tents also do very well for camp, but you need a second set of staves or poles for rigging them if you want to leave the camp standing while you are out scouting.

You can also make your own tents during the winter months — and this, perhaps, is the best way of all, as it comes cheapest in the end. And if, while you are about it, you make one or two extra ones, you may be able to sell them at a good profit.

Camp Equipment

When you have decided what kind of camp you intend to have and whereabouts, your next point is to look to the equipment — that is to say, what you will need in the way of buckets, brooms, tools, and so on. Here is a rough list of things that are useful in a standing camp, but they will not all be necessary in a bivouac or shifting camp: —

For Tent. — Bucket, lantern, and candles, matches, mallet, tin basin, spade, axe, pick, hank of cord, flag, and pole-strap for hanging things on.

FOR KITCHEN. — Saucepan or stewpot, fry-pan, kettle, grid-iron, matches, bucket, butcher's knife, ladle, cleaning rags, empty bottles for milk, bags for rusks, potatoes, etc.

FOR EACH SCOUT. — Waterproof sheet, two blankets, cord or strap for tying them up, straw mattress (to be made in camp — twine and straw required), ration bags (one for sugar and tea, one for pepper and salt, one for flour and baking powder).

CLOTHING — Each scout, in addition to the suit of clothing which he is wearing, should take to camp the following things. If you are going for a tramping camp you need only those marked with a *.

Old greatcoat or waterproof coat.
*One flannel shirt.
One extra flannel shirt.
One pair drawers.
*Two pair socks or stockings.
One vest.
Flannels or sleeping suit.
One pair stout walking boots or shoes.
*One pair canvas shoes.
One sweater or old jacket.
One pair bathing drawers.
*Hairbrush.
*Soap and towel.
*Toothbrush.
Two handkerchiefs.

PERSONAL EQUIPMENT. — Haversack, billy, staff, knife, fork, and spoon, matches, whistle, portion of tent.

FOOD. — Food is often a difficulty. Though it may seem strange to a tenderfoot, scouts know that neither bread nor meat are wholly necessary to keep them in good condition. Personally, I very seldom eat either myself. Biscuits are good for camp food, and can be carried in your pocket or haversack, for which bread is useless.

The best kind of bread for camp is what the Boers and most South African hunters use, and that is "rusks." Rusks are easily made. You buy a stale loaf at the baker's, cut it up into thick slices or square "junks," and then bake these in an oven or toast them before a hot fire till they are quite hard like biscuits. They can then be carried in a spare haversack or bag, and do very well instead of bread. Soft bread easily gets damp and sour and stale in camp.

Canned meat, eggs, rice, and porridge are easier to keep and to cook than fresh meat, when in camp, and are just as good food. Fruit is easy to stew and good to eat. Cakes of chocolate are very useful in camp and on the march. I have often gone a whole day on an army biscuit and a cake of chocolate.

The amount of food that is needed can be made out from the following list, which shows a good ration for a boy for one day. You have to multiply this amount by the number of boys in camp to see how much to provide each day. The most necessary are marked *.

*Oatmeal, rice, or macaroni, 2½ oz.; or potatoes, ½ lb.; or onions, 1½ oz. *Biscuits, bread, or rusks, ½ lb. *Chocolate and sugar, 2 oz. Fruit ¼ lb.; or jam or syrup, 1½ oz. Cocoa, ½ oz. Meat, ½ lb.; or fish, 6 oz.; or cheese, 1½ oz. *Milk, 2 pints. Butter, 1 oz. Also required: salt, pepper, currants, raisins, flour, suet, and so on. I omit tea because it is no good to a boy, and is expensive.

Pitching Camp

Having chosen the spot for your camp, pitch your tent with the door away from the wind. Dig a small trench about three inches deep all round it to prevent it getting flooded if heavy rain comes on. This trench should lead the water away downhill. Dig a small hole the size of a teacup alongside the foot of the pole into which to shift it if rain comes on. This enables you to slack up all ropes at once to allow for their shrinking when wet.

In scout camps the tents are not pitched in lines and streets as in military camps, but are dotted about, fifty or a hundred yards apart or more, in a big circle round the scoutmaster's tent, which, with the mess marquee, if there is one, is generally in the centre. This keeps each patrol separate as a unit.

WATER SUPPLY. — If there is a spring or stream, the best part of it must be strictly kept clear and clean for drinking water. Farther down-stream a place may be appointed for bathing, washing clothes, and so on. The greatest care is always taken by scouts to keep their drinking-water supply very clean, otherwise they are very likely to get sickness among them.

All water has a large number of tiny animals floating about in it, too small to be seen without the help of a microscope. Some of them are poisonous, some are not; you can't tell whether the poisonous ones are there, so the safest way is to kill them all before you drink any water; and the way to kill them is to boil the water, and let it cool again before drinking it. In boiling the water don't let it merely come to a boil and then take it off, but let it boil fully for a quarter of an hour, as these little beasts, or microbes, as they are called, are very tough, and take a lot of boiling before they are killed.

KITCHENS. — The cooking-fire is made to leeward, or down-wind of the camp, so that the smoke and sparks from the fire don't blow into the tents. Cooking-fires are described on page 114.

Old scouts always take special care to keep the kitchen par-ticularly clean, as, if scraps are left lying about, flies collect and smells arise which are very likely to poison slightly the food while it is being got ready for a meal, and this brings sickness to the scouts.

So keep the camp-kitchen and ground round it very clean at all times.

Dig a small pit a couple of feet deep near the kitchen, and throw all refuse that won't burn into this and fill in the pit with earth every night.

LATRINES. — Another very important point for the health of the scouts is to dig a trench to serve as a latrine. The trench should be two or three feet deep and quite narrow — one foot wide — so that the user can squat astride of it, one foot on each side. A thick sprinkling of earth should be thrown in after use, and the whole trench carefully filled in with earth after a few days' use. The cross screens are necessary for decency, about which scouts are always very careful.

TRENCH-LATRINE, WITH SCREENS ACROSS

Even in a one-night camp, scouts should dig a latrine trench. And when rearing away from camp a scout will always dig a small pit of a few inches, which he will fill in again after use.

Neglect of this not only makes a place unhealthy, but also it makes farmers and landowners disinclined to give the use of their ground for scouts to camp on or to work over. So don't forget it, scouts.

Camp Routine

As a large number of inquiries have reached me as to what I consider a good routine for a camp, I cannot do better than tell you what was done at my camp at Humshaugh in 1908. Here is the time-table for the day: —

6.30 A.M. Turn out, air bedding, coffee and biscuit.

7 to 7.30 A.M. Parade for prayers, and physical exercise, or instruction parade.

7.30 A.M. Stow tents and wash.

8 A.M. Breakfast.

9 A.M. Scouting practice.

11 A.M. Biscuit and milk.

11 A.M. to 1.30 P.M. Scouting games.

1.30 P.M. Dinner.

2 to 3 P.M. Rest (compulsory). No movement or talking allowed in camp.

3 to 5.30 P.M. Scouting games in the neighborhood.

5.30 P.M. Tea.

6 to 7.30 P.M. Recreation, camp games.

7.30 to 9 P.M. Camp fire; or, from 8 till 11, night practices.

9 P.M. Biscuit and milk; turn in.

9.30 P.M. Lights out.

No night work or night attacks or sentry duty should go on after 11.30.

Cleaning Camp-ground

Never forget also that the state of an old camp-ground, after the camp has finished, tells exactly whether the patrol or troop which has used it was a smart one or not. No scouts who are any good ever leave a camp-ground dirty; they sweep up and bury or burn every scrap of rubbish. This is done on service to prevent the enemy reading any information from what is left.

Thus, supposing you left some bits of old bandages, a few tunic buttons, old food scraps, etc., an enemy could tell which regiments were in the force, and that there were wounded men, and that the men were reduced to certain shifts for food.

In peace camps it is quite as important to get into this habit of cleaning up your camp-ground before leaving it, as then farmers don't have the trouble of having to clean their ground after you leave, and they are, therefore, all the more willing to let you use it again.

Payment

Another point to remember is that when you use a farmer's ground you ought to repay him for the use of it. If you do not do this with money, you can do it in other ways. You can and ought to do jobs that are useful for him. You can mend his fences or gates, or herd his cows, cut thistles or dig up weeds, and so on. You should always be doing " good turns " both to the farmer and to the people living near your camp, so that they will be glad to have you there.

Trespassing

Especially be careful to get leave from the owners of land in the neighborhood before you go on to it. You have no right to go anywhere off the roads without leave, but most owners will give you this if you go and tell them who you are and what you want to do.

When going over their land remember above all things: —
1. To shut all gates after you.
2. To disturb animals and game as little as you possibly can.
3. To do no damage to fences, crops, or trees.

Any firewood that you require you must ask for before taking.

Loafers in Camp

A camp is a roomy place, but there is no room in it for one boy, and that is the one who does not want to take his share in the many little odd jobs that have to be done; there is no room for the shirker or the *grouser* — well, there is no room for him in the Boy Scouts at all, but least of all when in camp.

Every boy must help, and help cheerily, in making it comfortable for all. In this way comradeship grows. On service, if one boy is out on night duty getting wet through, one of those left in the tent will be sure to get ready a cup of hot cocoa for him when he comes in, and that is the kind of thing every scout should think of and carry out.

Note to Parents

Camping-out is the great point in scouting which appeals to the boy, and is the opportunity in which to teach him self-reliance and resourcefulness, besides giving him health and development.

Many parents who have never had experience of camp life

themselves look upon it with misgiving as possibly likely to be too rough and risky for their boys; but when they see them return well set up and full of health and happiness outwardly, and morally improved in the points of practical manliness and comradeship, they cannot fail to appreciate the good which comes from such an outing.

I sincerely hope, therefore, that no obstacle may be placed in the way of the boys taking their holiday on the lines suggested.

Camp Beds

There are many ways of making a comfortable bed in camp, but always, if possible, have some kind of covering over the ground between your body and the earth, especially after wet weather. Cut grass or straw or ferns are very good things to lay down thickly where you are going to lie, but if you cannot get any of these and are obliged to lie on the ground, do not forget before lying down to make a small hole about the size of a teacup in which your hip joint will rest when you are lying on your side; it makes all the difference for sleeping comfortably. A very comfortable bed, almost a spring mattress, is made by cutting a large number of tips of branches of the balsam-fir and laying them closely in layers overlapping each other, like shingles on a roof, so that when you lie down on them they form a comfortable and springy couch.

Remember when sleeping in camp the secret of keeping warm is to have as many blankets *underneath* you as you have above you. If a patrol were sleeping round a fire, you would all lie with your feet towards it like the spokes of a wheel. If your blankets do not keep you sufficiently warm, put straw or ferns over yourselves, and newspapers, if you have them. It is also a good idea in cold weather, if you have not sufficiently warm clothing, to put a newspaper under your coat or waistcoat up your back and round your body; it will be as good as an over-coat in giving you extra warmth.

BED

To make a bed, cut four poles — two of seven feet, two of three — lay them on the ground, so as to form the edges.

Cut four pegs, two feet long, and sharpen, drive them into the ground at the four corners to keep the poles in place.

Cut down a fir tree, cut off all branches, and lay them overlapping each other like slates on a roof till a thick bed of them is made; the outside ones underlapping the poles. Cover with a blanket.

To make a mattress you first set up a camp loom (see " Hints to Instructors," at end of this Camp Fire Yarn), and weave a mattress out of ferns, straw, or grass, etc., six feet long, and two feet nine inches across.

With this same loom you can make grass or straw mats, with which to form tents, or shelters, or walls, or carpets, etc.

Camp candlesticks can be made by bending a bit of wire into a small spiral spring; or by using a cleft stick stuck in the wall; or by sticking the candle upright in a lump of clay or in a hole bored in a big potato; or a glass candle-shade can be made by cutting the bottom off a bottle and sticking it upside down in the ground with a candle stuck in the neck.

The bottom of the bottle may be cut off, either by putting about an inch or an inch and a half of water into the bottle, and

CAMP CANDLESTICKS

then standing it in the embers of the fire till it gets hot and cracks at the water-level. Or it can be done by passing a piece of string round the body of the bottle, and drawing it rapidly to and fro till it makes a hot line round the bottle, which then breaks neatly off with a blow, or on being immersed in cold water.

Camp forks can also be made out of wire sharpened at the points.

It is something to know how to sit down in a wet camp. You " squat " instead of sitting. Natives in India squat on their

CAMP FORK

heels, but this is a tiring way, if you have not done it as a child; though it comes easy if you put a sloping stone or block of wood under your heels.

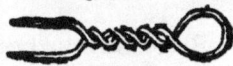

Boers and other camp men squat on one heel. It is a little tiring at first.

Buttons are always being lost in camp, and it adds greatly to your comfort to know how to make buttons out of bootlaces or string. This is shown on page 244. Scouts should also be able to carve collar studs out of wood, bone, or horn.

A great secret of sleeping comfortably in camp is to have a canvas bag about two feet long by one foot wide, into which you pack odds and ends — or carry empty, and fill up with grass or underclothing to form your pillow at night.

Camp Fires — The Right Way of Making Them

Before lighting your fire remember always to do as every backwoodsman does, and that is to cut away or burn all ferns, leaves, grass, etc., round the fire, to prevent its setting light to the surrounding grass or bush. Many bad bush-fires have been caused by young tenderfoots fooling about with blazes which they imagined to be camp fires. In burning the grass for this purpose, or " ring-burning," as it is called, burn only a little at a time, and have branches of trees or old sacks ready with which you can beat it out again at once when it has gone far enough.

Scouts should always be on the lookout to beat out a bush-fire or a prairie-fire that has been accidentally started at any time, as a " good turn " to the owner of the land or to people who may have herds and crops in danger.

It is no use to learn how to light a fire by hearsay; the only way is to pay attention to the instructions given you, and then practise laying and lighting a fire yourself.

In the book called " Two Little Savages," instructions for laying a fire are given in the following rhyme: —

" First a curl of birch-bark as dry as it can be,
    Then some twigs of soft wood dead from off a tree,
    Last of all some pine knots to make a kettle foam,
    And there's a fire to make you think you're sitting right at home."

Remember to begin your fire with a small amount of very small chips or twigs of really dry, dead wood lightly heaped together, and a little straw or paper to ignite it; about this should be put little sticks leaning together in the shape of a pyramid, and above this bigger sticks similarly standing on end. When the fire is well alight bigger sticks can be added, and finally logs of wood. A great thing for a cooking-fire is to get a good pile of red-hot wood ashes, and if you use three large logs, they should be placed lying on the ground, star-shaped, like the spokes of a wheel, with their ends centred in the fire. A fire made in this way need never go out, for as the logs burn away you keep pushing them

STAR FIRE READY TO LIGHT

towards the centre of the fire, always making fresh red-hot ashes there. This makes a good cooking-fire, and also one which gives very little flame or smoke for the enemy to detect from a distance.

To leave your fire alight at night, cover it over with a heap of ashes, and it will smoulder all night ready for early use in the morning, when you can easily blow it into a glow.

If you want to keep a fire going all night to show or to warm you, put good-sized logs end to end star-shaped — and one long one reaching to your hand, so that you can push it in, from time to time, to the centre, without the trouble of getting up to stoke the fire.

Above all things be careful, as all real backwoodsmen are, to put out every spark of your fire before leaving camp.

If coals or wood are difficult to get for making fires at home, don't forget that old boots, which you often find lying about on dust-heaps, make very good fuel.

You can do a good turn to any poor old woman in winter time by collecting old boots and giving them to her for firing.

Here is a good way to make a cooking-fire. Drive two stout stakes into the ground about four feet apart, both leaning a bit backwards. Cut down a young tree with a trunk some fifteen feet high and ten inches thick; chop it into five-foot lengths; lay three logs, one on top of another, leaning against the upright stakes. This forms the back of your fire-place. Two short logs are then laid as fire-dogs, and a log laid

CAMP GRATE

across them as front bar of the fire. Inside this " grate " you build a pyramid-shaped fire, which then gives out great heat. The " grate " must, of course, be built so that it faces the wind.

Tongs are useful about a camp fire, and can be made from a rod of beech or other tough wood, about four feet long and one inch thick. Shave it away in the middle to about half its proper thickness, and put this part into the hot embers of the fire for a few moments, and bend the stick over till the two ends come together. Then flatten away the inside edges of the ends so that they have a better grip, and there are your tongs.

A broom is also useful for keeping the camp clean, and can easily be made with a few sprigs of birch bound tightly round a stake.

Drying Clothes

You will often get wet through on service, and you will see tenderfoots remaining in their wet clothes until they get dry again; no old scout would do so, as that is the way to catch fever and get ill. When you are wet, take the first opportunity of getting your wet clothes off and drying them, even though you may not have other clothes to put on, as happened to me many a time. I have sat naked under a wagon while my one suit of clothes was drying over a fire. The way to dry clothes over a fire is to make a fire of hot ashes, and then build a small beehive-shaped cage of sticks over the fire, and then hang your clothes all over this cage, and they will very quickly dry. Also, in hot weather it is dangerous to sit in your clothes when they have got wet from your perspiration. On the west coast of Africa I always carried a spare shirt, hanging down my back, with the sleeves tied round my neck; so soon as I halted I would take off the wet shirt I was wearing, and put on the dry, which had been hanging out in the sun on my back. By this means I never got fever when almost every one else went down with it.

Tidiness

The camp-ground should at all times be kept clean and tidy, not only, as I have pointed out, to keep flies away, but also because if you go away to another place, and leave an untidy ground behind you, it gives so much important information to the enemy's scouts. For this reason scouts are always tidy, whether in camp or not, as a matter of habit. If you are not tidy at home, you won't be tidy in camp; and if you're not tidy in camp, you will be only a tenderfoot and no scout.

A scout is tidy also in his tent, bunk, or room, because he may yet be suddenly called upon to go off on an alarm, or something unexpected; and if he does not know exactly where to lay his hand on his things, he will be a long time in turning out, especially if called up in the middle of the night. So on going to bed, even when at home, practise the habit of folding up your clothes and putting them where you can at once find them in the dark, and get into them quickly.

SHOE LACED IN THE SCOUT'S WAY

One end of the lace is knotted under the lowest outside hole, and the lace is brought through and threaded downwards through the opposite hole; it is then taken up to the top. The dotted part of the lace is the part which lies underneath the shoe and is not visible.

A scout even ties his shoe-laces neatly — in fact, they are not tied, but are woven through the eyelet holes from the top of the boot downwards, and so need no tying.

HINTS TO INSTRUCTORS

CAMP ORDERS

In going into camp it is essential to have a few "Standing Orders" published, which can be added to from time to time, if necessary. These should be carefully explained to patrol leaders, who should then be held fully responsible that their scouts carry them out exactly.

Such orders might point out that each patrol will camp separately from the others, and there will be a comparison between the respective cleanliness and good order of tents and surrounding ground.

Each patrol usually has a tent to itself, well away from any others, but within call of the scoutmaster's tent. The patrol leader may make his own little tent or shelter outside this patrol tent, but close to it.

Patrol leaders to report on the good work or otherwise of their scouts, which will be recorded in the scoutmaster's book of marks.

Rest time for one hour and a half in middle of day.

Bathing under strict supervision to prevent non-swimmers getting into dangerous water.

"Bathing picket of two good swimmers will be on duty while bathing is going on, and ready to help any boy in distress. This picket will be in the boat (undressed) with greatcoats on. They may only bathe when the general bathing is over, and the last of the bathers has left the water." The observance of this rule has saved the life of more than one scout already.

Orders as to what is to be done in case of fire alarm.

Orders as to boundaries of grounds to be worked over, damages to fences, property, good drinking-water, etc.

PRACTICES

To MAKE A CAMP LOOM. — Plant a row (1) of five stakes, 2 ft. 6 in., firmly in the ground; opposite to them, at a distance of 6 ft. to 7 ft., drive in a row of two and a crossbar or five

CAMP LOOM, FOR MAKING MATS AND MATTRESSES

stakes (2). Fasten a cord or gardener's twine to the head of each stake in No. 1 row, and stretch it to the corresponding stake in No. 2 and make it fast there, then carry the continuation of it back over No. 1 row for some 5 ft. extra, and fasten it to a loose crossbar or " beam " at exactly the same distances apart from the next cord as it stands at the stakes. This beam is then moved up and down at slow intervals by one scout, while the remainder lay bundles of fern or straw, etc., in layers, alternately under and over the stretched strings, which are thus bound in by the rising or falling on to them.

If in camp, practise making different kinds of beds.

If indoors, make camp candlesticks, lamps, forks, tongs, buttons, brooms.

If outdoors, practise laying and lighting fires.

Make scouts lace shoes neatly on the principle given.

CAMP FIRE YARN. No. 10

CAMP COOKING

Cooking — Bread-making — Cattle-driving — Cleanliness — Hints — Camp games.

Cooking

EVERY scout must, of course, know how to cook his own meat and vegetables, and to make bread for himself, without regular cooking utensils. For boiling water a scout would usually have his tin " billy," and in that he can boil vegetables or stew his meat; but often he will want it for drinking, and will cook his meat in some other way. This would usually be done by sticking it on sharp sticks and hanging it close to the fire, so that it gets broiled; or the lid of an old biscuit tin can be used as a kind of frying-pan. Put grease or water in it to prevent the meat getting burnt before it is cooked.

Meat can also be wrapped in a few sheets of wet paper, or in a coating of clay, and put in the red-hot embers of the fire, where it will cook itself. Birds and fish can also be cooked in this manner, and there is no need to pluck the bird before doing so if you use clay, as the feathers will stick to the clay when it hardens in the heat, and when you break it open the bird will come out cooked, without its feathers, like the kernel out of a nutshell.

Another way is to clean out the inside of the bird, get a pebble about the size of its inside, and heat it till nearly red-hot; place it inside the bird, and put the bird on a gridiron, or on a wooden spit over the fire.

Birds are most easily plucked immediately after being killed. Don't do as I did once when I was a tenderfoot. It was my turn to cook, so I thought I would vary the dinner by giving them soup. I had some pea-flower, and I mixed it with water and boiled it up, and served it as pea-soup; but I did not put in any stock or meat juice of any kind. I didn't know that it was necessary or would be noticeable. But they noticed it directly, called my beautiful soup a " wet pease-pudding," and told me I might eat it myself — not only told me I *might*, but they *made* me eat it. I never made the mistake again.

To boil your " billy," or camp kettle, you can either stand it on the logs (where it often falls over unless care is taken), or, better, stand it on the ground among the hot embers of the fire; or else rig up a triangle of three green poles over the fire, tying them together at the top, and hanging the pot by a wire or chain from the poles. But in making this tripod do not, if there is an old scout in camp, use poplar sticks for poles, because, although they are easy to cut and trim for the purpose, old-fashioned scouts have a fancy that they bring bad luck to the cooking. Any other kind of wood will do better.

This is as good a kind of camp kitchen as any: it is made with two lines of sods, bricks, stones, or thick logs, flattened at the top, about six feet long, slightly splayed from each other, being

CAMP KITCHEN

four inches apart at one end and eight inches at the other — the big end towards the wind.

Another way, when there are several " billies " to cook, is to put them in two lines a few inches apart, one end of the line facing towards the wind. Lay your fire of small wood between the two lines, and put a third row of "billies" standing on top of the

first two rows — so that a small tunnel is made by the " billies."
In the windward end of this tunnel start your fire; the draught
will carry its heat along the tunnel, and this will heat all the pots
The fire should be kept up with small split chunks of wood.

When boiling a pot of water on the fire do not jam the lid on
too firmly, as, when the steam forms inside the pot, it must have
some means of escape, or it will burst the pot.

To find out when the water is beginning to boil, you need not
take off the lid and look, but just hold the end of a stick or knife,
etc., to the pot, and if the water is boiling you will feel it trembling.

KABOBS. — Cut your meat up into a slice about half or three-
quarters of an inch thick; cut this up into small pieces about one
to one and a half inches across. String a lot of these chunks on
to a stick or iron rod, and plant it in front of the fire, or suspend
it over the hot embers for a few minutes till the meat is roasted.

HUNTER'S STEW. — Chop your meat into small chunks about
an inch or one and a half inches square.

Scrape and chop up any vegetables, such as potatoes, carrots,
onions, etc., and put them into your " billy."

Add clean water or soup till it is half full.

Mix some flour, salt, and pepper together, and rub your .neat
well in it, and put this in the " billy."

There should be enough water just to cover the food — no
more.

Let the " billy " stand in the embers and simmer for about
one hour and a quarter.

The potatoes take longest to cook. When these are soft
(which you try with a fork) enough not to lift out, the whole stew
is cooked.

Bread-making

" The three B's of life in camp are the ability to cook bannocks, beans, and bacon."

To make bread, or bannocks, the usual way is for a scout to
take off his coat, spread it on the ground, with the inside upper-
most (so that any mess he makes in it will not show outwardly
when he wears his coat afterwards). Then he washes his hands
thoroughly. Then he makes a pile of flour on the coat, and
scoops out the centre until it forms a cup for the water, which
he then pours in; he then mixes the dough with a pinch or two
of salt, and of baking powder or of Eno's Fruit Salt, and kneads
and mixes it well together until it forms a lump of well-mixed

dough. Then, with a little fresh flour sprinkled over the hands to prevent the dough sticking to them, he pats it and makes it into the shape of a large bun or several buns.

Then he puts it on a gridiron over hot ashes, or sweeps part of the fire to one side, and on the hot ground left there he puts his dough, and piles hot ashes round it and lets it bake itself.

Only small loaves, or bannocks, like buns, can be made in this way.

If real bread is required, a kind of oven has to be made, either by using an old earthenware pot or tin box, and putting it into the fire and piling fire all over it, or by making a clay oven, lighting a fire inside it, and then, when it is well heated, raking out the fire and putting the dough inside, and shutting up the entrance tightly till the bread is baked.

Another way is to cut a stout club, sharpen its thin end, peel it, and heat it in the fire. Make a long strip of dough, about two inches wide and half an inch thick; wind it spirally down the club; then plant the club close to the fire and let the dough toast itself, just giving the club a turn now and then.

RATION BAGS. — Very often on service they serve you out with a double handful of flour instead of bread or biscuits, a bit of meat, a spoonful of salt, one of pepper, one of sugar, one of baking-powder, and a handful of coffee or tea. It is rather fun to watch a tenderfoot get this ration and see how he carries it away to his bivouac.

How would you do it?

Of course you could put the pepper into one pocket, the salt into another, the sugar into another, the flour into your hat, and carry that in one hand, the bit of beef in the other hand, and the coffee in the other.

Only if you are in your shirt-sleeves, as you generally are, you haven't many pockets, and if, like some people, you have only two hands, it is a difficult job.

The old campaigner, therefore, always has his three " ration bags " — little bags which he makes himself out of bits of shirt-tails or pocket-handkerchiefs, or other such luxuries; and into one he puts the flour and baking-powder, into No. 2 his coffee and sugar, into No. 3 his salt and pepper.

Very often just after we had got our rations we would have to march at once. How do you suppose we made our flour into bread in one minute?

We just mixed it with a lot of water in a mug, and drank it ! It did just as well in the end.

Cattle-driving and Slaughtering

Before you cook your hare you've got to catch him.   So with mutton or beef — you have to bring the sheep or ox to the place where you want him.   Then you have to kill him and cut him up before you can cook him and eat him.

Scouts ought to know how to drive sheep and cattle and horses.   Tenderfoots always forget to send some one in front of the herd to draw them on.

Sheep are apt to crowd up too much together, so that those in the middle of the flock soon get half suffocated in dust and heat, and then they faint.   It is always, therefore, advisable for one driver to keep moving in the centre of the flock to make an occasional opening for air, and it keeps the whole flock moving better. If you come to an obstacle like a fence or wall with sheep, lift one or two over it and the rest will soon follow, but they should not be too hurried.

Scouts should also know how to kill and cut up their cattle.

Cattle are generally poleaxed, or a spike is driven into the forehead with a mallet, or a shot or blank cartridge is fired into the forehead, or a big, sharp knife is driven into the spine just behind the horns, the animal's head having first been securely tied down to a cart-wheel or fence.

Sheep are generally killed either by being laid on the back and having the head drawn back and throat cut with a big sharp knife, or by being shot in the forehead with a revolver or blank cartridge of a rifle.

If you are a beginner in slaughtering with the knife, it is sometimes useful first to drop the animal insensible by a heavy blow with a big hammer or back of a felling-axe on the top of the head.

After being killed the animal should then be gutted by having the belly slit open and the inside taken out, liver and kidneys being kept.

To skin the beast lay the carcass on its back and slit the skin down the centre with a sharp knife, slit up the inside of the legs, and pull the skin off, helping it with the knife where it sticks to the body, first one side and then the other, down to the backbone.

In the case of a sheep the carcass should be securely hung up by the hind legs, and, after slitting round the head and legs and down the centre, the fleece can be pulled off like an overcoat.

The carcass is split in half in the case of a big beast; with a sheep it is cut into two, and the forequarters and hindquarters are then again divided into joints.

A scout should know how to milk a cow or a goat, else he may go thirsty when there is lots of milk available. A goat is not so easy to milk as you might think. You have to keep hold of its head with one hand, its hind leg with the other, and milk it with the other if you have a third. The way a native does it is to catch hold of its hind leg between his big toe and the next, and thus he has a hand to spare to milk with.

Cleanliness

One thing to remember in camp is that if you get sick you are no use as a scout, and are only a burden to others, and you generally get ill through your own fault. Either you don't change into dry clothes when you get wet, or you let dirt get into your food, or you drink bad water.

So, when cooking your food, always be careful to clean your cooking-pots, plates, forks, etc., very thoroughly.

Flies are most dangerous, because they carry about seeds of disease on their feet, and if they settle on your food they will often leave the poison there for you to eat — and then you wonder why you get ill. Flies generally live best where there is dirt and scraps of food are left lying about.

For this reason you should be careful to keep your camp very clean, so that flies won't come there. All slops and scraps should be thrown away into a properly dug hole, where they can be buried, and not scattered about all over the place. Patrol leaders must be very careful to see that this is always done.

For the same reason it is very dangerous to drink out of streams, and especially out of ponds, when you feel thirsty, for you may suck down any amount of poison in doing so. If a pond is your only water-supply, it is best to dig a small well, three feet deep, about ten feet away from the pond, and the water will ooze through into it, and will be much more healthy to drink.

We did this in Mafeking when the Boers cut off our regular water supply, and so had no sickness from bad water.

Sulphate of copper, one part to a million of water, is used in South America for purifying lakes and ponds.

HINTS TO INSTRUCTORS

Practise mixing dough and baking; it is useful. If possible, get a baker to give a lesson. But let each scout mix his own dough with the amount of water he thinks right. Let him make his mistakes at first to get experience.

A visit to a slaughter-house and butcher's shop to see the cutting up is useful for boys.

Get scouts to make their own linen ration bags.

Issue raw rations, and let each scout make his own fire and cook his own meal.

Camp Games

Baseball, football, basketball, which is practically football played only with the hands, with a basket seven feet above ground as goal. A small bit of ground or room or court will do for the game.

" Bang the Bear " (from Mr. Thompson Seton's " Birchbark of the Woodcraft Indians "). One big boy is bear, and has three bases in which he can take refuge and be s fe. He carries a small air balloon on his back. The other boys are armed with clubs of straw rope twisted, with which they try to burst his balloon while he is outside the base. The bear has a similar club, with which he knocks off the hunters' hats. The hat represents the hunter's life. A good game for introducing strange or shy boys to each other.

Songs, recitations, small plays, etc., can be performed round the camp fire, and every scout should be made to contribute something to the programme, whether he thinks he is a performer or not. A different patrol may be told off for each night of the week to provide for the performance; they can thus prepare it beforehand.

BOOKS TO READ

" Woodcraft," by Nessmuk. Price 5s. (Forest and Stream, New York.)

" Active Service Pocket Book," by Lt. B. Stewart. Price 4s. nett.

CHAPTER IV

TRACKING

HINTS TO INSTRUCTORS

Instruction in the art of observation and deduction is difficult to lay down in black and white. It must be taught by practice. One can give only a few instances and hints, the rest depends upon your own powers of imagination and local circumstances.

The importance of the power of observation and deduction to the young citizen is great. Children are proverbially quick in observation, but it dies out as they grow older, largely because first experiences catch their attention, which they fail to do on repetition.

OBSERVATION *is, in fact, a habit to which a boy has to be trained.* TRACKING *is an interesting step towards gaining it.* DEDUCTION *is the art of subsequently reasoning out and extracting the meaning from the points observed.*

When once observation and deduction have been made habitual in the boy, a great step in the development of " character " has been gained.

CAMP FIRE YARN. No. 11.

OBSERVATION OF "SIGN"

Noticing "Sign" — Details of People — Sign round a Dead
Body — Details in the Country — Use of Eyes, Ears, and
Nose by Scouts — Night Scouting — Games in Observation.

Noticing "Sign"

" Sign " is the word used by scouts to mean any little details,
such as footprints, broken twigs, trampled grass, scraps of food,
a drop of blood, a hair, and so on; anything that may help as
clues in getting the information they are in search of.

Mrs. Walter Smithson, when travelling in Kashmir last year,
was following up with some native Indian trackers the " pugs "
of a panther which had killed and carried off a young buck. He
had crossed a wide, bare slab of rock which, of course, gave no
mark of his soft feet. The tracker went at once to the far side
of the rock where it came to a sharp edge; he wetted his finger,
and just passed it along the edge till he found a few buck's hairs
sticking to it. This showed him where the panther had passed
down off the rock, dragging the buck with him. Those few hairs
were what scouts call " sign."

Mrs. Smithson's tracker also found bears by noticing small
" sign." On one occasion he noticed a fresh scratch in the bark
of a tree, evidently made by a bear's claw, and on the other he
found a single black hair sticking to the bark of a tree, which
told him that a bear had rubbed against it.

One of the most important things that a scout has to learn,
whether he is a war scout or a peace scout or a hunter, is *to let
nothing escape his attention;* he must notice small points and
signs, and then make out the meaning of them; but it takes a
good deal of practice before a tenderfoot can get into the habit
of really noting everything and letting nothing escape his eye.
It can be learned just as well in a town as in the country.

And in the same way you should notice any strange sound or
any peculiar smell and think for yourself what it may mean.
Unless you learn to notice " signs " you will have very little of
" this and that " to put together, and so you will be no use as
a scout. It comes by practice.

Remember, a scout always considers it a great disgrace if an
outsider discovers a thing before he has seen it for himself,

whether that thing is far away in the distance or close by under his feet.

If you go out with a really trained scout, you will see that his eyes are constantly moving, looking out in every direction, near and far, noticing everything that is going on, just from habit, not because he wants to show off how much he notices.

I was walking with one the other day in Hyde Park in London. He presently remarked, " That horse is going a little lame " — there was no horse near us, but I found he was looking at one far away across the Serpentine; the next moment he picked up a peculiar button lying by the path. His eyes, you see, were looking both far away and near.

In the streets of a strange town a scout will notice his way by the principal buildings and side-streets, and in any case he will notice what shops he passes and what is in their windows; also what vehicles pass him and such details as whether the horses' harness and shoes are all right; and most especially what people he passes, what their faces are like, their dress, their boots, and their way of walking, so that if, for instance, he should be asked by a policeman, " Have you seen a man with dark overhanging eyebrows, dressed in a blue suit, going down this street? " he should be able to give some such answer as " Yes — he was walking a little lame with the right foot, wore peculiar looking boots, was carrying a parcel in his hand; he turned down Gold Street, the second turning on the left from here, about three minutes ago."

Information of that kind has often been of the greatest value in tracing out a criminal, but so many people go along with their eyes shut and never notice things.

In the story of " Kim," by Rudyard Kipling, there is an account of two boys being taught " observation " in order to become detectives, or scouts, by means of a game in which a trayful of small objects was shown to them for a minute and was then covered over and they had to describe all the things on it from memory.

We will have that game, as it is excellent practice for scouts.

There was a revolutionary society in Italy called the Camorra, who used to train their boys to be quick at noticing and remembering things. When walking through the streets of the city, the Camorrist would suddenly stop and ask his boy — " How was the woman dressed who sat at the door of the fourth house on the right in the last street? " or, " What were the two men talking about whom we met at the corner of the last street but three?" or, "Where was the cab ordered to drive to, and what was its number?" "What is the height of that house and what is the width of its upper-floor window?" and so on. Or the boy was given a minute to look in a shop window, and then he had to describe all that was in it. Captain Cook, the great explorer and scout, was trained in the same way as a boy, and so was Houdin, the great conjurer.

Every town scout should know, as a matter of course, where is the nearest drug-store (in case of accidents), the nearest police "fixed point," police station, hospital, fire alarm, telephone, ambulance station, etc.

The scout must also have his eyes on the ground, especially along the edge of the pavement against the houses or in the gutter. I have often found valuable trinkets that have been dropped, and which have been walked over by numbers of people, and swept to one side by ladies' dresses without being noticed.

Details of People

When you are travelling by train or street car always notice every little thing about your fellow-travellers; notice their faces, dress, way of talking, and so on, so that you could describe them each pretty accurately afterwards; and also try and make out from their appearance and behavior whether they are rich or poor (which you can generally tell from their boots), and what is their probable business, whether they are happy, or ill, or in want of help.

HOW THE WEARING OF A HAT SHOWS CHARACTER

But in doing this you must not let them see you are watching them, else it puts them on their guard. Remember the shepherd-boy who noticed the gypsy's boots, but did not look at him, and so did not make the gypsy suspicious of him.

Close observation of people and ability to read their character and their thoughts are of immense value in trade and commerce, especially for a clerk or salesman in persuading people to buy goods, or in detecting would-be swindlers.

It is said that you can tell a man's character from the way he wears his hat. If it is slightly on one side, the wearer is good-natured; if it is worn very much on one side, he is a swaggerer; if on the back of his head, he is bad at paying his debts; if worn straight on the top, he is probably honest but very dull.

The way a man, or a woman, walks is often a good guide to character — witness the fussy, swaggering little man paddling along with short steps with much arm-action; the nervous man's hurried, jerky stride; the slow slouch of the loafer; the smooth, quick, and silent step of the scout, and so on.

I was once accused of mistrusting men with waxed mustaches. Well, so, to a certain extent, I do. It often means vanity, and sometimes drink.

Certainly the lock of hair which some lads wear on their forehead is a sure sign of silliness. The shape of the face gives a good guide to the man's character.

Perhaps you can tell the characters of these gentlemen?

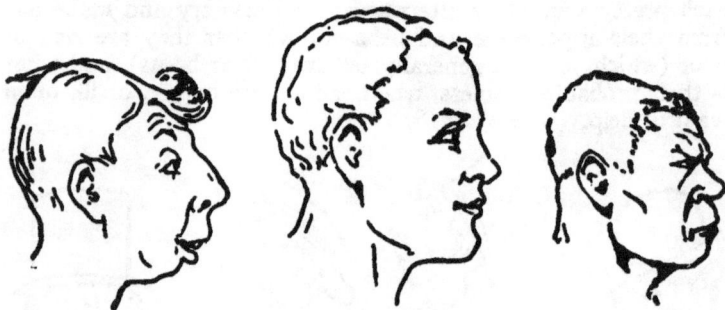

Practise Observation

A well-known detective, Mr. Justin Chevasse, describes how, with a little practice in observation, you can tell pretty accurately a man's character from his dress.

The boots are very generally the best test of all the details of clothing. I was with a lady the other day in the country, and a young lady was walking just in front of us. " I wonder who she is? " said my friend. "Well," I said, "I should be inclined to say I wonder whose maid she is." The girl was very well dressed, but when I saw her boots I guessed that the dress had belonged to some one else, had been given to her and refitted by herself — but that as regards boots she felt more comfortable in her own. She went up to the house at which we were staying — to the servants' entrance — and we found that she was the maid of one of the ladies staying there.

I was speaking with a detective not long ago about a gentleman we had both been talking to, and we were trying to make out his character. I remarked, " Well, at any rate, he is a fisherman "; but my companion could not see why — but then he was not a fisherman himself. I had noticed a lot of little tufts of cloth sticking up on the left cuff of his coat. A good many fishermen, when they take their flies off the line, stick them into their cap to dry; others stick them into their sleeve. When dry they pull them out, which often tears a thread or two of the cloth.

It is an amusing practice when you are in a railway train or a street car with other people to look only at their feet and guess, without looking any higher, what sort of people they are, old or young, well-to-do or poor, fat or thin, and so on, and then look up and see how near you have been to the truth.

Mr. Nat Goodwin, the American actor, once described to me how he went to see a balloon ascent at a time when he happened to be suffering from a stiff neck. He was able only to look down instead of up, and he could see only the feet of the people round him in the crowd. So he chose among the feet those that he felt sure belonged to an affable, kind-hearted man, who would describe to him what the balloon was doing.

I once was able to be of service to a lady who was in poor circumstances, as I guessed it from noticing, while walking behind her, that though she was well dressed the soles of her shoes were in the last stage of disrepair. I don't suppose she ever knew how I guessed that she was in a bad way.

But it is surprising how much of the sole of the boot you can see when behind a person walking — and it is equally surprising how much meaning you can read from that boot. It is said that to wear out soles and heels equally is to give evidence of business capacity and honesty; to wear your heels down on the outside means that you are a man of imagination and love of adventure; but heels worn down on the inside signify weakness and indecision of character, and this last sign is more infallible in the case of man than in that of woman.

Remember how " Sherlock Holmes " met a stranger and noticed that he was looking fairly well-to-do, in new clothes with a
mourning band on his sleeve, with a soldierly bearing, and a
sailor's way of walking, sunburnt, with tattoo marks on his hands,
and he was carrying some children's toys in his hand.   What
should you have supposed that man to be?   Well, Sherlock
Holmes guessed, correctly, that he had lately retired from the
Royal Marines as a Sergeant, and his wife had died, and he had
some small children at home.

" Sign " Round a Dead Body

It may happen to some of you that one day you will be the first
to find the dead body of a man, in which case you will remember
that it is your duty to examine and note down the smallest signs
that are to be seen on and near the body before it is moved or the
ground disturbed and trampled down.   Besides noticing the
exact position of the body (which should, if possible, be photo-
graphed exactly as found)'the ground all round should be very
carefully examined — without treading on it yourself more than is
absolutely necessary, for fear of spoiling existing tracks.   If you
can also draw a little map of how the body lay and where the
signs round it were, it might be of value.

Twice, lately, bodies have been found which were at first supposed to be those of people who had hanged themselves; but
close examination of the ground round them—in one case some
torn twigs and trampled grass, and in the other a crumpled
carpet — showed that murder had been committed, and that the
bodies had been hung after death to make it appear as though
they had committed suicide.

Finger-marks should especially be looked for on any likely
articles, and if they do not correspond to those of the murdered
man, they may be those of his murderer, who could then be
identified by comparing the impression with his fingers.   Such
a case occurred in India, where a man was found murdered and
a bloody finger-mark on his clothes.   The owner of the finger-
mark was found, tried, and convicted.

Dr. Gross relates the story of a learned old gentleman who
was found dead in his bedroom with a wound in his forehead
and another in his left temple.

Very often, after a murder, the murderer, with his hands bloody
from the deed and running away, may catch hold of the door,
or a jug of water to wash his hands.

In the present case a newspaper lying on the table had the marks of three blood-stained fingers on it.

The son of the dead man was suspected, and was arrested by the police.

But careful examination of the room and the prints of the finger-marks showed that the old gentleman had been taken ill in the night — had got out of bed to get some medicine, but getting near the table a new spasm seized him and he fell, striking his head violently against the corner of the table, and made the wound on his temple, which just fitted the corner. In trying to get up he had caught hold of the table and the newspaper on it, and had made the bloody finger-marks on the newspaper in doing so. Then he had fallen again, cutting his head a second time on the foot of the bed.

The finger-marks were compared with the dead man's fingers, and were found to be exactly the same. Well, you don't find two men in 64,000,000,000,000 with the same pattern on the skin of their fingers. So it was evident there had been no murder, and the dead man's son was released as innocent.

In St. Petersburg in Russia a banker was found murdered. Near the body was found a cigar-holder with an amber mouthpiece. This mouthpiece was of peculiar shape, and could be held in the mouth only in one position, and it had two teeth marks in it. These marks showed that the two teeth were of different lengths.

The teeth of the murdered man were quite regular, so the cigar-holder was evidently not his. But his nephew had teeth which corresponded to the marks on the mouthpiece, so he was arrested, and then further proof came up and showed that he was the murderer.

[*Compare the story in " Sherlock Holmes' Memoirs " called " The Resident Patient," in which a man was found hanging and was considered to be a suicide till Sherlock Holmes came in and showed various signs, such as cigar ends bitten by different teeth, footprints, and that three men had been in the room with the dead man for some time previous to his death and had hanged him.*]

Details in the Country

If you are in the country you should notice landmarks, that is, objects which help you to find your way or prevent you getting lost, such as distant hills, church towers, and nearer objects, such as peculiar buildings, trees, gates, rocks, etc.

And remember in noticing such landmarks that you may want to use your knowledge of them some day for telling some one else how to find his way, so you must notice them pretty closely so as to be able to describe them unmistakably and in their proper order. You must notice and *remember* every by-road and foot-path.

Then you must also notice smaller signs, such as birds getting up and flying hurriedly, which means somebody or some animal is there; dust shows animals, men, or vehicles moving.

Of course, when in the country you should notice, just as much as in town, all passers-by very carefully — how they are dressed, what their faces are like, and their way of walking, and examine their footmarks — and jot down a sketch of them in your note-book, so that you would know the footmark again if you found it somewhere else (as the shepherd boy did in the story at the beginning of this book).

And notice all tracks — that is, footmarks of men, animals, birds, wheels, etc., for from these you can read the most important information, as Captain d'Artagnan did in the story of the secret duel, in my " Yarns for Boy Scouts," is.

This track-reading is of such importance that I shall give you a lecture on that subject by itself.

Using your Eyes

Let nothing be too small for your notice; a button, a match, a cigar ash, a feather, or a leaf might be of great importance.

Remember too that there are a number of people now who wear the Scouts' Badge of Thanks, and it would be a great disgrace to a scout if he let one of these people pass him without noticing it, and asking if he could be of any service.

A scout must look not only to the front, but also to either side and behind him; he must have "eyes at the back of his head," as the saying is.

Often, by suddenly looking back, you will see an enemy's scout or a thief showing himself in a way that he would not have done had he thought you would look round.

There is an interesting story by Fenimore Cooper called " The Pathfinder," in which the action of an Indian scout is well described. He had " eyes at the back of his head," and after passing some bushes he caught sight of a withered leaf or two among the fresh ones, which made him suspect that somebody might have put the leaves there to make a better hiding-place, and so he discovered some hidden fugitives.

Night Scouting

A scout has to be able to notice small details just as much by night as by day, and this he has to do chiefly by listening, occasionally by feeling or smelling.

In the stillness of the night sounds carry farther than by day. If you put your ear to the ground or place it against a stick, or especially against a drum, which is touching the ground, you will hear the shake of horses' hoofs or the thud of a man's footfall a long way off. Another way is to open a knife with a blade at each end, stick one blade into the ground and hold the other between your teeth, and you will hear all the better. The human voice, even though talking low, carries to a great distance, and is not likely to be mistaken for any other sound.

I have often passed through outposts at night after having found where the pickets were posted by hearing the low talking of the men or the snoring of those asleep.

A BOOK TO READ ON OBSERVATION

"Aids to Scouting." Price 1s. nett. (Gale and Polden.)

HINTS TO INSTRUCTORS

How to Teach Observation in Practice—Practices

IN TOWNS: *Practise your boys first in walking down a street to notice the different kinds of shops as they pass and to remember them in their proper sequence at the end.*

Then to notice and remember the names on the shops.

Then to notice and remember the contents of a shop window after two minutes' gaze. Finally to notice the contents of several shop windows in succession, with half a minute at each.

The boys must also notice prominent buildings as landmarks, the number of turnings off the street they are using; names of other streets; details of horses and vehicles passing by; and, especially, details of the people as to dress, features, gait; numbers on motor cars, policemen, etc.

Take them the first time to show them how to do it; and after that send them out and on their return question them, as below.

Make them learn for themselves to notice and remember the

whereabouts of all drug-stores, fire alarms, police fixed points, am-bulances, etc.

IN THE COUNTRY: *Take the patrol out for a walk and teach the boys to notice distant prominent features as landmarks, such as hills, church steeples, and so on; and as nearer landmarks, such things as peculiar buildings, trees, rocks, gates, etc.; by-roads or paths, nature of fences, crops; different kinds of trees, birds, animals, tracks, etc., also people, vehicles, etc. Also any peculiar smells of plants, animals, manure, etc.*

Then send them out a certain walk, and on their return have them in one by one and examine them verbally, or have them all in and let them write their answers on, say, six questions which you give them with reference to certain points which they should have noticed.

It adds to the value of the practice if you make a certain num-ber of small marks in the ground beforehand, or leave buttons or matches, etc., for the boys to notice or to pick up and bring in (as a means of making them examine the ground close to them, as well as distant objects).

TELLING CHARACTER: *Send scouts out for half an hour to look for, say, a brutish character, or a case of genteel poverty, etc.*

The scout must on his return be able to describe the person accurately, and give the reasons which made him think the person was of the character he reports.

He should also state how many other characters he passed in his search, such as silly, good-natured, deceitful, swaggering, and so on, judging of course by their faces, their walk, their boots, hats, clothing, etc.

Games in Observation

THIMBLE-FINDING (Indoors)

Send the patrol out of the room.

Take a thimble, ring, coin, bit of paper, or any small article, and place it where it is perfectly visible, but in a spot where it is not likely to be noticed. Let the patrol come in and look for it. When one of them sees it he should go and quietly sit down without indicating to the others where it is.

After a fair time he should be told to point it out to those who have not succeeded in finding it.

[This ensures his really having seen it.]

SHOP WINDOW (Outdoors in town)

Umpire takes a patrol down a street past six shops. Gives them half a minute at each shop, then, after moving them off to some distance, he gives each boy a pencil and card, and tells him to write from memory, or himself takes down what they noticed in, say, the third and fifth shops. The one who sets down most articles correctly wins. It is useful practice to match one boy against another in heats — the loser competing again, till you arrive at the worst. This gives the worst scouts the most practice.

SIMILAR GAME (Indoors)

Send each scout in turn into a room for half a minute; when he comes out take down a list of furniture and articles which he notices. The boy who notices most wins.

The simplest way of scoring is to make a list of the articles in the room on your scoring-paper with a column for marks for each scout against them, which can then easily be totalled up at foot.

SPOTTING THE SPOT (Indoors — town or country)

Show a series of photographs or sketches of objects in the neighborhood such as would be known to all the scouts if they kept their eyes open — such, for instance, as cross-roads, curious window, gargoyle or weathercock, tree, reflection in the water (guess the building causing it), and so on.

A pair of scouts can play most of the above competitions off between themselves, if they like, as a matter of practice.

Patrol leaders can match one pair of their scouts against another pair in the game, and thus get them really practised at it, and when they become really good he can challenge other patrols to compete against his.

FOLLOW THE TRAIL

Send out a " hare," either walking or cycling, with a pocketful of corn, nutshells, confetti paper or buttons, etc., and drop a few here and there to give a trail for the patrol to follow.

Or go out with a piece of chalk and draw the patrol sign on walls, gateposts, pavements, lamp-posts, trees, etc., every here and there, and let the patrol hunt you by these marks. Patrols should wipe out all these marks as they pass them for tidiness, and so as not to mislead them for another day's practice.

The other road signs should also be used, such as closing up certain roads as not used, and hiding a letter at some point, giving directions as to the next turn.

Scout's Nose (Indoors)

Prepare a number of paper bags, all alike, and put in each a different-smelling article, such as chopped onion in one, tan in another, rose leaves, leather, aniseed, violet powder, orange peel, etc. Put these packets in a row a couple of feet apart, and let each competitor walk down the line and have five seconds' sniff at each. At the end he has one minute in which to write down or to state to the umpire the names of the different objects smelled, from memory, in their correct order.

Far and Near (For town or country)

Umpire goes along a given road or line of country with a patrol in patrol formation. He caries a scoring card with the name of each scout on it.

Each scout looks out for the details required, and directly he notices one he runs to the umpire and informs him or hands in the article, if it is an article he finds. The umpire enters a mark accordingly against his name. The scout who gains most marks in the walk wins.

Details like the following should be chosen, to develop the scout's observation and to encourage him to look far and near, up and down, etc.

The details should be varied every time the game is played; and about eight or ten should be given at a time.

Every match found	1 point
Every button found	1 "
Birds' foot tracks	2 points
Patch noticed on stranger's clothing or boots	2 "
Gray horse seen	2 "
Pigeon flying	2 "
Sparrow sitting	1 point
Ash-tree	2 points
Broken chimney-pot	2 "
Broken window	1 point

CAMP FIRE YARN. No. 12

SPOORING

Men's Tracks—Animals' Tracks—How to learn " Spooring."

Men's Tracks

GENERAL DODGE, of the United States Army, describes how he once had to pursue a party of Indians who had been murdering some people.

The murderers had nearly a week's start, and had gone away on horseback. But General Dodge got a splendid tracking-scout named Espinosa to help him. The Indians were all riding unshod horses, except one, and after Espinosa had been tracking them for many miles he suddenly got off his horse and pulled four horseshoes out of a hidden crevice in the rocks. The Indian had evidently pulled them off so that they should not leave a track.

For six days they pursued the band, and for a great part of the time there was no sign visible to an ordinary eye, and after going for 150 miles they eventually overtook and captured the whole party. But it was all entirely due to Espinosa's good tracking.

On another occasion some United States troops were following up a number of Indians, who had been raiding and murdering whites, and they had some Indian scouts to assist them in tracking. In order to make a successful attack, they marched by night, and the trackers found the way in the darkness by feeling the tracks of the enemy with their hands, and they went at a fairly good pace for many miles, merely touching the track with their fingers; but suddenly they halted and reported that the track they had been following had been crossed by a fresh track, and on the commanding officer going up, he found the Indians still holding the track with their hands, so that there should be no mistake. A light was brought, and it was found that the new track was that of a bear which had walked across the trail of the enemy! So the march continued without further incident, and the enemy were surprised and caught in the early hours of the morning.

The scout, Burnham, in South Africa, who was with Wilson's party when they were massacred on the Shangani River in Matabeleland, was sent away with a despatch shortly before they were surrounded. He travelled during the night to escape the observation of the enemy. He found his way by feeling for the tracks left in the mud by the column when it marched up there in the morning.

I myself led a column through an intricate part of the Matopo Mountains in Rhodesia by night to attack the enemy's stronghold which I had reconnoitred the previous day. I found the way by feeling my own tracks, sometimes with my hands and sometimes through the soles of my shoes, which had worn very thin; and I never had any difficulty in finding the line.

Tracking, or following up tracks, is called by different names in different countries. Thus, in South Africa you would talk only of " spooring," that is, following up the " spoor "; in India it would be following the " pugs," or " pugging "; in Canada it is "trailing."

It is one of the principal ways by which scouts gain information and hunters find their game. But to become a good tracker you must begin young, and practise it at all times when you are out walking, whether in town or country.

If at first you constantly remind yourself to do it, you will soon find that you do it as a habit without having to remind yourself. And it is a very useful habit, and makes the dullest walk interesting.

Hunters, when they are looking about in a country to find game, first look for any tracks, old or new, to see if there are any animals in the country; then they study the newer marks to find out where the animals are hiding themselves; then, after they have found a fresh track, they follow it up till they find the animal and kill him; and afterwards they often have to retrace their own tracks to find their way back to camp. And war scouts do much the same as regards their enemies.

First of all you must be able to distinguish one man's footmark from that of another, by its size, shape, and nails, etc. And similarly the prints of horses and other animals.

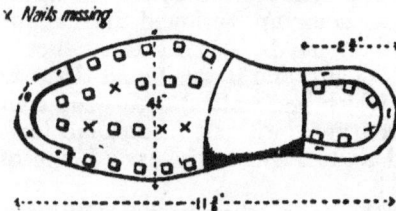

x Nails missing

The way in which the diagram of a boot-track should be drawn

From a man's track, that is, from the size of his foot and the length of his stride, you can tell, to a certain extent, his height.

In taking notes of a track you should pick out a well-marked print, very carefully measure its length, length of heel, with widest point of tread, width at waist, width of heel, number of rows of nails, and number of nails in each row, heel and toe-plates or nails, shape of nail-heads, etc.

It is best to make a diagram of the footprint thus — nails missing.

You should also measure very carefully the length of the man's stride from the toe of one foot to the heel of the other.

NOTE TO INSTRUCTOR: *Make each scout take off his own boot and draw a diagram of it on paper, putting in all nails and other points. Or, out-of-doors, give each scout the outline ready drawn of a footmark, and then let him find a footmark (or make his own) and fill in the details of nail-marks, etc.*

Also he should note down the length of stride taken, and how much the feet point outwards from the straight direction of their path.

A man was once found drowned in a river. It was supposed that he must have fallen in accidentally, and that the cuts on his head were caused by stones, etc., in the river. But some one took a drawing of his boots, and after searching the river-bank came on his tracks, and followed them up to a spot where there had evidently been a struggle, the ground being much trampled and bushes broken down to the water's edge, and the track of two other men's feet. And though these men were never found, it showed the case to be one of probable murder, which would not otherwise have been suspected.

A scout must learn to recognize at a glance at what pace the maker of the tracks was going, and so on.

A man walking puts the whole flat of his foot on the ground, each foot a little under a yard from the other. In running the toes are more deeply dug into the ground, and a little dirt is kicked up, and the feet are more than a yard apart. Sometimes men walk backwards in order to deceive any one who may be tracking, but a good scout can generally tell this at once by the stride being shorter, the toes more turned in, and the heels being tightly impressed.

With animals, if they are moving fast, their toes are more deeply dug into the ground, and they kick up the dirt, and their paces are longer than when going slowly.

You ought to be able to tell the pace at which a horse has been going directly you see the tracks.

At a walk the horse makes two pair of hoof-prints — the near (left) hind foot close in front of near fore foot mark, and the off (right) fore foot similarly just beyond the print of the off hind foot.

At a trot the track is similar, but the stride is longer.

The hind feet are generally longer and narrower in shape than the fore feet.

Horse's Tracks

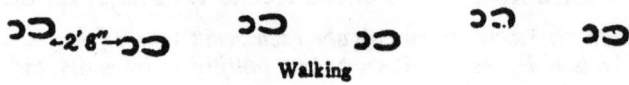

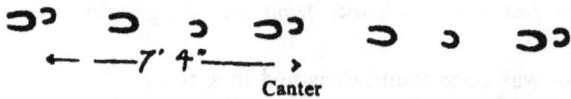

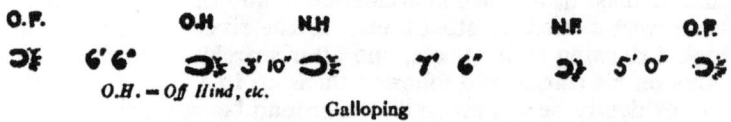

Walking

Trotting

Canter

O.F.   O.H   N.H   N.F.   O.F.

O.H. — Off Hind, etc.

Galloping

Lame Horse Walking : Which leg is he lame in?
N.B. — *The long feet are the hind feet.*

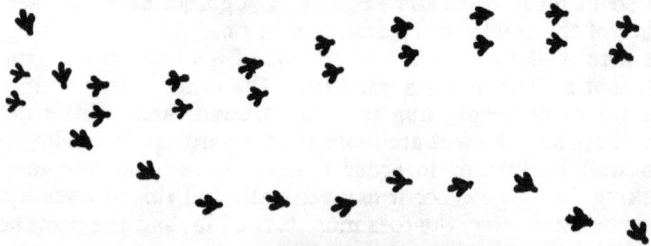

These are the tracks of two birds on the ground. One lives generally on the ground, the other in bushes and trees. Which track belongs to which bird?

Native trackers boast that not only can they tell a person's sex and age by their tracks, but also their characters. They say that people who turn out their toes much are generally " liars."

It was a trick with highwaymen of old, and with horse-stealers more recently, to put their horses' shoes on wrong way round in order to deceive trackers who might try to follow them up, but a good tracker would not be taken in. Similarly, thieves often walk backwards for the same reason, but a clever tracker will very soon recognize the deception.

Wheel tracks should also be studied till you can tell the difference between the track of a gun, a carriage, a country car, motor car, or a bicycle, *and the direction they were going in.* [*See diagram.*]

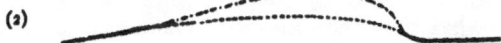

(2) *The direction of a bicycle is further shown by the loops made in the track where the rider has made a turn or wobble; the thinner end of the loop points in the direction he was going.*

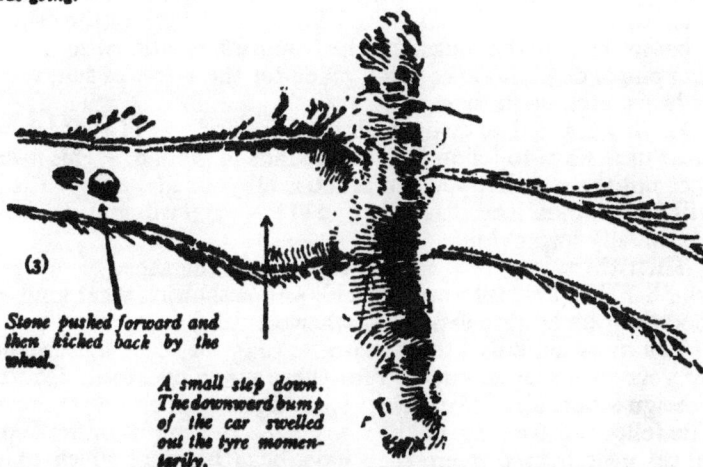

Stone pushed forward and then kicked back by the wheel.

A small step down. The downward bump of the car swelled out the tyre momentarily.

TRACK OF (1) (2) BICYCLE AND (3) MOTOR

In addition to learning to recognize the pace of tracks, you must get to know how old they are. This is a most important point, and requires a very great amount of practice and experience before you can judge it really well.

So much depends on the state of the ground and weather, and its effects on the spoor. If you follow one track, say on a dry, windy day, over varying ground, you will find that when it is on light, sandy soil, it will look old in a very short time, because any damp earth that it may kick up from under the surface will dry very rapidly to the same color as the surface dust, and the sharp edges of the footmarks will soon be rounded off by the breeze playing over the dry dust in which they are formed. When it gets into damp ground, the same track will look much fresher, because the sun will have only partially dried up the upturned soil, and the wind will not, therefore, have bevelled off the sharp edges of the impression, and if it gets into damp clay, under shade of trees, etc., where the sun does not get at it, the same track, which may have looked a day old in the sand, will here look quite fresh.

Of course, a great clew to the age of tracks will often be found in spots of rain having fallen on them since they were made (if you know at what time the rain fell), dust or grass seeds blown into them (if you noticed at what time the wind was blowing), or the crossing of other tracks over the original ones, or, where the grass has been trodden down, the extent to which it has since dried or withered. In following a horse, the length of time since it passed can also be judged by the freshness, or otherwise, of the droppings, due allowance being made for the effect of sun, rain, or birds, etc., upon them.

Having learned to distinguish the pace and age of spoor, you must next learn to follow it over all kinds of ground. This is an accomplishment that you can practise all your life, and you will still find yourself learning at the end of it — you will find yourself continually improving.

Then there is a great deal to learn from the ashes of fires — whether they are still warm or cold, scraps showing what kind of food the people were eating, whether plentiful or scarce.

You must not only keep a sharp lookout for scout signs made by your own scouts, but also for those made by hostile scouts. Foreign scouts also have their private signs — as also do tramps. The following are some of the signs made by tramps on walls or fences near houses where they have been begging, which they chalk up to warn others of their class: —

⊙ Very bad: they give you in charge here.

⋋ No good.

△ Too many tramps have been here already.

▢ Bad people.

There are very good native trackers in the Soudan and Egypt, and I saw some of their work there.

The colonel of the Egyptian Cavalry had had some things stolen out of his house, so a tracker was sent for from the neighboring Jaalin tribe. He soon found the footprints of the thief and followed them a long way out on to the desert, and found the spot where he had buried the stolen goods. His tracks then came back to the barracks. So the whole of the regiment was paraded without shoes on for the tracker to examine. And at the end, when he had seen every man walk, he said, " No, the thief is not there." Just then the colonel's native servant came up to him with a message, and the tracker, who was standing by, said to the colonel, " That is the man who buried the stolen goods." The servant, surprised at being found out, then confessed that it was he who had stolen his master's property, thinking that he would be the last man to be suspected.

Mr. Deakin, the ex-premier of Australia, told me how he travelled on board ship with a number of natives of Australia who were on the sea for the first time in their lives. When the ship got out to sea he noticed all these natives had got into the bows and were lying flat on the deck with their heads over the side staring intently into the water ahead of the ship. So interested were they in the water that for some time he could not get any reply to his question as to what they were looking at, till at length one of them said: " We cannot understand how the ship is finding its way across the sea; we cannot see the trail that it is following; we know that our eyes are sharp enough on shore, and often when we are guiding white men along a trail they say they cannot see the tracks which to us are clear enough — their eyes are different to ours. But here·at sea the English sailors evidently can see tracks ahead of them, otherwise they would not know which way to send the ship, and yet we, who are so good at seeing on shore, cannot see any sign of a track or mark on the water."

When getting on to very fresh spoor of man or beast, the old scout will generally avoid following it closely, because the hunted animal will frequently look back to see if it is being followed. The tracker therefore makes a circle, and comes back on to where he would expect to find the spoor again. If he finds it, he makes another circle farther ahead till he finds no spoor. Then he knows he is ahead of his game, so he gradually circles nearer and nearer till he finds it, taking care of course not to get to windward of the animal when within scenting distance.

Hints on Spooring

Some trackers of Scinde followed up a stolen camel from Karachi to Sehwan, 150 miles over sand and bare rock. The thieves, to escape detection, drove the camel up and down a crowded street, in order to get the trail mixed up with others — but the trackers foresaw this, and made a " cast " round the town, and hit on the outgoing spoor on the far side, which they successfully followed up.

In tracking where the spoor is difficult to see, such as on hard ground, or in grass, note the direction of the last footprint that you can see, then look on in the same direction, but well ahead of you, say twenty or thirty yards, and in grass you will generally see the blades bent or trodden, and on hard ground, possibly stones displaced or scratched, and so on, small signs which, seen in a line one behind the other, give a kind of track that otherwise would not be noticed. I once tracked a bicycle on a hard macadam road where it really made no impression at all, but by looking along the surface of the road for a long distance ahead of me, under the rising sun, as it happened, the line it had taken was quite visible through the almost invisible coating of dew upon the ground. Standing on the track and looking upon it close to my feet I could not see the slightest sign of it. The great thing is to look for a difficult track *against* the sun, so that the slightest dent in the ground throws a shadow.

If you lose sight of the track you must make a " cast " to find it again. To do this put your handkerchief, staff, or other mark, at the last footmark that you noticed, then work round it in a wide circle, say 30, 50, or 100 yards away from it as a centre— choosing the most favorable ground, soft ground if possible, to find signs of the outward track. If you are with a patrol it is generally best for the patrol to halt while one or perhaps two men make the cast. If everybody starts trying to find the spoor, they very soon defeat their object by treading it out or confusing it with their own footmarks — too many cooks easily spoil the broth in such a case.

In making a cast use your common sense as to which direction the enemy has probably taken, and try it there. I remember an instance of tracking a boar which illustrates what I mean. The boar had been running through some muddy, inundated fields, and was easy enough to follow until he turned off over some very hard and stony ground, where, after a little while, not a sign of his spoor was to be seen. A cast had accordingly to be made.

The last footmark was marked, and the tracker moved round a wide circle, examining the ground most carefully, but not a sign was found. Then the tracker took a look round the country, and, putting himself in place of the pig, said, " Now which direction would I have gone in? " Some distance to the front of him, as the original track led, stood a long hedge of prickly cactus; in it were two gaps. The tracker went to one of these as being the line the boar would probably take. Here the ground was still very hard, and no footmark was visible, but on a leaf of the cactus in the gap was a pellet of wet mud; and this gave the desired clew; there was no mud on this hard ground, but the pig had evidently brought some on his feet from the wet ground he had been travelling through. This one little sign enabled the tracker to work on in the right direction to another and another, until eventually he got on to the spoor again in favorable ground, and was able to follow up the boar to his resting-place.

I have watched a tracker in the Soudan following tracks where for a time they were quite invisible to the ordinary eye in this way. While the track was clear he made his own stride exactly to fit that of the track, so that he walked step for step with it, and he tapped the ground with his staff as he walked along — ticking off each footprint, as it were. When the footprints disappeared on hard ground, or had been buried by drifting sand, he still walked on at the same pace, tap-tapping the ground

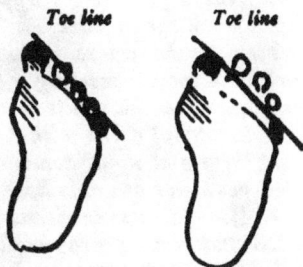

Toe line   Toe line

with his staff at the spot where there ought to have been a footprint. Occasionally he saw a slight depression or mark, which showed that there had been a footprint there, and thus he knew he was still on the right line.

It is very puzzling for a beginner to tell the difference between a lot of footmarks of bare feet — they all look so much alike; but this is the way that the police trackers in India do it. It may come in useful some day for a scout to know it in South Africa or Egypt, or other places where people go barefooted.

When measuring the footprint of the man you are after draw a line from the tip of the big toe to the tip of the little toe, and then notice where the other toes come with regard to this line, and note it down in your pocket-book. Then when you come to a number of tracks you have only to try this same line on one or two of them till you find the one you want; all people vary a little in the position of their toes.

Try it with the other scouts in your patrol, each of you making a footprint with his bare foot, and then noting how it is different from the others when the toe line is drawn.

HINTS TO INSTRUCTORS

PRACTICES IN TRACKING

1. The instructor should make his scouts prepare a well-rolled or flattened piece of ground (about ten or fifteen yards square) and make one boy walk across it, then run, and then bicycle across it. Part of the ground should be wet as if by rain, the other part dr

He can then explain the difference in the tracks, so that scou can tell at once from any tracks they may see afterwards whether a person was walking or running.

If possible, a day later, make fresh tracks alongside the old and notice the difference in appearance, so that the scouts can learn to judge the age of tracks.

Then make tracks of various kinds overrunning each other, such as a bicycle meeting a boy on foot, each going over the other's tracks, and let the scouts read the meaning.

2. Send out a boy with " tracking irons " on and let the patrol track him and notice when any other tracks override his, showing what people or animals have passed since.

N.B. — Tracking irons are an invention of Mr. Thompson Seton and can be strapped on to the soles of a scout's boots (like a pair of skates), so that wherever he goes he leaves a track similar to that of a deer. Instead of tracking irons you can easily use a few extra nails screwed into the sole or heel of your boots or into the butt of your staff in such a pattern as to make an unmistakable track.

Practices and Games in Spooring

TRACK MEMORY

Make a patrol sit with their feet up, so that other scouts can study them. Give the scouts, say, three minutes to study the boots. Then leaving the scouts in a room or out of sight, let one of the patrol make some footmarks in a good bit of ground. Call up the scouts one by one and let them see the track and say who made it.

TRACK DRAWING

Take out a patrol; set them on to one foot-track. Award a prize to the scout who makes the most accurate drawing of one of the footprints of the track. The scouts should be allowed to follow up the track till they get to a bit of ground where a good impression of it can be found.

SPOT THE THIEF

Get a stranger to make a track unseen by the scouts. The scouts study his track so as to know it again.

Then put the stranger among eight or ten others are let them all make their tracks for the boys to see, going by in rotation. Each scout then in turn whispers to the umpire which man made the original track — describing him by his number in filing past The scout who answers correctly wins; if more than one answers correctly, the one who then draws the best diagram from memory of the footprint, wins.

" SMUGGLERS OVER THE BORDER "

The " border " is a certain line of country about four hundred yards long, preferably a road or wide path or bit of sand, on which foot-tracks can easily be seen. One patrol watches the border with sentries posted along this road, with a reserve posted farther inland. This latter about halfway between the border and the " town "; the " town " would be a base marked by a tree, building, or flags, etc., about half a mile distant from the border. A hostile patrol of smugglers assembles about half a mile on the other side of the border. They will all cross the border, in any formation they please, either singly or together or scattered, and make for the town, either walking or running, or at scout's pace. Only one among them is supposed to be smuggling, and he wears tracking irons, so that the sentries walk up and down their beat (they may not run till after the " alarm "), waiting for the tracks of the smuggler. Directly a sentry sees the track, he gives the alarm signal to the reserve and starts himself to follow up the track as fast as he can. The reserve thereupon co-operate with them and try to catch the smuggler before he can reach the town. Once within the boundary of the town he is safe and wins the game.

ALARM: "CATCH THE THIEF"

Like "Hostile Spy," in the "Birchbark Roll of Woodcraft Indians," by Mr. Thompson Seton. A red rag is hung up in the camp or room in the morning; the umpire goes round to each scout in turn, while they are at work or play, and whispers to him, "There is a thief in the camp"; but to one he whispers, "There is a thief in the camp, and you are he — Marble Arch," or some other well-known spot about a mile away. That scout then knows that he must steal the rag at any time within the next three hours, and bolt with it to the Marble Arch. Nobody else knows who is to be the thief, where he will run and when he will steal it. Directly any one notices that the red rag is stolen, he gives the alarm, and all stop what they may be doing at the time, and dart off in pursuit of the thief. The scout who gets the rag, or a bit of it, wins. If none succeed in doing this, the thief wins. He must carry the rag tied round his neck, and not in his pocket or hidden away.

BOOKS TO READ ON SPOORING

"Lectures in Tracking"; *Cavalry Journal* for October, 1907. Price 2s. 6d. nett.

"Scouting and Reconnaissance in Savage Countries," by Captain Stigand. Price 5s. nett. (H. Rees.)

"Tracks of Wild Animals," by Captain Stigand.

"Footprints," by G. W. Gayer, Indian Police.

CAMP FIRE YARN. No. 13

READING "SIGN" OR DEDUCTION

Putting This and That Together — Sherlock-Holmesism — Instances of Deduction

Putting This and That Together

WHEN a scout has learned to notice "sign," he must then learn to "put this and that together," and so read a *meaning* from what he has seen. This is called "deduction." Here is an example of what I mean which was lately given in the *Forest and Stream*, which shows how the young scout can read the meaning from "sign" when he has been trained to it.

A cavalry soldier had got lost and some of his comrades were hunting all over the country to find him, when they came across a native boy, and asked him if he had seen the lost man. He immediately said: "Do you mean a very tall soldier, riding a roan horse that was slightly lame?"

They said: "Yes; that was the man. Where did you see him?"

The boy replied: "I have not seen him, but I know where he has gone."

Thereupon they arrested him, thinking that probably the man had been murdered and made away with, and that the boy had heard about it.

But eventually he explained that he had seen tracks of the man which he could point out to them.

Finally, he brought them to a place where the signs showed that the man had made a halt. The horse had rubbed itself against a tree, and had left some of its hairs sticking to the bark, which showed that it was a roan horse; its hoof-marks showed that it was lame; that is, one foot was not so deeply indented on the ground and did not take so long a pace as the other feet. That the rider was a soldier was shown by the imprint of his boot, which was an army boot. Then they asked the boy, "How could you tell that he was a tall man?" and the boy pointed to where the soldier had broken a branch from the tree, which would have been out of reach of a man of ordinary height.

Deduction is exactly like reading a book.

A boy who has never been taught to read, and who sees you reading from a book, would ask, "How do you do it?" and you would point out to him that a number of small signs on a page are letters; these letters when grouped form words, and words form sentences, and sentences give information.

Similarly, a trained scout will see little signs and tracks; he puts them together in his mind, and quickly reads a meaning from them such as an untrained man would never arrive at.

And from frequent practice he gets to read the meaning at a glance, just as you do a book, without the delay of spelling out each word, letter by letter.

I was one day, during the Matabele War [*show on map*] with a native out scouting near to the Matopo Hills over a wide, grassy plain. Suddenly we crossed a track freshly made in grass, where the blades of grass were still green and damp, though pressed down; all were bending one way, which showed the direction in which the people had been travelling; following up the track for a bit it got on to a patch of sand, and we then saw that it was the spoor of several women (small feet with straight edge, and short steps) and boys (small feet, curved edge, and longer strides), walking, not running, towards the hills, about five miles away, where we believed the enemy to be hiding.

Then we saw a leaf lying about ten yards off the track. There were no trees for miles, but we knew that trees having this kind of leaf grew at a village fifteen miles away, in the direction from which the footmarks were coming. It seemed likely, therefore, that the women had come from that village, bringing the leaf with them, and had gone to the hills.

On picking up the leaf we found it was damp, and smelled of native beer. The short steps showed that the women were carrying loads. So we guessed that according to the custom they had been carrying pots of native beer on their heads, the mouths of the pots being stopped up with bunches of leaves. One of these leaves had fallen out; but we found it ten yards off the track, which showed that at the time it fell a wind was blowing. There was no wind now, *i.e.*, seven o'clock, but there had been some about five o'clock.

So we guessed from all these little signs that a party of women and boys had brought beer during the night from the village fifteen miles away, and had taken it to the enemy on the hills, arriving there soon after six o'clock.

The men would probably start to drink the beer at once, as it goes sour in a few hours, and would, by the time we could get there, be getting sleepy and keeping a bad lookout, so we should have a favorable chance of looking at their position.

We accordingly followed the women's tracks, found the enemy, made our observations, and got away with our information without any difficulty.

And it was chiefly done on the evidence of that one leaf. So you see the importance of noticing even a little thing like that.

Instances of Deduction

Mr. Tighe Hopkins, writing in *World's Work*, describes how, by noticing very small signs, detectives have discovered crimes.

In one case a crime had been committed, and a stranger's coat was found which gave no clew to the owner. The coat was put into a stout bag and beaten with a stick. The dust was collected from the bag and examined under a powerful magnifying glass, and was found to consist of fine sawdust, which showed that the owner of the coat was probably a carpenter, or sawyer, or joiner. The dust was then put under a microscope, and it was then seen that it also contained some tiny grains of gelatine and powdered glue. These things are not used by carpenters or sawyers, so the coat was shown to belong to a joiner, and the police got on the track of the criminal.

Dust out of pockets, or in the recesses of a pocket-knife, and so on, if closely examined, tells a great deal.

Dr. Bell, of Edinburgh, is said to be the original from whom Sir Conan Doyle drew his idea of Sherlock Holmes.

The doctor was once teaching a class of medical students at a hospital how to doctor people. A patient was brought in, so that the doctor might show how an injured man should be treated. The patient in this case came limping in, and the doctor turned to one of the students and asked him: —

" What is the matter with this man? "

The student replied: " I don't know, sir. I haven't asked him."

The doctor said: " Well, there is no need to ask him, you should see for yourself — he has injured his right knee; he is limping on that leg; he injured it by burning it in the fire; you see how his trouser is burnt away at the knee. This is Monday morning. Yesterday was fine; Saturday was wet and muddy. The man's trousers are muddy all over. He had a fall in the mud on Saturday night."

Then he turned to the man and said: " You drew your wages on Saturday and got drunk, and in trying to get your clothes dry by the fire when you got home, you fell on the fire and burnt your knee — isn't that so? "

" Yes, sir," replied the man.

I saw a case in the paper once where a judge at the county court used his powers of " noticing little things," and " putting this and that together." He was trying a man as a debtor.

The man pleaded that he was out of work, and could get no employment.

The judge said: " Then what are you doing with that pencil behind your ear if you are not in business? "

The man had to admit that he had been helping his wife in her business, which, it turned out, was a very profitable one, and the judge thereupon ordered him to pay his debt.

Dr. Reiss, of the Police Department of the University of Lausanne, records how the police read spoor.

A burglary had taken place in a house, and the thief's footprints were found in the garden. Those going towards the house were not so deeply impressed as those coming away from it, nor were they so close together; from this the police gathered that the burglar had carried away with him a heavy load, which made him take short steps, and he was fully weighted down, so that they sank deeply in the ground.

True Scouting Stories

Captain Stigand in " Scouting and Reconnaissance in Savage Countries " gives the following instances of scouts reading important meanings from small signs.

When he was going round outside his camp one morning he noticed fresh spoor of a horse which had been walking. He knew that all his horses went only at a jog-trot, so it must have been a stranger's horse. So he recognized that a mounted scout of the enemy had been quietly looking at his camp in the night.

Coming to a village in Central Africa from which the inhabitants had fled, he could not tell what tribe it belonged to till he found a crocodile's foot in one of the huts, which showed that the village belonged to the Awisa tribe, as they eat crocodiles, and the neighboring tribes do not.

A man was seen riding a camel over half a mile away. A native who was watching him said: " It is a man of slave blood." " How can you tell at this distance? " " Because he is swinging his leg. A true Arab rides with his leg close to the camel's side."

General Joubert, who was commander-in-chief of the Boer Army in the Boer War, 1900, told me (some years before that) that in the previous Boer War, 1881, it was his wife who first noticed that the British troops were occupying Majuba Mountain. The Boers were at that time camped near the foot of the mountain, and they generally had a small party of men on the top as a lookout. On this particular day they had intended moving away early in the morning, so the usual picket had not been sent up on to the mountain.

While they were getting ready to start, Mrs. Joubert, who evidently had the eyes of a scout, looked up and said: " Why, there is an Englishman on the top of Majuba ! " The Boers said: " No — it must be our own men who have gone up there, after all." But Mrs. Joubert stuck to it, and said: " Look at the way he walks, that is no Boer — it is an Englishman." And so it was; she was right. An English force had climbed the mountain during the night, but by the stupidity of this man showing himself up on the sky-line their presence was immediately detected by the Boers, who, instead of being surprised by them, climbed up the mountain unseen under the steep crags, and surprised the British, and drove them off with heavy loss.

An officer lost his field-glasses during some manœuvres on the desert five miles from Cairo, and he sent for the native trackers to look for them.

They came and asked to see the tracks of his horse; so the horse was brought out and led about, so that they could see his footprints. These they carried in their minds, and went out to where the manœuvres had been; there, among the hundreds of hoof-marks of the cavalry and artillery, they very soon found those of the officer's horse, and followed them up wherever he had ridden, till they found the field-glasses hung where they had dropped out of their case on the desert.

These trackers are particularly good at spooring camels. To any one not accustomed to them the footmark of one camel looks very like that of any other camel, but to a trained eye they are all as different as people's faces, and these trackers remember them very much as you would remember the faces of people you had seen.

About a year ago a camel was stolen near Cairo. The police tracker was sent for and shown its spoor. He followed it for a long way until it got into some streets, where it was entirely lost among other footmarks. But the other day, a year later, this police tracker suddenly came on the fresh track of this camel; he had remembered its appearance all that time. It had evidently been walking with another camel whose footmark he knew was one which belonged to a well-known camel thief. So without trying to follow the tracks when they got into the city he went with a policeman straight to the man's stable, and there found the long missing camel.

The " Gauchos," or native cowboys, of South America are fine scouts. Though the cattle lands are now for the most part enclosed, they used formerly to have to track stolen and lost beasts for miles, and were therefore very good trackers. The story is told that one of these men was sent to track a stolen horse, but failed to follow it up. Ten months later, when in a different part of the country, he suddenly noticed the fresh spoor of this horse on the ground. He had remembered its appearance all that time. He at once followed it up and recovered it for his master.

HINTS TO INSTRUCTORS

How to teach Deduction in Practice

Read aloud a story in which a good amount of observation of details occurs, with consequent deductions, such as in either the " Memoirs " or the " Adventures of Sherlock Holmes."

Then question the boys afterwards as to which details suggested certain solutions, to see that they really have grasped the method.

Follow up ordinary tracks and deduce their meaning. For examples of daily practice see my book of " Aids to Scouting."

Example of Practice in Deduction

A simple deduction from signs noticed in my walk one morning on a stormy mountain path in Kashmir.

Sign Observed. — Tree-stump, about three feet high, by the path. A stone about the size of a cocoanut lying near it, to which were sticking some bits of bruised walnut rind, dried up. Some walnut rind also lying on the stump. Farther along the path, 30 yards to the south of the stump, were lying bits of walnut shell of four walnuts. Close by was a high sloping rock, alongside the path. The only walnut tree in sight was 150 yards north of the stump.

At the foot of the stump was a cake of hardened mud which showed the impression of a grass shoe

What would you make out from those signs? My solution of it was this: —

A man had gone southwards on a long journey along the path two days ago carrying a load, and had rested at the rock while he ate walnuts.

My deductions were these: —

It was a man carrying a load, because carriers when they want to rest do not sit down, but rest their load against a sloping rock and lean back. Had he had no load, he would probably have sat down on the stump, but he preferred to go 30 yards further to where the rock was. Women do not carry loads there, so it was a man. But he first broke the shells of his walnuts on the tree-stump with the stone, having brought them from the tree 150 yards north. So he was travelling south, and he was on a long journey, as he was wearing shoes, and not going barefooted, as he would be if only strolling near his home. Three days ago there was rain, the cake of mud had been picked up while the ground was still wet but it had not been since rained upon, and was now dry.   The walnut rind was also dry, and confirmed the time that had elapsed.

There is no important story attached to this, but it is just an example of every-day practice which should be carried out by scouts.

GAMES AND COMPETITIONS IN DEDUCTIONS

Get some people who are strangers to the boys to come along as passers-by in the street or road, and let the boys separately notice all about them; and after an interval ask each for a full description of each of the passers-by as to appearance, peculiar recognizable points, and what he guesses his business to be; or let each boy have two minutes' conversation with your friend, and try to find out what he can about him in that time by questioning and observation.

Set a room or prepare a piece of ground with small signs, tracks, etc.; read aloud the story of the crime up to that point and let each boy or each patrol in turn examine the scene for a given time, and then privately give each his solution of it.

The very simplest, most elementary schemes should be given at first and they can gradually be elaborated.   For instance, take a number of footmarks and spent matches by a tree, showing where a man had difficulty in lighting his pipe, etc.

For a more finished theme take a mystery like that in "Memoirs of Sherlock Holmes" called "The Resident Patient." Set a room to represent the patient's room where he was found hanging, with footprints of muddy boots on the carpet, cigar ends bitten or cut in the fireplace, cigar ashes, screw-driver and screws, etc.   Put down a strip or " stepping stones " of stuff, handkerchiefs, or paper, on which the competitors shall walk (so as not to confuse existing tracks).   Let each scout (or patrol) come in separately, and have three minutes in which to investigate.   Then to go out and give in his solution, written or verbal, half an hour later.

Let one patrol make tracks by carrying out such a series as that which D'Artagnan elucidated.   The other patrol then act as detectives, and endeavor to unravel the mystery from the tracks and other sign.

"TRACK THE ASSASSIN." — The assassin escapes after having stabbed his victim, carrying in his hand the dripping dagger. The remainder, a minute later, start out to track him by the drops of blood (represented by beans or peas) which fall at every third pace.   His confederate (the umpire) tells him beforehand where to make for, and if he gets there without being touched by his pursuers, over eight minutes ahead of them, he wins. If they never reach his confederate, neither side wins.

Play

Any one of the Sherlock Holmes stories makes a good play.

BOOKS TO READ

"Memoirs of Sherlock Holmes." Price 3s. 6d. and 6d.
"Adventures of Sherlock Holmes." Price 3s. 6d. and 6d.
"The Thinking Machine," which contains a number of stories like Sherlock Holmes. Price 6s. (Chapman & Hall.)
"Criminal Investigation," by Dr. Gross. Edited by J. Adam. (Specialist Press, London.)

CHAPTER V

WOODCRAFT

or

Knowledge of Animals and Nature

CAMP FIRE YARN. No. 14

HINTS TO INSTRUCTORS

HOW TO TEACH NATURAL HISTORY

If you are in a city or town where there is a Zoölogical Garden or a Museum of Natural History, take your scouts there. Take them to certain animals on which you are prepared to lecture to to them. About half a dozen animals would be quite enough for one day.

If in the country, get leave from a farmer or carter to show the boys how to put on harness, etc., and how to feed and water the horse; how he is shod, etc. How to catch hold of a runaway horse in harness. How to milk a cow.

Study habits of cows, rabbits, birds, water-voles, trout, etc., by stalking them and watching all that they do.

Take your scouts to any menagerie, and explain the animals.

STALKING

As an Aid to Observation — How to hide Yourself — How to learn Stalking — Games — Books on Stalking.

AT some manœuvres lately, two hostile patrols of soldiers were approaching, looking for each other, till the ground between them became very open, and it seemed hopeless for a scout to cross it without being seen. However, a small ditch of about two feet deep and overgrown with bushes ran across part of the open plain from the point where one patrol was lying hidden. They noticed two calves which came out on to the plain from the opposite side, and walked across the open till they got to the end of this ditch, and here they stopped and separated and began browsing.

A scout now started to make use of this ditch by crawling along it till he should get to the far end near the calves, and there he hoped to find some way of getting on farther, or of at least peeping out and getting a nearer view of the possible position of the enemy. When about halfway along the ditch he was suddenly fired at by an enemy's scout already there, in the ditch.

When the umpire rode up and asked him how he had got there without being seen, the hostile scout said that finding he could not reach the ditch without being seen if he went across the plain, he seized two calves which he had found among the bushes where his patrol was hiding, and stepping between them, he drove the pair of them, by holding their tails, across to the open ditch; there he let them go, and slid himself into the ditch without being noticed.

How to Hide Yourself

When you want to observe wild animals you have to stalk them; that is, to creep up to them without their seeing or smelling you.

A hunter when he is stalking wild animals keeps himself entirely hidden, so does the war scout when watching or looking for the enemy; a policeman does not catch pickpockets by standing about in uniform watching for them; he dresses like one of the crowd, and as often as not gazes into a shop window and sees all that goes on behind him reflected as if in a looking-glass.

If a guilty person finds himself being watched, it puts him on his guard, while an innocent person becomes annoyed. So when you are observing a person, don't do so by staring openly at him, but notice the details you want to at one glance or two, and if you want to study him further, walk behind him; you can learn just as much from a back view, in fact more than you can from a front view, and, unless he is a scout and looks round frequently, he does not know that you are observing him.

War scouts and hunters stalking game always carry out two important things when they don't want to be seen.

One is — they take care that the ground behind them, or tree or buildings, etc., is of the same color as their clothes.

And the other is — if an enemy or a deer is seen looking for them, they remain perfectly still without moving so long as he is there.

In that way a scout, even though he is out in the open, will often escape being noticed.

In choosing your background, consider the color of your clothes; thus, if you are dressed in khaki, don't go and stand in front of a whitewashed wall, or in front of a dark-shaded bush, but go where there is khaki-colored sand or grass or rocks behind you — and remain perfectly still. It will be very difficult for an enemy to distinguish you, even at a short distance.

If you are in dark clothes, get among dark bushes, or in the shadow of trees or rocks, but be careful that the ground beyond you is also dark — if there is light-colored ground beyond the trees under which you are standing, for instance, you will stand out clearly defined against it.

If you are in red, try and get against red-brick buildings, or red earth or rocks, and so on.

In making use of hills as lookout places be very careful not to show yourself on the top or sky-line. That is the fault which a tenderfoot generally makes.

It is quite a lesson to watch a Zulu scout making use of a hill-top or rising ground as a lookout place. He will crawl up on all fours, lying flat in the grass; on reaching the top he will very slowly raise his head, inch by inch, till he can see the view. If he sees the enemy on beyond, he will have a good look, and, if he thinks they are watching him, will keep his head perfectly steady for a very long time, hoping that he will be mistaken for a stump or a stone. If he is not detected, he will very gradually lower his head, inch by inch, into the grass again, and crawl quietly away. Any quick or sudden movement of the head on the sky-line would be very likely to attract attention, even at a considerable distance.

At night keep as much as possible in low ground, ditches, etc., so that you are down in the dark, while an enemy who comes near will be visible to you outlined against the stars on higher ground.

By squatting low in the shadow of the bush at night, and keeping quite still, I have let an enemy's scout come and stand within three feet of me, so that when he turned his back towards me I was able to stand up where I was, and fling my arms round him.

A point also to remember in keeping hidden while moving, especially at night, is to walk quietly; the thump of an ordinary man's heel on the ground can be heard a good distance off, but a scout or hunter always walks lightly, on the ball of his foot, not on his heels; and this you should practise whenever you are walking, by day or by night, indoors as well as out, so that it becomes a habit with you — so as to walk as lightly and silently as possible. You will find that as you grow into it your power of walking long distances will grow, you will not tire so soon as you would if clumping along in the heavy-footed manner of most people.

Remember always that to stalk a wild animal, or a good scout, you must keep down wind of him, even if the wind is so slight as to be merely a faint air.

Before starting to stalk your enemy, then, you should be sure which way the wind is blowing, and work up against it. To

SCOUT STALKING SCOUT
From "Sketches in Mafeking and East Africa"
By permission of Messrs. Smith, Elder, & Co.

find this out you should wet your thumb all round with your tongue, and then hold it up and see which side feels coldest, or you can throw some light dust, or dry grass or leaves in the air, and see which way they drift.

The Red Indian scouts, when they wanted to reconnoitre an enemy's camp, used to tie a wolf's skin on their backs and walk on all fours, and, imitating the howl of a wolf, prowl round the camps at night.

In Australia the natives stalk emus — which are great birds

something like an ostrich — by putting an emu's skin over themselves, and walking with body bent and one hand held up to represent the bird's head and neck.

American scouts, when peeping over a ridge or any place where the head might be seen against the sky-line, put on a cap made of wolf's-head skin with ears on it — so that they may be mistaken for a wolf, if seen.

Our scouts also, when looking out among grass, etc., tie a string or band round the head, and stick a lot of grass in it, some upright, some drooping over the face, so that the head is very invisible.

When hiding behind a big stone or mound, etc., they don't look over the top, but round the side of it.

How to teach Stalking

Demonstrate the value of adapting color of clothes to background by sending out one boy about 500 yards to stand against different backgrounds in turn, till he gets one similar in color to his own clothes.

The rest of the patrol to watch and to notice how invisible he becomes when he gets a suitable background. E.g., a boy in a gray suit standing in front of dark bushes, etc., is quite visible — but becomes less so if he stands in front of a gray rock or house; a boy in a dark suit is very visible in a green field, but not when he stands in an open doorway against dark interior shadow.

Games in Stalking

SCOUT HUNTING

One scout is given time to go out and hide himself, the remainder then start to find him; he wins if he is not found, or if he can get back to the starting-point within a given time without being touched.

DESPATCH RUNNING

A scout is told to bring a note into a certain spot or house from a distance within a given time: other hostile scouts are told to prevent any message getting to this place, and to hide themselves at different points to stop the despatch carrier getting in with it.

To count as a capture two scouts must touch the despatch runner before he reaches the spot for delivering the message.

RELAY RACE

One patrol pitted against another to see who can get a message sent a long distance in shortest time by means of relays of runners (or cyclists). The patrol is ordered out to send in three successive notes or tokens (such as sprigs of certain plants), from a point, say, two miles distant or more. The leader, in taking his patrol out to the spot, drops scouts at convenient distances, who will then act as runners from one post to the next and back. If relays are posted in pairs, messages can be passed both ways.

STALKING

Instructor acts as a deer — not hiding, but standing, moving a little now and then if he likes.

Scouts go out to find, and each in his own way tries to get up to him unseen:

Directly the instructor sees a scout he directs him to stand up as having failed. After a certain time the instructor calls "Time," all stand up at the spot which they have reached, and the nearest wins.

The same game may be played to test the scouts in stepping lightly — the umpire being blindfolded. The practice should preferably be carried out where there are dry twigs lying about, and gravel, etc. The scout may start to stalk the blind enemy at 100 yards' distance, and he must do it fairly fast — say in one minute and a half — to touch the blind man before he hears him.

STALKING AND REPORTING

The umpire places himself out in the open and sends each scout or pair of scouts away in different directions about half a mile off. When he waves a flag, which is the signal to begin, they all hide, and then proceed to stalk him, creeping up and watching all he does. When he waves the flag again, they rise, come in, and report each in turn all that he did, either by handing in a written report or verbally, as may be ordered. The umpire meantime has kept a lookout in each direction, and, every time he sees a scout, he takes two points off that scout's score. He, on his part, performs small actions, such as sitting down, kneeling up, looking through glasses, using handkerchief, taking hat off for a while, walking round in a circle a few times, to give scouts something to note and report about him. Scouts are given three points for each act reported correctly. It saves time if the umpire makes out a scoring card beforehand, giving the name of each scout, and a number of columns showing each act of his, and what mark that scout wins, also a column of deducted marks for exposing himself.

BOOK ON STALKING

" Deer Stalking." Badminton Library Series. 6s. nett.

" Spider and Fly "

A bit of country or section of the town about a mile square is selected as the web, and its boundaries described, and an hour fixed at which operations are to cease.

One patrol (or half-patrol) is the " spider " which goes out and selects a place to hide itself.

The other patrol (or half-patrol) goes a quarter of an hour later as the " fly " to look for the " spider." They can spread themselves about as they like, but must tell their leader anything that they discover.

An umpire goes with each party.

If within the given time (say about two hours) the fly has not discovered the spider, the spider wins. The spiders write down the names of any of the fly patrol that they may see; similarly, the flies write down the names of any spiders that they may see, and their exact hiding-place.

The two sides should wear different colors or be differently dressed (e.g., one side in shirt-sleeves).

Throwing the Assegai

Target, a thin sack, lightly stuffed with straw, or a sheet of cardboard, or canvas stretched on a frame.

Assegais to be made of wands, with weighted ends sharpened, or with iron arrow-heads on them.

Flag Raiding

(From " Aids to Scouting," 1s. Gale and Polden.)

Two or more patrols on each side.

Each side will form an outpost within a given tract of country to protect three flags (or at night three lanterns two feet above ground), planted not less than 200 yards (100 yards at night) from it. The protecting outpost will be posted in concealment either all together or spread out in pairs. It will then send out scouts to discover the enemy's position. When these have found out where the outpost is, they try and creep round out of sight till they can get to the flags and bring them away to their own line. One scout may not take away more than one flag.

This is the general position of a patrol on such an outpost: —

†   †   †
 †   †   †

Pair of Scouts Pair of Scouts Pair of Scouts

†
Patrol Leader

P P P
Flags

Any scout coming within fifty yards of a stronger party will be put out of action if seen by the enemy; if he can creep by without being seen it is all right.

Scouts posted to watch as outposts cannot move from their ground, but their strength counts as double, and they may send single messengers to their neighbors or to their own scouting party.

An umpire should be with each outpost and with each scouting patrol.

At a given hour operations will cease, and all will assemble at the given spot to hand in their reports. The following points might be awarded: —

For each flag or lamp captured and brought in	5 points
For each report or sketch of the position of the enemy's outposts......................	up to 5 points
For each report of movement of enemy's scouting patrols..............................	2 points

The side which makes the biggest total wins.

CAMP FIRE YARN. No. 15

ANIMALS

The Calling of Wild Animals — Animals — Birds — Reptiles — Fish — Insects — Practical Instruction about Animals — Games — Books to Read.

Scouts in many parts of the world use the calls of wild animals and birds for communicating with each other, especially at night or in thick bush, or in fog, etc., but it is also very useful to be able to imitate the calls if you want to watch the habits of the animals. You can begin by calling chickens; or by talking to dogs in dog language, and you very soon find you can give the angry growl or the playful growl of a dog. Owls, thrushes, chickadees, woodchucks, squirrels, and other birds and animals, are very easily called.

In India I have seen a certain tribe of gypsies who eat jackals. Now a jackal is one of the most suspicious animals that lives, and is very difficult to catch in a trap, but these gypsies catch them by calling them in this way.

Several men with dogs hide themselves in the grass and bushes round a small field. In the middle of this open place one gypsy imitates the call of the jackals calling to each other: he gets louder and louder till they seem to come together ; then they begin to growl and finally tackle each other

INDIAN GYPSY CALLING JACKALS

with violent snapping, snarling, and yelling, and at the same time he shakes a bundle of dried leaves, which sounds like the animals dashing about among grass and reeds. Then he flings himself down on the ground, and throws up dust in the air, so that he is completely hidden in it, still growling and fighting. If any jackal is within sound of this, he comes tearing out of the jungle, and dashes into the dust to join in the fight. When he finds a man there, he comes out again in a hurry; but meantime the dogs have been loosed from all sides, and they quickly catch him and kill him.

Mr. William Long, in his very interesting book called " Beasts of the Field," describes how he once called a moose. The moose inhabits the forests of Canada and the Northern United States. He is a shy beast and very hard to get near, but inclined to be dangerous when he is angry.

Mr. Long was in a canoe fishing when he heard a bull moose calling in the forest — so just for fun he went ashore and cut a strip of bark off a birch tree and rolled it up into a cone or trumpet shape so as to make a kind of megaphone (about fifteen inches long, five inches wide at the larger end, and about an inch or two at the mouthpiece).   With this he proceeded to imitate the roaring grunt of the bull moose.   The effect was tremendous; the old moose came tearing down and even came into the water and tried to get at him — and it was only by hard paddling that in the end he got away.

One of the best things in scouting is the hunting of big game — that is, going after elephants, lions, rhinoceros, wild boar, deer, and those kinds of animals; and a man has to be a pretty good scout if he hopes to succeed at it.

You get plenty of excitement and plenty of danger, too; and all that I have told you about observation and tracking and hiding yourself comes in here.   And in addition to these you must know all about animals and their habits and ways if you want to be successful.

I have said the " hunting " or " going after big game is one of the best things in scouting."   I did not say shooting or killing the game was the best part; for as you get to study animals you get to like them more and more, and you will soon find that you don't want to kill them for the mere sake of killing, and that the more you see of them the more you see the wonderful work of God in them.

All the fun of hunting lies in the adventurous life in the jungle, the chance in many cases of the animal hunting *you* instead of you hunting the animal, the interest of tracking him up, stalking him and watching all that he does and learning his habits.   The actual shooting the animal that follows is only a very small part of the fun.

No scout should ever kill an animal unless there is some real reason for doing so, and in that case he should kill it quickly and effectively, so as to give it as little pain as possible.

In fact, many big-game hunters nowadays prefer to shoot their game with the camera instead of with the rifle — which gives just as interesting results — except when you and your natives are hungry, then you must, of course, kill your game.

My brother was lately big-game shooting in East Africa and had very good sport with the camera, living in the wilds, and tracking and stalking, and finally snap-shotting elephants, rhinoceros, and other big animals.

One day he had crept up near to an elephant and had set up his camera and had got his head under the cloth, focussing it, when his native cried, " Look out, sir ! " and started to run.

My brother poked his head out from under the cloth and found a great elephant coming for him, only a few yards off. So he just pressed the button, and then ran too. The elephant rushed up to the camera, stopped, and seemed to recognize that it was only a camera after all, and smiling at his own irritability, lurched off into the jungle again.

Mr. Schillings' book, "With Flashlight and Rifle in Africa," is a most interesting collection of instantaneous photos of wild animals, most of them taken by night by means of flashlight, which was set going by the animals themselves striking against wires which he had put out for the purpose. He got splendid photos of lions, hyenas, deer of all sorts, zebras, and other beasts. There is one of a lion actually in the air springing on to a buck.

The boar is certainly the bravest of all animals; he is the real "King of the Jungle," and the other animals all know it. If you watch a drinking pool in the jungle at night, you will see the animals that come to it all creeping down nervously, looking out in every direction for hidden enemies. But when the boar comes he simply swaggers down with his great head and its shiny tusks swinging from side to side; he cares for nobody, but everybody cares for him; even a tiger drinking at the pool will give a snarl and sneak quickly out of sight.

I have often lain out on moonlight nights to watch the animals, especially wild boars, in the jungle; and it is just as good fun as merely going after them to kill them.

And I have caught and kept a young wild boar and a young panther, and found them most amusing and interesting little beggars. The boar used to live in my garden, and he never became really tame, though I got him as a baby.

He would come to me when I called him — but very warily; he would never come to a stranger, and a native he would "go for" and try and cut him with his little tusks.

He used to practise the use of his tusks while turning at full speed round an old tree stump in the garden, and he would gallop at this and round it in a figure of eight continuously for over five minutes at a time, and then fling himself down on his side panting with his exertions.

My panther was also a beautiful and delightfully playful beast, and used to go about with me like a dog; but he was very uncertain in his dealings with strangers.

I think one gets to know more about animals and to understand them better by keeping them as pets at first, and then going and watching them in their wild natural life.

But before going to study big game in the jungles everybody must study all animals wild and tame at home. It would be a very good thing if every scout kept some kind of animal, such as a pony or a dog, birds, or rabbits, or even live butterflies.

Every boy scout ought to know all about the tame animals which he sees every day. You ought to know all about grooming, feeding, and watering a horse, about putting him into harness or taking him out of harness and putting him in the stable, and know when he is going lame and should not therefore be worked.

And when you harness a horse I hope you will show more knowledge of the animal and more kindness towards him than do some men — by not putting bearing-reins on him.

H.R.H. the Prince of Wales was reported some time ago to have said as follows: —

" When I am King I shall make three laws: —
1. That no one shall cut puppies' tails, because it must hurt them so.
2. That there shall be no more sin in the country.
3. That nobody shall use bearing-reins, because they hurt the horses."

These laws not only show us that King Edward VIII will be a kind and humane monarch, but that he is far-seeing, for the last one, at any rate, might well be a law of the country now. It is much needed.

Bearing-reins are small extra reins which are hooked on to the horse's back-pad to hold up his head. They are generally put on so tightly as to cause him pain the moment he drops his head at

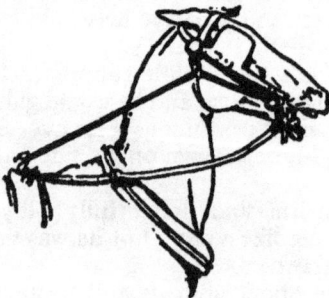

TORTURE
(*Note the bearing rein.*)

COMFORT

all; when put on loosely they do not cause him to hold up his head, and therefore are not of any use.

Sometimes you see them used on horses in heavy wagons; they are then called "Hame reins" — but they are cruel on the horse if tightly tied. A horse when pulling a heavy wagon wants to lean forward with his head down, just as you or I would do when pulling a garden roller; but this hame rein pulls at the corners of his mouth and forces him to keep his head up.

I saw lately a man in charge of a loaded wagon whose horse was thus tied up. He wanted to get the wagon through some heavy mud and the horse tried to lean forward to pull, but could not. The man beat him for not trying. The poor beast in his pain and terror reared up on his hind legs, and the man beat him again for "showing temper."

When I saw it I felt inclined to beat the man, but I went up and said I thought I could make the horse do it. The man grinned while I was undoing the hame rein and said I should have to get another horse to do it, then. But when the horse found his head free and I smacked him on the back, he flung the whole of his weight into the collar with his head well down, and, with both hind toes dug into the ground, he heaved the cart forward a few inches, and then again a few more, and not many seconds later had it all safe on the hard road.

Often you can help a horse struggling with a load on a slippery road by scattering a few handfuls of sand or ashes. Miss Lisette Rest used to do this in London, and when she died she left money for that purpose.

Other tame animals to understand are, of course, dogs. And a good dog is the very best companion for a scout, who need not think himself a really good scout till he has trained a young dog to do all he wants of him. It requires great patience and kindness, and genuine sympathy with the dog.

A dog is the most human of all animals, and therefore the best companion for a man. He is always courteous, and always ready for a game — full of humor, and very faithful and loving.

Every scout who was present at the funeral of our late King Edward will remember the sadness of his little terrier Cæsar, who followed the coffin.

Of course a scout who lives in the country has much better chances of studying animals and birds than in a town.

In a number of Canadian cities there is a Natural History Museum, where a boy can learn the appearance and names of

many animals; and you can do a lot of observing in the parks
or by starting a feeding-box for birds at your own window.
And, best of all, by going out into the country whenever you
can get a few hours for it by train, or bicycle, or on your own
flat feet, and there stalk such animals as rabbits, hares, water-
rats, birds, fish, etc., and watch all they do, and get to know
their different kinds and their names, and also what kind of
tracks they make on the ground, their nests and eggs, and so on.

If you are lucky enough to own a camera, you cannot possibly
do better than start making a collection of photographs of animals and birds taken from life.　Such a collection is ten times
more interesting than the ordinary boy's collection of stamps, or
crests, or autographs, which any one can accomplish by sitting at
home and bothering other people to give.

The following are some of the wild animals that are found in
Canada and the United States:—

Deer	Raccoons	Hares
Elk	Skunks	Muskrats
Moose	Weasels	Squirrels
Bears	Minks	Chipmunks
Wolves	Beavers	Rats
Foxes	Woodchucks	Mice
Lynx	Porcupines	Moles
	Bats	

As a scout you should study the habits of as many of these
animals as you can.

Every animal is interesting to watch, and it is just as difficult
to stalk a weasel as it is to stalk a lion.　Even the humble hedgehog can be a hero among animals.　Here is a description of a
fight between a hedgehog [1] and a viper by Mr. Millais in his book
on the " Mammals of Great Britain and Ireland."　(Mammals
mean animals that have " Mammas " — that is, they are born
alive, not like chickens in eggs, that have to be hatched; birds
are not mammals.)

" Every one knows that the hedgehog is a sworn enemy of reptiles in general, and of the viper in particular; but few, perhaps,
are aware in what way he overcomes so dangerous an enemy.

"My keeper was going his rounds this summer in a wood
which was infested by vipers when he espied an enormous one
asleep in the sun.　He was on the point of killing it with a

[1] A hedgehog is covered with spines or quills much in the same way as the
American porcupine.

charge of shot when he perceived a hedgehog coming cautiously over the moss and noiselessly approaching the reptile. He then witnessed a curious sight. As soon as the hedgehog was within reach of his prey he seized it by the tail with his teeth and as quick as thought rolled himself into a ball. The viper, awakened by the pain, at once turned and made a terrific dart at him. The hedgehog did not wince. The viper, infuriated, extends itself, hisses and twists in fearful contortions. In five minutes it is covered with blood, its mouth one large wound (from the spines of the hedgehog), and it lies exhausted on the ground.

" A few more starts, and then a last convulsive agony, and it expires.

" When the hedgehog perceived that it was quite dead he let go his hold and quietly unrolled himself. He was just about to begin his meal and devour the reptile, when the sight of my keeper, who had approached during the struggle, alarmed him, and he rolled himself up again till the man had retreated into the wood."

We are apt to think that all animals are guided in their conduct by instinct, that is, by a sort of idea that is born in them. For instance, we imagine that a young muskrat, or an otter, swims naturally directly he is put into water, or that a young deer runs away from a man from a natural inborn fear of him.

Mr. W. Long, in his book " School of the Woods," shows that animals owe their cleverness largely to their mothers, who teach them while yet young. Thus he has seen an otter carry two of her young upon her back into the water, and, after swimming about for a little while, she suddenly dived from under them, and left them struggling in the water. But she rose near them and helped them to swim back to the shore. In this way she gradually taught them to swim.

I once saw a lioness in East Africa sitting with her four little cubs all in a row watching me approaching her. She looked

TEACHING THE YOUNGSTERS

exactly as though she were teaching her young ones how to act in the case of a man coming.

She was evidently saying to them, " Now, cubbies, I want you all to notice what a white man is like. Then, one by one, you must jump up and skip away, with a whisk of your tail. The moment you are out of sight in the long grass you must creep and crawl till you have got to leeward (down-wind) of him; then follow him, always keeping him to windward, so that you can smell whereabouts he is, and he cannot find you."

In " The School of the Woods," Long writes: —

" Watch, say, a crow's nest. One day you will see the mother bird standing near the nest and stretching her wings over her little ones. Presently the young stand up and stretch their wings in imitation. That is the first lesson.

" Next day, perhaps, you will see the old bird lifting herself to tiptoe and holding herself there by vigorous flapping. Again the young imitate, and soon learn that their wings are a power to sustain them. Next day you may see both parent birds passing from branch to branch about the nest, aided by their wings in the long jumps. The little ones join and play, and lo ! they have learned to fly without even knowing that they were being taught."

Birds

A man who studies birds is called an ornithologist. Mark Twain says: " There are fellows who write books about birds and love them so much that they'll go hungry and tired to find a new kind of bird — and kill it.

" They are called ' ornithologers.'

" I could have been an ' ornithologer ' myself, because I always loved birds and creatures. And I started out to learn how to be one. I saw a bird sitting on a dead limb of a high tree, singing away with his head tilted back and his mouth open — and before I thought I fired my gun at him; his song stopped all suddenly, and he fell from the branch, limp like a rag, and I ran and picked him up — and he was dead: his body was warm in my hand, and his head rolled about this way and that, like as if his neck was broke, and there was a white skin over his eyes, and one drop of red blood sparkled on the side of his head — and — laws ! I couldn't see nothing for the tears. I haven't ever murdered no creature since then that warn't doing me no harm — and I ain't agoing to neither."

A good scout is generally a good " ornithologer," as Mark Twain calls him. That is to say, he likes stalking birds and watching all that they do. He discovers, by watching them, where and how they build their nests.

He does not, like the ordinary boy, want to go and rob them of their eggs, but he likes to watch how they hatch out their young and teach them to feed themselves and to fly. He gets to know every species of bird by its call and by its way of flying; and he knows which birds remain all the year round and which come only at certain seasons; and what kind of food they like best, and how they change their plumage; what sort of nests they build, where they build them, and what the eggs are like.

In Canada and the eastern United States there are over 300 different kinds of birds. Here are some of the commoner birds which a scout should know by sight and sound.

Grebe	Cuckoo	Tanager
Loon	Kingfisher	Grosbeck
Gull	Woodpecker	Swallow
Duck	Nighthawk	Waxwing
Heron	Whippoorwill	Shrike
Bittern	Chimney Swift	Vireo
Snipe	Flycatcher	Warbler
Sandpiper	Horned Lark	Wren
Plover	Meadowlark	Catbird
Partridge	Crow	Brown Thresher
Quail	Blue Jay	Brown Creeper
Hawk	Blackbird	Nuthatch
Eagle	Oriole	Kinglet
Owl	Sparrow	Thrush
Junco	Snow-Bunting	Robin
	Chickadee	Bluebird

A good deal of natural history can be studied even by keeping birds in your houses, or watching them in your neighborhood, especially if you feed them daily in winter. It is interesting to note, for instance, their different ways of singing, how some sing to make love to the hen birds, while others, like the barn-door cock, crow or sing to challenge another to fight. Then it is interesting to watch how the young birds hatch out: some appear naked, with no feathers, and their eyes shut and their mouths open. Others, with fluffy kind of feathers all over them, are full of life and energy. Young chickens start running about and hunting flies within a very few minutes after they are hatched, while a young sparrow is useless for days, and has to be fed and coddled by his parents.

A good many birds are almost dying out because so many boys steal all their eggs when they find their nests.

Bird's-nesting is very like big-game shooting — you look out in places that, as a hunter, you know are likely places for the bird you want; you watch the birds fly in and out and you find the nest. But do not then go and destroy the nest and take the eggs. And, above all, don't pull the nest about, otherwise the parent birds will desert it, and all those eggs, which might have developed into young birds, will be wasted.

Far better than taking the eggs is to take a photograph, or make a sketch of the hen sitting on her nest, or to make a collection of pictures of the different kinds of nests made by the different kinds of birds.

Aberdeen, in Scotland, is supposed to be specially well off for skylarks for the following reason.

A few years ago there came a very severe gale and snowstorm late in March, and all the high ground inland was so buried under snow and ice that the birds were all driven to the lower land near the coast. The fields by the seashore were covered with them.

Numbers of people went out to catch them with birdlime, nets, snares, and guns. Large numbers were taken alive to be sent to market in London and other places.

One gentleman found a man selling a big cage full of them. They were crowded up to a fearful extent, and all fluttering with terror at their imprisonment, struggling over each other in their frantic desire to escape. He felt so sorry for them that he bought the whole lot, and took them to his warehouse, where he was able to give them plenty of room and food and water.

Then he offered to buy all the larks that were being captured for the market at market prices. In this way he received over a thousand; and these he put in a big room, where they had comparative freedom and plenty of food. It is said that the noise of their singing in the morning was almost deafening, and crowds of birds used to gather over the house to hear them.

At last the bad weather passed off, the sun shone out again, and the fields became green and bright, and then the kind man who had housed the birds opened the windows of the room and all the birds flew out in a happy crowd, chirping and singing as they mounted into the bright warm air or fluttered off to the adjoining fields and woods. And there they built their nests and hatched out their young, so that to-day the song of the lark is to be heard everywhere round Aberdeen.

Through ignorance of natural history many farmers and others see no difference between those hawks and owls which are beneficial and those which are harmful. The screech owl, for instance, lives principally on field mice and rarely interferes with the farmers' chickens, but the great horned owl is a hen-thief. Among the hawks, too, there are only two kinds that interfere to any extent with the farmers' poultry — the Cooper's and the sharp-shinned. The others do very little harm, while some of them do a great deal of good.

The more usual reptiles found in Canada and the eastern United States are snakes and turtles. Our common snakes are the garter snake, the water snake, the grass snake, the milk snake, the little brown snake, and the black snake. None of these snakes are poisonous. The poisonous species, the rattlesnake and the copperhead, are rarely found.

Our common turtles are the snapping turtle, the pond turtle, and the box turtle.

Animals that spend part of their lives in water and part on land are known as amphibia. The amphibia include frogs, toads, tree toads, salamanders, and mud puppies.

Fishes

The common fishes are

White Fish	Maskinonge	Mackerel
Salmon Trout	Pike	Cod
Brook Trout	Pickerel	Haddock
Herrings	Perch	Halibut
Sucker	Bass	Flounder
Catfish	Sunfish	Sturgeon

Every scout ought to be able to fish in order to get food for himself. A tenderfoot who starved on the bank of a river full of fish would look very silly, yet it might happen to one who had never learned to catch fish.

And fishing brings out a lot of the points in scouting, especially if you fish with a fly. To be successful you must know a lot about the habits and ways of the fish, what kind of haunt he frequents, in what kind of weather he feeds, and at what time of day, which kind of food he likes best, how far off he can see you, and so on. Without knowing these you can fish away until you are blue in the face and never catch one.

A fish generally has his own particular haunt in the stream, and when once you discover a fish at home you can go and creep near and watch all that he does.

Then you have to be able to tie very special knots with delicate gut, which is a bit of a puzzler to any boy whose fingers are
all thumbs.

And you have to have infinite patience; your line gets caught
up in bushes and reeds, or your clothes — or when it can't find
any other body it ties itself up in a knot round itself. Well, it's
no use getting angry with it. There are only two things to do
— the first is to grin a smile, and the second is to set to work very
leisurely to undo it. Then you will have loads of disappointments in losing fish through the line breaking, or other mishaps;
but remember those are what happen to everybody when they
begin fishing, and are the troubles that in the end make it so very
enjoyable when you have got over them.

And when you catch your fish do as I do — only keep those you
specially want for food or as specimens; put back the others
the moment you have landed them. The prick of the hook in
th ir leathery mouths does not hurt them for long, and they
swim off quite happily to enjoy life in their water again.

If you use a dry fly, that is, keeping your fly sitting on top
of the water instead of sunk under the surface, you have really to
stalk your fish, just as you would deer or any other game, for
a trout is very sharp-eyed and shy.

A scout, of course, has to look at animals of all sorts, partly
with an eye to their being useful to him sometime or another
for food. Reptiles don't look tempting as food, but, once you
have tasted frogs' legs nicely cooked, you will want more of them.

I believe that fried snake, like fried eel, is not half bad.

I have eaten the huge kind of lizard called an iguana. He
had his head and tail cut off to enable him to go into the cooking
pot, and when he was boiled and put on the table he looked
exactly like a healthy baby with his arms and legs and little
hands. And when we ate him he tasted just like a baby, too.
Well — you know what a baby tastes like — sort of soft chicken
flavored with violet powder !

Of course a scout ought to know about snakes, because in
almost all wild countries you come across plenty of them and
many of them dangerous. But as far as snakes go there are
not, fortunately, many poisonous ones in America. The only
poisonous snakes that we have in eastern North America are
the rattlesnake and the copperhead, and they are found only
in unfrequented, rocky parts of the country.

Snakes have a horrid knack of creeping into tents and under
blankets, or into boots. You will always notice an old hand

in camp before he turns in at night look very carefully through his blankets, and in the morning before putting on his boots he will carefully shake them out. I even find myself doing it now in my bedroom at home, just from habit.

Snakes don't like crawling over anything rough as a rule; so in India you often construct a kind of path, made of sharp, jagged stones, all round a house to prevent snakes crawling into it from the garden.

And on the prairie hunters lay a hair rope on the ground in a circle round their blankets.

A hair rope has so many tiny spikes sticking out of it that it tickles the snake's stomach to such an extent he cannot go over it.

I used to catch snakes when I was at school by using a long stick with a small fork at the end of it. When I saw a snake I stalked him, jammed the fork down on his neck, and then tied him up the stick with strips of old handkerchief, and carried him back to sell to anybody who wanted a pet. But they are not good things to make pets of as a rule, because so many people have a horror of them, and it is not fair, therefore, to have them about in a house where others of your family or your friends might get frightened by them.

Poisonous snakes carry their poison in a small kind of bag inside their mouths. They have two fangs or long pointed teeth, which are on a kind of hinge; they lie flat along the snake's gums till he gets angry and wants to kill something; then they stand on end, and he dives his head forward and strikes them into his enemy. As he does so the poison passes out of the poison bag, or gland, as it is called, into the two holes in your skin made by the fangs. This poison then gets into the veins of the man who has been bitten and is carried by the blood all over the body in a few seconds, unless steps are at once taken to stop it by sucking the wound and binding the veins up very tightly. It does no harm when swallowed.

Insects

Insects are very interesting animals to collect, or to watch, or to photograph.

Also for a scout who fishes, or studies birds or reptiles, it is most important that he should know a certain amount about the insects which are their favorite food at different times of the year or different hours of the day.

The usual insects about which a scout ought to know something are: —

Moths	Ants	Beetles
Grasshoppers	Butterflies	Cicadas
Mosquitoes	Bees and Wasps	Spiders
Dragon Flies	Fireflies	Plant Lice
Gnats	Crickets	

About bees alone whole books have been written — for they have wonderful powers in making their honeycomb, in finding their way for miles — sometimes as far as six miles — to find the right kind of flowers for giving them the sugary juice for making honey, and getting back with it to the hive.

They are quite a model community, for they respect their queen and kill their unemployed.

Then some insects are useful as food. Ants make a substitute for salt. Locusts — a big kind of grasshopper — are eaten in India and South Africa. We were very glad to get a flight or two of them over Mafeking. When they settled on the ground we went and, with empty sacks, beat them down as they tried to rise. They were then dried in the sun and pounded up and eaten.

HINTS TO INSTRUCTORS

PRACTICES

Set your scouts to find out by observation, and to report on such points as these: —

IN COUNTRY: *When a lot of rabbits are alarmed does a rabbit merely run because the others do, or does he look round and see what is the danger before he goes, too?*

Does a woodpecker break the bark away to get at insects on a tree trunk, or does he pick them out of holes, or how does he get at them?

Does a trout when disturbed by people passing along the bank go up or down stream? Does he go away altogether or return to his place? How long does he stay away? etc.

IN TOWN: *Make your scouts go out and report if they see a lame horse, or one with collar gall, or sore mouth, or tight bearing-rein.*

Patrol to make a beehive or two, and put in queen bees or swarms, and start bee-farming for profit.

For tests for Stalkers' Badge, see page 34.

Lion Hunting

A lion is represented by one scout, who goes out with tracking irons on his feet, and a pocketful of corn or peas, and six lawn-tennis balls or rag balls. He is allowed half an hour's start, and then the patrol go after him, following his spoor, each armed with one tennis ball with which to shoot him when they find him. The lion may hide or creep about or run, just as he feels inclined, but whenever the ground is hard or very greasy he must drop a few grains of corn every few yards to show the trail.

If the hunters fail to come up to him, neither wins the game. When they come near to his lair the lion fires at them with his tennis balls, and the moment a hunter is hit he must fall out dead and cannot throw his tennis ball. If the lion gets hit by a hunting tennis ball he is wounded, and if he gets wounded three times, he is killed.

Tennis balls may only be fired once; they cannot be picked up and fired again in the same fight.

Each scout must collect and hand in his tennis balls after the game. In winter, if there is snow, this game can be played without tracking irons, and using snowballs instead of tennis balls.

BOOKS TO READ

" Modern Nature Study," by Silcox and Stevenson. 75 cents. (Morang Educational Company Limited.)

" Animal Artisans," by C. J. Cornish. 6s. 6d. nett. (Longmans.)

" Every Boy's Book of British Natural History," by W. P. Westall. 3s. 6d. (Religious Tract Society, London.)

" Woodcraft for Scouts," by Owens Jones and Marcus Woodward. 1s. nett.

" Duty," by Samuel Smiles. (Chaps. XIII, XIV.) 2s. nett.

" Beasts of the Field," by William J. Long. 7s. 6d. nett.

" Countryside," weekly. Illustrated. 1d.

" Wild Sports of the Highlands," by C. St. John. 3s. 6d. (Murray.)

" I Go A Walking through Lanes and Meadows," by Rev. C. Johns. Photos and short account of English birds. 3s. 6d. nett. (Foulis.)

" The Jungle Book," by Rudyard Kipling. Price 6s.

" Jock of the Bushveld," by Sir Percy FitzPatrick. A story of big game hunting in S. Africa, and the active part that " Jock " the terrier played in it. Price 3s. (Longmans.)

Play

" The Wild Animal Play," by Mrs. E. Thompson Seton. A musical play, in which the parts of Lobo, Waahb, and Vixen are taken by boys and girls. Price 6d. (Doubleday, New York.)

CAMP FIRE YARN. No. 16

PLANTS

Trees and their Leaves — Eatable Plants — Practices and Games connected with Plants — Books about Plants.

Trees [1]

ALTHOUGH they are not animals, trees are things about which scouts should know something. Very often a scout has to describe country which he has seen, and if he says it is " well wooded," it would often be of great importance that the reader

OAK

of his report should know what kind of trees the woods were composed of.

For instance, if the wood were of fir or larch trees it would mean you could get poles for building bridges; if it were palm trees you know you could get cocoanuts (or dates if they were date palms), and the palm juice for drinking. Willow trees mean water close by.

Or if pine woods or sugar bush or gum trees it would mean lots of good fuel. And he must know a poplar tree by sight, so as not to use poplar wood in camp if there are any old scouts present — they have a superstition that poplar brings bad luck.

[1] Much interesting and valuable information about the more common Canadian trees is given in " Modern Nature Study," by Silcox and Stevenson, published by Morang Educational Company Limited, Toronto.

A scout should therefore make a point of learning the names and appearances of the trees in his country.

He should get hold of a leaf of each kind and compare it with the leaf on the tree; and then get to know the general shape and appearance of each kind of tree, so as to be able to recognize it at a distance — and not only in summer, but also in winter.

Horse chestnut is not so called because horses like the chestnuts, but because it has on the bark of its smaller branches small marks like horseshoes, with all the nails in them.

The common trees in eastern North America which a scout should know by sight are: —

Maple	Poplar	Catalpa	Beech
Oak	Pine	Horse	Ironwood
Elm	Sycamore	Chestnut	Birch
Cedar	(Buttonwood)	Ash	Walnut
Fir	Larch	Basswood	Hickory
Spruce	Willow	Mountain	Butternut
Hemlock		Ash	

But especially you ought to know what kinds of plants are useful to you in providing you with food. Supposing you were out in a jungle without any food, as very often happens; if you knew nothing about plants you would probably die of starvation, or of poisoning, from not knowing which fruit or roots were wholesome and which dangerous to eat.

There are numbers of berries, nuts, roots, barks, and leaves and fungi that are good to eat.

The same with crops of different kinds of grain and seed, vegetable roots, and even grasses and vetches. Seaweed is much eaten in Ireland (sloke) and Scotland. Certain kinds of moss are also used as food.

HINTS TO INSTRUCTORS

PRACTICES

Take out scouts to get specimens of leaves, fruits, or blossoms of various trees, shrubs, etc., and observe the shape and nature of the tree both in summer and in winter.

Collect leaves of different trees; let scouts make tracings of them and write the name of the tree on each.

In the country make scouts examine crops in all stages of their growth, so that they know pretty well by sight what kind of crop is coming up.

Start gardens, if possible, either a patrol garden or individual scout's garden. Let them grow flowers and vegetables for profit to pay for their equipment, etc.

Show all the wild plants which may be made use of for food.

Games

PLANT RACE

Start off your scouts, either cycling or on foot, to go in any direction they like, to get a specimen of any ordered plant, say a piece of Indian turnip, a bunch of mountain ash berries, a horseshoe mark from a chestnut tree, a brier rose, or something of that kind, whichever you may order, such as will tax their knowledge of plants and will test their memory as to where they noticed one of the kind required, and will also make them quick in getting there and back.

BOOKS TO READ

" School Gardening," by W. E. Watkins. 2s. 6d. (Philip & Son.)

Play

THE DIAMOND THIEF

(Best performed in the open air and in dumb show.)

A party of prospectors have been out into the wild country in South Africa and have found a magnificent diamond. They are now making their way back to civilization with it. Horse-sickness has killed off their horses, and so they are doing their journey on foot, carrying their blankets, food, and cooking-pots.

As the heat of the day comes on they camp for the day, meaning to push on again at night. They rig up blanket-tents and light fires and cook their food, weave mattresses, sing songs of home, play cards, etc. The diamond is taken out of the sardine tin in which it is kept for all to look at and admire. It is then put carefully back. The box is placed out in the open where it can be seen, and one man is told off as sentry to guard it. The remainder have their food, and then gradually lie down to sleep. When the camp is all still the sentry gets tired of standing, and presently sits down and begins to nod.

While he is dozing the diamond thief sneaks into sight, creeps near to the camp, and crouches, watching the sleeping man; when the sentry wakes up for a moment with a start the thief crouches flat.

Eventually the sentry reclines and goes to sleep. Inch by inch the thief creeps up, till he stealthily removes the sentry's gun (or pistol) out of his reach; then he swiftly glides up to the diamond box, seizes it, and sneaks quietly away without being discovered, dodges about, walks backwards, and wipes out his tracks as he goes in order to confuse pursuers.

The leader wakes with a yawn, and, looking round, starts when he sees there is no sentry standing about. He springs up, rushes to the sleeping sentry, shakes him up, and asks him where is the diamond. Sentry wakes up confused and scared. Remainder wake and crowd angrily together, threatening and questioning the sentry.

Then one suddenly sees the footprints of the thief; it follows in jerks of a few paces along the trail; the rest follow and help to pick it up, first one and then another finding it, till they go off the scene. The leader is about to follow them when he stops and waves them onward, and then turns back to the sentry, who is standing stupefied. He hands him a pistol, and hints to him that, having ruined his friends by his faithlessness, he may as well shoot himself. The leader then turns to follow the rest, looking about for them. A shout is heard in the distance just as the guilty sentry is putting the pistol to his head. The leader stops him from shooting himself, and both stand listening to shouts in the distance.

Remainder of the men return, bringing in with them the thief and the diamond all safe.

They then sit round in a semicircle, the leader on a mound or box in the centre, with the diamond in front of him. The thief, standing with arms bound, is tried and condemned to be shot. He goes away a few paces and sits down with his back to the rest and thinks over his past life.

They then try the sentry, and condemn him as a punishment for his carelessness to shoot the thief.

All get up. They start to dig a grave. When ready the thief is made to stand up, his eyes are bound. The sentry takes a pistol and shoots him. Remainder then bring a blanket and lift the dead man into it and carry him to the grave — to the opposite side from the audience, so that every one can see the " body " lowered into the grave. They then withdraw the blanket, fill in the grave, and trample the earth down. All shake hands with the sentry to show that they forgive him.

They then pack up camp and continue their journey with the diamond.

Or another alternative is to hang the thief on a tree and to leave him hanging.

At the foot of the tree which is to form the gallows dig a small trench beforehand; carefully conceal it with grass, etc., and hide in it a dummy figure made to look as much as possible like the scout who is to be hanged.

When the prisoner is taken to execution, make him lie down to be pinioned close to this trench. While the scouts are busy round him in binding him and putting on the noose, they of course substitute the dummy for the real boy, who then slides into the ditch and hides there.

N.B. — The grave is managed thus. A hole must be previously prepared near to the edge of the arena. Then a tunnel is made by which the " corpse " can creep out of the grave and get away underground. This is done by digging a trench and roofing it with boards or hurdles and covering it over with earth and turf again, so that the spectators will not notice it. The grave, too, is made in the same way, but shallower, and partly filled up with sods; the diggers remove the top earth, then, hidden by the rest crowding round, they remove the board and pile up the sods on the surface. As soon as the corpse is lowered into the grave he creeps away down the tunnel, and so goes off the scene. The diggers throw in some earth, jump down and trample it, then pile up the sods on top till they make a nice looking grave.

The whole thing wants careful rehearsing beforehand, but is most effective when well done, especially if accompanied by sympathetic music.

It is a good thing to use for an open-air show to attract a crowd when raising funds for your troop.

CHAPTER VI

ENDURANCE FOR SCOUTS

Or, How to be Strong

HINTS TO INSTRUCTORS

HOW TO HELP IN A GREAT NATIONAL WORK

Recent reports on the deterioration of our race in the British Isles ought to act as a warning to be taken in time, before it goes too far.

One cause which contributed to the downfall of the Roman Empire was the fact that the soldiers fell away from the standard of their forefathers in bodily strength.

The standard of height in the British Army was 5 ft. 6 in. in 1845; it was FOUR INCHES less in 1895. In 1900 forty-four men in every thousand recruits weighed under 110 lbs.; in 1905 this deficiency had increased to seventy-six per thousand.

In 1908 the recruits were two inches below the standard height of men of their age, viz. eighteen to nineteen, and six pounds under the average weight.

Three thousand men were sent home from the South African War on account of bad teeth.

The reports of Boards of Education and educational institutions show that much PREVENTABLE deterioration is being allowed to creep in among the rising generation, largely owing to ignorance on the part of parents and of the children themselves.

Then there is also prevalent a great amount of illness result-

ing from self-abuse and venereal disease, as well as from drink. Also much pauper overpopulation due to lack of self-restraint on the part of men and women.

The training of Boy Scouts would be therefore incomplete if it did not endeavor to help in remedying these evils where they exist. Some idea is much needed among boys of their personal hygiene. It has been stated on good authority that half our losses in the Boer War from sickness might have been avoided had our men and officers had any knowledge of personal care of their health.

No doubt it is the same in peace time, as numbers of men are thrown out of work by sickness, which might be avoided if they knew how to look after themselves, and took reasonable precautions. Sir Victor Horsley computes that Great Britain loses annually 20 million weeks of work through sickness, and 60,000 workers by premature death.

Total abstainers suffer 6.4 weeks' sickness; non-abstainers 10.9 weeks.

Since most of these cases of physical decay are preventable, they open to instructors a field for doing a work of national value. I venture to hope that they will therefore make a special feature of the instructions suggested in the three following camp yarns.

For these reasons the following chapter suggests the instruction of boys in being PERSONALLY RESPONSIBLE for their own Strength, Health, and Sanitary Surroundings.

CAMP FIRE YARN. No. 17.

HOW TO GROW STRONG

Need for Scouts to be Strong — Exercises — Care of Body — Nose — Ears — Eyes — Teeth — Nails — Practices.

A Scout's Endurance

A SCOUT lay sick in hospital in India with that most fatal disease called cholera. The doctor told the native man in attendance on him that the only chance of saving his life was to warm up his feet violently and keep the blood moving in his body by constantly rubbing him. The moment the doctor's back was turned the native gave up rubbing and squatted down to have a quiet smoke. The poor patient, though he could not speak, understood all that was going on, and he was so enraged at the conduct of the native attendant that he resolved then and there that he would get well if only to give the native a lesson. Having made up his mind to get well he *got* well.

A scout's motto is, " Never say die till you're dead " — and if he acts up to this, it will pull him out of many a bad place when everything seems to be going wrong with him. It means a mixture of pluck, patience, and strength, which we call " endurance."

The great South African hunter and scout, F. C. Selous, gave a great example of scouts' endurance when on a hunting expedition in Barotseland, north of the Zambesi River, some years ago. In the middle of the night his camp was suddenly attacked by a hostile tribe, who fired into it at close range and charged in.

He and his small party of natives scattered at once into the darkness and hid themselves away in the long grass. Selous himself had snatched up his rifle and a few cartridges and got safely into the grass. But he could not find any of his men, and, seeing that the enemy had got possession of his camp, and that there were still a few hours of darkness before him in which to make his escape, he started off southwards, using the stars of the Southern Cross as his guide.

He crept past an outpost of the enemy whom he overheard talking, and then swam across a river and finally got well away, dressed only in a shirt, and shorts, and shoes. For the next few days and nights he kept walking southwards, having frequently to hide to avoid hostile natives. He shot deer for food.

But one night, going into what he thought was a friendly village, he had his rifle stolen from him, and was again a fugitive, without any means of protecting himself or of getting food. However, he was not one to give in while there was a chance of life left, and he pushed on and on till at length he reached a place where he met some of his men who had also escaped, and after further tramping they got safely back into friendly country.

But what a terrible time they must have had !

Three weeks had passed since the attack, and the great part of that time Selous had been alone, hunted, starving — and bitterly cold at night, and in sweltering heat by day.

None but a scout with extraordinary endurance could have lived through it, but then Selous is a man who as a lad had made himself strong by care and exercise; and he neither drinks nor smokes. And he kept up his pluck all the time.

It shows you that if you want to get through such adventures safely when you are a man, you must train yourself up to be strong, healthy, and active as a boy.

Exercises and their Object

There is a great deal of nonsense done in the way of bodily exercises; so many people seem to think that their only object is to make huge muscle. But to make yourself strong and healthy it is necessary to begin with your inside and to get the blood into good order and the heart to work well; that is the secret of the whole thing, and exercises of the body do it for you. This is the way: —

(a) MAKE THE HEART STRONG in order to pump the blood properly to every part of the body, and so to build up flesh, bone, and muscle.

Exercise: The "Struggle" and "Wrist Pushing." See page 195.

(b) MAKE THE LUNGS STRONG in order to provide the blood with fresh air.

Exercise: "Deep breathing." See page 208.

(c) MAKE THE SKIN PERSPIRE to get rid of the dirt from the blood.

Exercise: Bath, or dry rub with a damp towel every day.

(d) MAKE THE STOMACH WORK to feed the blood.

Exercise: "Cone," or "Body Bending," and "Twisting." See page 198.

(e) MAKE THE BOWELS ACTIVE to remove the remains of food and dirt from the body.

Exercise: "Body Bending" and "Kneading the Abdomen." Drink plenty of good water. Regular daily "rear."

(f) WORK MUSCLES IN EACH PART OF THE BODY to make the blood circulate to that part, and so increase your strength.

Exercise: Running and Walking, and special exercises of special muscles, such as "Wrist Pushing" (page 195), etc.

The secret of keeping well and healthy is to keep your blood clean and active. These different exercises will do that if you will use them every day. Some one has said, "If you practise body exercises every morning you will never be ill; and if you also drink a pint of hot water every night you will never die."

The blood thrives on simple good food, plenty of exercise, plenty of fresh air, cleanliness of the body both *inside* and out, and proper rest of body and mind at intervals.

The Japanese are very strong and healthy, as was shown in the late war with Russia. There was very little sickness among them, and those who were wounded generally very quickly recovered, because their skin was clean and their blood was in a healthy, sound condition. They are the best example that we can copy. They keep themselves very clean by having two or three baths every day.

They eat very plain food, chiefly rice and fruit, and not much of it. They drink plenty of water, but no ˙irits. They take lots of exercise. They make themselves good-tempered and do not worry their brain. They live in fresh air as much as possible day and night. Their particular exercise is " Ju-Jitsu," which is more of a game than drill, and is generally played in pairs. And pupils get to like the game so much that they generally go on with it after their course of instruction has finished.

By Ju-Jitsu, the muscles and body are developed in a natural way, in the open air as a rule. It requires no apparatus, and once the muscles have been formed by it, they do not disappear again when you cease the practices, as is the case in ordinary gymnastics.

Admiral Kamimura, the great Japanese admiral, strongly recommends all young men and boys to practise Ju-Jitsu, as it makes them not only strong, but also quick in the mind.

The Nose

A scout must be able to smell well, in order to find his enemy by night. If he always breathes through the nose, and not through the mouth, this helps him considerably. But there are other reasons more important than that for always breathing through the nose. Fifty years ago, Mr. Catlin, in America, wrote a book called " Shut your Mouth and Save your Life," and he showed how the Indians for a long time had adopted that method with their children to the extent of tying up their jaws at night, to ensure their breathing only through their nose.

Breathing through the nose prevents germs of disease getting from the air into the throat and stomach; it also prevents a growth in the back of the throat called " adenoids," which are apt to stop the breathing power of the nostrils, and also to cause deafness.

For a scout nose-breathing is also specially useful.

By keeping the mouth shut you prevent yourself from getting thirsty when you are doing hard work. And also at night, if you are in the habit of breathing through the nose, it prevents snoring, and snoring is a dangerous thing if you are sleeping anywhere in an enemy's country. Therefore practise keeping your mouth shut and breathing through your nose at all times.

Ears

A scout must be able to hear well. Generally the ears are very delicate, and once damaged are apt to become incurably deaf. People are too apt to fiddle about with their ears in cleaning them by putting the corners of handkerchiefs, hairpins, and so on into them, and also stuffing them up with hard cotton wool, all of which are dangerous with such a delicate organ as the ear, the drum of the ear being a very delicate, tightly-stretched skin which is easily damaged. Very many children have had the drums of their ears permanently injured by getting a box on the ear.

Eyes

A scout, of course, must have particularly good eyesight; he must be able to see anything very quickly, and to see at a long way off. By practising your eyes in looking at things at a great distance, they will grow stronger. While you are young you should save your eyes as much as possible, or they are not strong when you get older; therefore avoid reading by lamplight as much as possible, and also sit with your back or side to the light when doing any work during the day; if you sit facing the light it strains your eyes.

The strain of the eyes is a very common failure with growing boys, although very often they do not know it, and headaches come most frequently from the eyes being strained; frowning on the part of a boy is very generally a sign that his eyes are being strained.

A scout, besides having good eyesight, must be able to tell the color of things which he sees. Color-blindness is a great infliction which some boys suffer from. It takes away a pleasure from them, and it often makes them useless for certain trades and professions.

For instance, a railway signalman or engine-driver or a sailor would not be much good if he couldn't tell the difference between red and green.

It can very often be cured, and a simple way of doing this, if you find you are rather color-blind, is to get a collection of little bits of wool, or paper, of every different kind of color, and pick out which you think is red, blue, yellow, green, and so on, and then get some one to tell you where you were right and where wrong. Then you go at it again, and in time you will find yourself improving, until you have no difficulty in recognizing the right colors. It is better still to practise by looking at colored lights at night in drug stores, railway signals, etc.

Teeth

A would-be recruit came up to the recruiting officer to be enlisted during the Boer War. He was found to be a sufficiently strong and well-made man, but when they came to examine his teeth they found that these were in bad condition, and he was told that he could not be accepted as a soldier. To this he replied: "But, sir, that seems hard lines. Surely we don't have to eat the enemy when we've killed them, do we?"

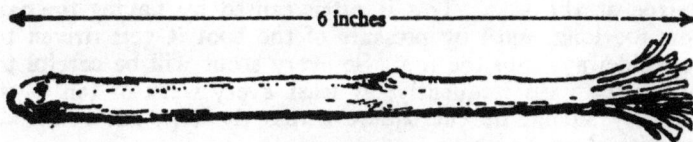

CAMP TOOTH-BRUSH

A scout with bad teeth is no use at all for scouting work, because he has to live on hard biscuits and hard meat, which he cannot possibly eat or digest if his teeth are not good; and good teeth depend upon how you look after them when you are young, which means that you should keep them very carefully clean. At least twice a day they should be brushed, when you get up in the morning and when you go to bed, both inside and out, with a tooth-brush and tooth powder; and should be rinsed with water, if possible, after every meal, but especially after eating fruit or acid food.

Scouts in the jungle cannot always find tooth-brushes, but they make substitutes out of dry sticks, which they fray out at the end, and make an imitation of a brush.

Three thousand men had to be sent away from the war in South Africa because their teeth were so bad that they could not chew the hard biscuits, etc., on which they had to live there.

In the western part of America, cowboys are generally supposed to be rather rough customers, but they are in reality peace scouts of a high order. They live a hard life, doing hard and dangerous work far away from towns and civilization — where nobody sees them. But there is one civilized thing that they do — they clean their teeth every day, morning and evening.

Years ago I was travelling through Natal on horseback, and I was anxious to find a lodging for the night, when I came across a hut evidently occupied by a white man, but nobody was about. In looking around inside the hut, I noticed that though it was very roughly furnished, there were several tooth-brushes on what served as a wash-hand stand, so I guessed that the owner must be a decent fellow, and I made myself at home until he came in, and I found that I had guessed aright.

Nails

Soldiers, as well as other people, very often suffer great pain and lameness from the nail of their big toe growing down into the toe at the side. This is often caused by having the nail grow too long, until by pressure of the boot it gets driven to grow sideways into the toe. So every scout will be careful to cut his toe nails frequently, at least every week or ten days, and they should be cut square across the top, not rounded, and with sharp scissors.

Finger nails should also be cut about once a week with sharp scissors, to keep them in good order. Biting the nails is not good for them.

HINTS TO INSTRUCTORS

PRACTICES IN DEVELOPING STRENGTH

MEASUREMENT OF THE BODY

It is of paramount importance to teach the young citizen to assume responsibility for his own development and health.

Physical drill is all very well as a disciplinary means of development, but it does not give the boy any responsibility in the matter.

It is therefore deemed preferable to tell each boy, according to his age, what ought to be his height, weight, and various measurements (such as chest, waist, arm, leg, etc.). He is then measured, and learns in which points he fails to come up to the standard. He can then be shown which exercises to practise for himself in order to develop those particular points. Encouragement must afterwards be given by periodical measurements, say every three months or so.

Cards may be obtained from the "Boy Scouts" Office, 116, Victoria Street, London, S.W., which, besides giving the standard measurements for the various ages, give columns to be filled in periodically, showing the boy's remeasurements and progress in development. If each boy has his card it is a great incentive to him to develop himself at odd times when he has a few minutes to spare.

Teach how to make camp tooth-brushes out of sticks. "Dragon-root" sticks for cleaning teeth can be had at drug stores as samples.

Games to Develop Strength

Boxing, wrestling, rowing. skipping, cock-fighting are all valuable health aids to developing strength.

"The Struggle." — Two players face each other about a yard apart, stretch arms out sideways, lock fingers of both hands, and lean towards each other till their chests touch, push chest to chest and see who can drive the other back to the wall of the room or on to a goal line. At first a very short struggle is sufficient to set their hearts pumping, but after practice for a few days the heart grows stronger, and they can go on for a long time.

"Wrist Pushing" by one man alone. Stand with both your arms to the front about level with the waist, cross your wrists so that one hand has knuckles up, the other knuckles down. Clench the fists.

Now make the lower hand press upwards and make the upper hand press downwards.

Press as hard as you can with both wrists gradually, and only after great resistance let the lower push the upper one upwards till opposite your forehead, then let the upper press the lower down, the lower one resisting all the time.

These two exercises, although they sound small and simple, if carried out with all your might, develop most muscles in your body, and especially those about the heart. They should not be carried on too long at a time, but should be done at frequent intervals during the day for a minute or so.

"Wrist Pushing" can also be played by two boys half facing each other, each putting out the wrist nearest to his opponent at arm's length; pressing it against the other's wrist, and trying to turn him round backwards.

Staff Exercises — to music if possible.

STAFF TOSSING. — With your right hand grasp your staff near the butt and hold it upright; then toss it straight up in the air a short distance at first, and catch it with the left hand near the butt as it comes down. Toss it straight up again with the left and catch it with the right, and so on, till you can do it one hundred times without dropping it.

"FOLLOW MY LEADER." — With a large number of boys this can be made a very effective display, and is easy to do — at a jog-trot, and occasional "knees up," with musical accompaniment. It can also be done at night, each boy carrying a Chinese lantern on top of his staff. If in a building, all lights would, of course, be turned down. A usual fault is that the exercise is kept on too long, till it wearies both spectators and performers.

An Easy Way to Grow Strong

It is possible for any boy, even though he may be small and weak, to make himself into a strong and healthy man if he takes the trouble to do a few body exercises every day. They take only about ten minutes, and do not require any kind of apparatus, such as dumb-bells, parallel bars, and so on.

They should be practised every morning, the first thing on getting up, and every evening before going to bed. It is best to do them with little or no clothing on, and in the open air, or close to an open window. The value of this exercise is much increased if you think of the object of each move while you are doing it, and if you are very particular to breath the air in through your nose and to breath out through your mouth — since breathing in through the nose prevents you from swallowing down all sorts of little seeds of poison or bad health, which are always floating about in the air — especially in rooms from which the fresh air is shut out; such rooms are very poisonous. A great many people who are pale and seedy are made so by living in rooms where the windows are seldom opened and the air is full of unwholesome gases or germs. Open your windows, especially at the top, every day to let the foul air out.

Here are some good exercises: —

No. 1. For the Head and Neck.
No. 2. For the Chest.
No. 3. For the Stomach.
No. 4. For the Body.
No. 5. For the Lower Body and Back of Legs.
No. 6. For the Legs, Feet, and Toes.

It strengthens the toes and feet to do these exercises bare-footed.

1. *Head*. — Rub the head, face, and neck firmly over several times with the palms and fingers of both hands. Thumb the muscles of the neck and throat — this is done by the Japs to such an extent as to make their necks so strong and muscular that they have no fear of being gripped by the throat, which otherwise is such a weak and tender spot.

Brush your hair, clean your teeth, wash out your mouth and nose, drink a cup of cold water, and then go on with the following exercises.

The movements should all be done as slowly as possible.

2. *Upper Body*. — From upright position bend to the front, arms stretched downwards, with back of the hands together in front of the knees. Breath out.

Raise the hands gradually over the head and lean back as far as possible, drawing a deep breath *through the nose* as you do so — that is,

FIG. 1

The right way   The wrong way

drinking God's air into your lungs and blood. Lower the arms gradually to the sides, breathing out the word " Thanks " (to God) through the mouth.

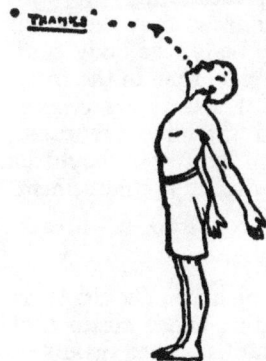

FIG. 2

Lastly, bend forwards again, breathing out the last bit of breath in you, and saying the number of times you have done it, in order to keep count.

Repeat this exercise twelve times.

Remember while carrying it out that the object of the exercise is to develop shoulders, chest, heart, and breathing apparatus inside you.

3. *For the Stomach*. — Standing upright, send out both arms, fingers extended, straight to the front, then slowly swing round to the right from the hips without moving the feet, and point the right arm as far round behind you as

you can, keeping both arms level with the shoulders. Then, after a pause, swing slowly round as far as you can to the left. Repeat this a dozen times.

This exercise is to move the inside organs, such as liver and intestines, and help their work, as well as to strengthen the outside muscles round the ribs and stomach.

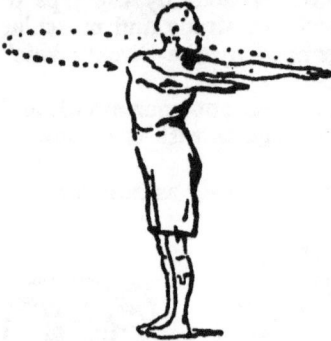

While carrying out this exercise, the breathing should be carefully regulated. Breathe in through the nose (not through the mouth), while pointing to the right rear; breathe out through the mouth as you come round and point to the left rear, and at the same time count aloud the number of the swing — or, what is better, thinking of it as part of your morning prayer with God, say aloud: " Bless Tim," " bless Father," and any of your family or friends in turn.

EXERCISE 3. BODY TWISTING

When you have done this six times to the right change the breathing to the other side: breath in when pointing to the left rear, and breath out to the right.

4. *For the Body and Back.* " Cone Exercise." — Standing at the " Alert," raise both hands as high as possible over the head, and link fingers, lean backwards, then sway the arms very slowly round in the direction of a cone, so that the hands make a wide circle above and around the body, the body turning from the hips, and leaning over to one side, then to the front, then to the other side, and then back; this is to exercise the muscles of the waist and stomach, and should be repeated, say, six times to either hand. With the eyes you should be trying to see all that goes on behind you during the movement.

NOTE. — The arrow → means when to draw in breath; the c→ means when to breathe out.

A meaning attached to this exercise, which you should think of while carrying it out, is this: The clasping hands means that you are knit together with friends — that is, other Scouts — all round you as you sway round to the right, left, before, and behind you; in every direction you are bound to friends. Love and friendship are the gift of God, so when you are making the upward move you look to Heaven and drink in the air and the good feeling, which you then breath out to your comrades all round.

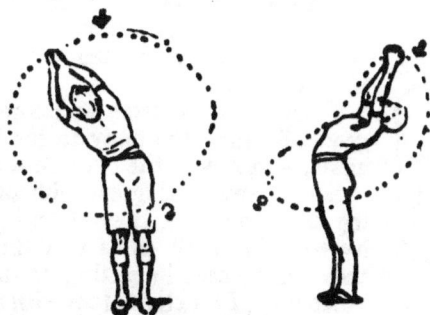

"CONE" EXERCISE

5. *For the lower part of the Body and back of Thighs.* — Like every one of the exercises, this is, at the same time, a breathing exercise by which the lungs and heart are developed, and the blood made strong and healthy. You simply stand up and reach as high as you can skywards, and then bend forwards and downwards till your fingers touch your toes *without bending your knees*.

Stand with feet slightly apart, touch your head with both hands, and look up into the sky, leaning back as far as you can, as in Fig. 1.

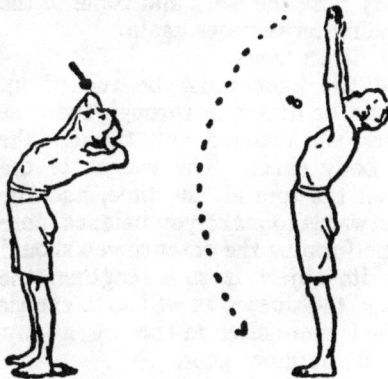

FIG. 1   FIG. 2

If you mingle prayer with your exercises, as I described to you before, you can, while looking up in this way, say to God: " I am yours from top to toe," and drink in God's air (through

your nose, not through the mouth). Then reach both hands
upwards as far as possible (Fig. 2), breathe out the number of
the turn that you are doing; then bend
slowly forwards and downwards, knees stiff,
till you touch your toes with yᵣ · finger-
tips (Fig. 3).

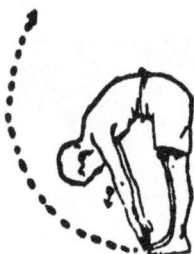

Then, keeping arms and knees still stiff,
gradually raise the body to the first position
again, and repeat the exercise a dozen times.

Some boys find great difficulty in touching their toes, but they should go on trying
by touching their shins first; in a few days
they will succeed in getting down to the toes

FIG. 3

Personally, I touch my toes with my knuckles,
which is rather harder than with the tips of the fingers, and
stretches the back sinews of the legs very nicely. See if you
can do it !

In the picture → means drawing in the breath through the
nose; o→ means breathing out through the mouth.

6. *For the Legs and Feet.* — Standing, barefooted, at the position of " Alert," put the hands on the hips, stand on tiptoe, turn
the knees outwards, and bend them slowly till you gradually
sink down to a squatting position, keeping the heels off the
ground the whole time.

Then gradually raise the body and come to the
position of standing on the toes again.

Repeat this a dozen times.

The small of the back must be tucked in.
The breath should be drawn in through the nose
as the body rises, and counted out, through the
mouth, as the body sinks. The weight of the
body must be on the toes all the time, and the
knees turned outwards to make you balance more
easily. While performing the practice you should
remember that its object is to strengthen the
thighs, calves, and toe-sinews, as well as to exercise the stomach,
so if you practise it more often in the day, at any odd moments,
it will do you all the more good.

And you can connect with this exercise, since it makes you
alternately stand up and squat down, that whether you are standing or sitting, at work or resting, you will hold yourself together
(as your hands on your hips are doing), and make yourself do
what is right.

These exercises are not intended merely as a way of passing time, but really to help a boy to grow big as well as to grow strong.

Eugen Sandow, the great athlete, has undertaken to help recruits who are under the size for the British Territorial Army, so that by exercises they can add, in a few weeks, from an inch to an inch and a half to their height, and as much as four or five inches round their chests.

Sandow himself was, as a boy, weak and small for his age, and you know from his portraits what he is now in the way of muscle and sinew and health. This was all got by exercising himself in the right way. So any boy can do it if he likes.

BOOKS TO READ

" The Syllabus of Physical Exercises for Elementary Schools." Board of Education, 1909. 9d.

" Annual Report of the Medical Officer of Board of Education," 1910. 9d.

" Cassell's Physical Educator," by E. Miles. A complete compendium of all kinds of Physical Training for boys and girls. 9s.

" Ju-Jitsu." 6d. (Richard Fox.)

" Playground Games," by T. Chesterton. 2s. 6d.

" Boxing," by A. J. Newton. 1s. (C. A. Pearson Limited.)

" Healthful Physical Exercises," by W. L. Rooper. Swedish system. 2s. 6d. (Newmann, 84 Newman Street.)

" Scout Charts." Nos. 1, 2, 3, 4, 5, 6, 7, 20. Post free, 3d. each, from "The Scout" Office, 28 Maiden Lane, London, W.C.

CAMP FIRE YARN. No. 18

HEALTH-GIVING HABITS

Keep Clean — Don't Smoke — Don't Drink — Keep Pur --
Rise Early — Laugh and Grow Fat.

How to Keep Healthy

ALL the great peace scouts who have succeeded in exploring or hunting expeditions in wild countries have been able to get on only by being pretty good doctors themselves; because diseases accidents, and wounds are always being suffered by them or their men, and they don't find doctors and drug stores in the jungles to cure them. So that a scout who does not know something about doctoring would never get on at all; he might just as well stay at home for all the good he will be.

Therefore, practise keeping healthy yourself, and then you will be able to show others how to keep themselves healthy too.

In this way you can do many good turns.

David Livingstone, the great missionary and peace scout, endeared himself to the natives by his cleverness as a doctor.

Also, if you know how to look after yourself you need never have to pay for medicines. The great English poet, Dryden, in his poem, " Cymon and Iphigenia," wrote that it was better to trust to fresh air and exercise than to pay doctors' bills to keep yourself healthy.

> " Better to hunt in fields for health unbought
> Than fee the doctor for a nauseous draught:
> The wise, for cure, on exercise depend;
> God never made his work for man to mend."

Keep Yourself Clean

In the war in South Africa we lost an enormous number of men from disease as well as from wounds. The Japs, in their war, lost very few from sickness, and a very small proportion of those who were wounded. What made the difference? Probably a good many things. Our men were not so particular as to what water they drank as the Japs were, and they ate more meat than the Japs; but, also, they did not keep themselves or their clothes very clean — it was often difficult to find water. The Japs, on the other hand, kept themselves very clean, with baths every day.

If you cut your hand when it is dirty, it is very likely to fester, and to become very sore; but if your hand is quite clean and freshly washed, no harm will come of it, it heals up at once. It was the same with wounds in the war; they become very bad in the case of men who had not kept themselves clean.

Cleaning your skin helps to clean your blood. The Japs say that half the good of exercise is lost if you do not have a bath immediately after it.

It may not be always possible for you to get a bath every day. but you can at any rate rub yourself over with a wet towel, or scrub yourself with a dry one, and you ought not to miss a single day in doing this if you want to keep in good condition.

You should also keep clean in your clothing, both your under clothing as well as that which shows. Beat it out with a stick every day before putting it on.

And to be healthy and strong you *must* keep your blood healthy and clean inside you. This is done by breathing in lots of pure, fresh air, by deep breathing, and by clearing out all dirty matter from inside your stomach, which is done by having a " rear " daily, without fail; many people are the better for having it twice a day. If there is any difficulty about it one day, drink plenty of good water, especially before and just after breakfast, and practise body-twisting exercises, and all should be well.

Never start work in the morning without some sort of food inside you, if it is only a cup of hot water.

There is no need to take all the drugs, pills, and medicines which you see so temptingly advertised; they often do you harm in the end.

Never bathe in deep water very soon after a meal ; it is very likely to cause cramp, which doubles you up, and so you get drowned.

Smoking

A scout does not smoke. Any boy can smoke; it is not such a very wonderful thing to do. But a scout will not do it because he is not so foolish. He knows that when a boy smokes before he is fully grown up it is almost sure to make his heart feeble, and the heart is the most important organ in a boy's body. It pumps the blood all over him to form flesh, bone, and muscle. If the heart does not do its work, the body cannot grow to be healthy. Any scout knows that smoking spoils his eyesight, and also his sense of smell, which is of greatest importance to him for scouting on active service.

Sir William Broadbent, the great doctor, and Professor Sims Woodhead have both told us what bad effects tobacco smoking has on the health of boys. Numerous well-known sportsmen and others in all kinds of professions have given up the use of tobacco, as they find they can do better without it. Lord Roberts and Lord Wolseley as soldiers, Lord Charles Beresford as a sailor, the Archbishop of Canterbury, the judge, Sir William Grantham, all do not smoke, nor do Dr. Grace, the cricketer, Noble and seven of the chief Australian cricketers, Eustace Miles, the champion tennis player, Basset, the football player, Weston, the pedestrian, Taylor, the golf player, Burnham, the scout, Selous, the hunter, and very many other celebrated men. They all are non-smokers.

The railway and post-office authorities in America will not employ boys who smoke. I know one big employer who not only does not smoke, but will not employ a boy who does. In Japan no boy under twenty is allowed to smoke, and if he does, his parents are taken up and fined.

A "Slopper." The boy who apes the man by smoking; he will never be much good.

A strong and healthy boy has the ball at his feet.

Dr. William Osler of Toronto. who is now professor of medicine at the University of Oxford, in speaking against tobacco, said it would be a good thing if all the beer and spirits in England could be thrown into the sea one day, and if, on the second day, you dumped all the tobacco there too, it would be very good for every one in England — although unhealthy for the fish.

No boy ever began smoking because he liked it, but generally because either he feared being laughed at by the other boys as afraid to smoke, or because he thought that by smoking he would look like a great man — when all the time he succeeds only in looking silly.

So don't let yourself be persuaded, but just make up your mind for yourself that you don't mean to smoke till you are grown up: and stick to it. That will show you to be a man much more than any slobbering about with a half-smoked cigarette between your lips. The other boys will in the end respect you much more, and will probably in many cases secretly follow your lead. If they do this, you will already have done a good thing in the world, although you are only a boy. From that small start you will most probably go on and do big things as you grow up.

Drinking

A priest in the East End of London has lately stated that out of a thousand cases of distress known to him only two or three were not caused by drink.

A soldierly looking man came up to me one night and brought out his discharge certificates, showing that he had served with me in South Africa. He said he could get no work, and he was starving. Every man's hand was against him, apparently because he was a soldier. My nose and eyes told me in a moment another tale, and that was the real cause of his being in distress.

A stale smell of tobacco and beer hung about his clothes, his finger-tips were yellow with cigarette smoke, he had even taken some kind of scented lozenge to try and hide the whiskey smell in his breath. No wonder nobody would employ him, or give him more money to drink with, for that was all that he would do with money if he got it.

Very much of the poverty and distress in all countries is brought about by men getting into the habit of wasting their money and time on drink. And a great deal of crime, and also of illness, and even madness, is due to the same habit of drinking too much. Liquor — that is, beer or spirits — is not at all necessary to make a man strong and well. Quite the contrary. The old saying, "Strong drink makes weak men," is a very true one.

It would be simply impossible for a man who drinks to be a scout. Keep off liquor from the very first, and make up your mind to have nothing to do with it. Water, tea, or coffee are quite good enough drinks for quenching your thirst or for making you feel better at any time, or if it is very hot, lemonade or a squeeze of lemon are much better refreshment.

A good scout trains himself pretty well to do without liquid. It is very much a matter of habit. If you keep your mouth shut when walking or running, or chew a pebble (which also makes you keep your mouth shut), you do not get thirsty as you do when you go along with your mouth open sucking in the air and dry dust. But you must also be in good hard condition. If you are fat from lack of exercise, you are sure to get thirsty and want to drink every mile. If you do not let yourself drink, the thirst wears off after a short time. If you keep drinking water on the line of march, or while playing games, it helps to tire you and spoils your wind.

It is often difficult to avoid taking strong drinks when you meet friends who want to treat you, but they generally like you all the better if you say you don't want anything, as then they don't have to pay for it; if they insist you can take a ginger-beer or something quite harmless. But it is a stupid fashion when, in order to prove that you are friends, you have to drink with each other. Luckily it is dying out now; the best men do not do it, because they know it does them no good. Good for nothing fellows like to stand about a bar talking and sipping — generally at the other man's expense — but they are of no use, either to themselves or to anybody else, and it is as well to keep out of their company, if you want to get on and have a good time.

Continence

Smoking and drinking are things that tempt some boys and not others, but there is one temptation that is pretty sure to come to you at one time or another, and I want just to warn you against it.

You would probably be surprised if you knew how many boys have written to me thanking me for what I have said in "Scouting for Boys" and elsewhere on this subject, so I expect there are more who will be glad of a word of advice against the secret vice which gets hold of so many boys.

It is called in our schools "beastliness," and that is about the best name for it.

Smoking and drinking and gambling are men's vices and therefore attract some boys, but this "beastliness" is not a man's vice; men have nothing but contempt for any one who gives way to it.

Some boys, like those who start smoking, think it a very fine and manly thing to tell or listen to dirty stories, but it shows only how foolish they are.

Yet such talk and the reading of trashy books or looking at lewd pictures are very apt to lead a thoughtless boy into the temptation of self-abuse. This is a most dangerous thing for him, for should it become a habit it quickly destroys both health and spirits; he becomes feeble in body and mind, and often ends in a lunatic asylum.

But if you have any manliness in you, you will throw off such temptation at once; you will stop looking at the books and listening to the stories, and will give yourself something else to think about.

Sometimes the desire is brought on by indigestion, or from eating too rich food, or from constipation. It can therefore be cured by correcting these, and by bathing at once in cold water, or by exercising the upper part of the body by arm exercises, boxing, etc.

It may seem difficult to overcome the temptation the first time, but when you have done so once it will be easier afterwards.

If you still have trouble about it, do not make a secret of it, but go to your scoutmaster and talk it over with him, and all will come right.

Bad dreams are another form of want of continence, which often come from sleeping in too warm a bed with too many blankets on, or from sleeping on your back; so try to avoid these causes.

Early Rising

The scout's time for being most active is in the early morning, because that is the time when wild animals all do their feeding and moving about; and also in war the usual hour for an attack is just before dawn, when the attackers can creep up unseen in the dark and get sufficient light to enable them to carry out the attack suddenly, while the other people are still asleep.

So a scout trains himself to the habit of getting up very early; and when once he is in the habit, it is no trouble at all to him, as it is to some fat fellows who lie asleep after the daylight has come.

The Emperor Charlemagne, who was a great scout in the old days, used always to get up in the middle of the night.

The Duke of Wellington, who, like Napoleon Bonaparte, preferred to sleep on a little camp bed, used to say, " When it is time to turn over in bed it is time to turn out."

Many men who manage to get through more work than others in a day do so by getting up an hour or two earlier. By getting up early you also can get more time for play.

If you get up one hour earlier than other people, you get thirty hours a month more of life than they do; while they have twelve months in the year you get 365 extra hours, or thirty more days — that is, thirteen months to their twelve.

The old rhyme has a lot of truth in it when it says —

> " Early to bed and early to rise
> Makes a man healthy, and wealthy, and wise."

Smile

Want of laughter means want of health.   Laugh as much as you can: it does you good; so whenever you can get a good laugh, laugh on.   And make other people laugh, too, when possible, as it does them good.

If you are in pain or trouble make yourself smile at it; if you remember to do this, and force yourself, you will find it really does make a difference.

If you read about great scouts like Captain John Smith, the " Pathfinder," and others, you will generally find that they were pretty cheery old fellows.

The ordinary boy is apt to frown when working hard at physical exercises, but the boy scout is required to smile all the time; he drops a mark off his score whenever he frowns.

How to keep Healthy Practices

DEEP BREATHING. — Deep breathing is of the greatest importance for bringing fresh air into the lungs to be put into the blood, and for developing the size of the chest, but it should be done carefully, according to instructions, and not overdone; otherwise it is liable to strain the heart.   The Japs always carry on deep breathing exercise for a few minutes when they first get up in the morning, and always in the open air.   It is done by sucking air in through the nose until it swells out your ribs as far as possible, especially at the back; then, after a pause, you breathe out the air slowly and gradually through the mouth until you have not a scrap of air left in you, then after a pause draw in your breath again through the nose as before.

Singing, if carried out on a system like that of Mr. Tomlins, develops simultaneously proper breathing and development of heart, lungs, chest, and throat, together with dramatic feeling in rendering the song.

For instance, his method of " Hooligan Taming " is to get a large crowd of wild lads together, and to start shouting a chorus to piano accompaniment — say, " Hearts of Oak."   He shouts the suggestion of a story as they go along with it; how they are marching boldly to attack a fort which they mean to carry in style for the glory of themselves and their country, when suddenly they become aware that the enemy does not know of their approach, so they must creep and crawl, "in a whisper," as they stealthily get nearer to the fort. Closer and closer they come, with gradually increasing tone. Now charge on up the hill, through shot and shell, a scramble, a rush and a fight, and the fort is theirs. But there are wounded to be picked up tenderly, and the dead to be laid out reverently with quiet and measured song, solemn and soft.

And then they pick up their arms again, and with the prisoners and spoils of war they march gayly away in triumph, at full power of their lungs.

Old English Morris Dances, too, are excellent practice for winter evenings, with their quaint music and movements.

BOOKS TO READ

"What's the Harm in Smoking?" by B. McCall Barbour. 1d. (S. W. Partridge.)

"A Note for Parents," by J. H. Bradley. 4 d. To be had direct only from Secretary, Moral Education Committee, Thurloe Square, Kensington, W. Suggestions for teaching children about reproduction.

"In Confidence," by H. Bisseker. (Adlard & Son.) $3\frac{1}{2}$ d., or 14s. per 1000, also publications by "The Alliance of Honor," 118 City Road, London, who can give the best advice and help.

CAMP FIRE YARN. No. 19

PREVENTION OF DISEASE

Camp Doctoring — Microbes, and how to fight Them — Proper Food — Clothing — Use of Drill and Exercise

Camp Doctoring

SOME years ago, when I was in Kashmir, Northern India, some natives brought to me a young man on a stretcher, who, they said, had fallen off a high rock, and had broken his back and was dying. I soon found that he had only dislocated his shoulder and had got a few bruises, and seemed to think that he ought to die.

So I pulled off my shoe, sat down alongside him, facing his head, put my heel in his armpit, got hold of his arm, and pulled with all my force till the bone jumped into its socket. The pain made him faint, and his friends thought I really had killed him. But in a few minutes he recovered and found his arm was all right. Then they thought I must be a great doctor, so they sent round the country for all the sick to be brought in to be

PULLING IN A DISLOCATED SHOULDER

cured; and I had an awful time of it for the next two days. Cases of every kind of disease were carried in, and I had scarcely any drugs with which to treat them, but I did the best I could, and I really believe that some of the poor creatures got better from simply *believing* that I was doing them a lot of good.

But most of them were ill from being dirty and letting their wounds get poisoned with filth; and many were ill from bad drainage, and from drinking foul water, and so on.

This I explained to the head men of the villages, and I hope that I did some good for their future health.

At any rate, they were most grateful and gave me a lot of help ever afterwards in getting good bear-hunting and in getting food, etc.

If I had not known a little doctoring I could have done nothing for these poor creatures.

Microbes, and How to Fight Them

Disease is carried about in the air and in water by tiny invisible insects called " germs " or " microbes," and you are very apt to breathe them in through the mouth or to get them in your drink or food and to swallow them, and then they breed disease inside you. If your blood is in really good order, it generally does not matter, no harm results; but if your blood is out of order from weakness or constipation — that is, not going regularly to the " rear " — these microbes will very probably make you ill. A great point is, therefore, to abolish the microbes, if possible. They like living in dark, damp, and dirty places. And they come from bad drains, old dustbins, and rotting flesh, etc.; in fact, generally where there is a bad smell. Therefore, keep your room, or your camp, and your clothes, clean, dry, and as sunny as possible, and well aired; and keep away from places that smell badly. Before your meals you should always wash your hands and finger nails, for they are very apt to harbor microbes which have come from anything that you may have been handling in the day.

You frequently see notices in street cars and in public places requesting you not to spit. The reason for this is that many people spit who have diseased lungs, and from their spittle the microbes of their diseases get in the air, and are breathed by healthy people into their lungs, and they become also diseased. Often you may have a disease in you for some years without knowing it, and if you spit you are liable to communicate that disease to sound people; so you should not do it for their sake.

But you need not be afraid of diseases if you breathe through your nose and keep your blood in good order. It is always well on coming out of a crowded theatre, church, or hall, to cough and blow your nose, in order to get rid of microbes which you might have breathed in from other people in the crowd. One in every thirty people that you meet has got the disease of consumption in him — and it is very catching. It comes very much from living in houses where the windows are kept always shut up. The best chance of getting cured of it if you get the disease is to sleep always out of doors.

A scout has to sleep a great deal in the open air; therefore, when he is in a house he sleeps with the windows as wide open as possible, otherwise he feels stuffy; and also if he gets accustomed to sleeping in warm atmosphere he would catch cold when he goes into camp, and nothing could be more ridiculous or more like a tenderfoot than a scout with a cold in his head. When once he is accustomed to having his windows open he will never catch cold in a room.

Food

A good many illnesses come from overeating or eating the wrong kind of food.

A scout must know how to take care of himself, else he is of no use. He must keep himself light and active. Once he has got the right kind of muscles on he can remain in good condition without further special exercising of those muscles, provided that he eats the right kind of food.

Eustace Miles, the tennis and racquet champion, does not go into training before he plays his matches; he knows he has got his muscles rightly formed, and he simply lives on plain, light food always, and so is always in condition to play a hard game. He never eats meat.

In the siege of Mafeking, when we were put on short rations, those of the garrison who were accustomed to eat very little at their meals did not suffer like some people, who had been accustomed to eating heartily in peace time; these became weak and irritable. Our food there towards the end was limited to a chunk of pounded-up oats, about the size of a penny bun, which was our whole bread supply for the day, and about a pound of meat and two pints of " sowens," a kind of stuff like bill-posters' paste that had gone wrong.

English people as a rule eat more meat than is necessary; in fact, they could do without it altogether if they tried, and would be none the worse. It is an expensive luxury. The Japanese are as strong as we are, but they do not eat any meat, and only eat small meals of other things.

The cheapest and best foods are dried peas, flour, oatmeal, potatoes, hominy, and cheese. Other good foods are fruit, vegetables, fish, eggs, nuts, rice, and milk, and one can live on these perfectly well without meat; bananas are especially good food, as they are cheap, have no seeds nor pips to irritate your inside, their skin protects them from germs of disease, and their flesh is of a wholesome kind and satisfying. The natives of the West Coast of Africa eat very little else all their lives and they are fat and happy.

If you have lots of fresh air you do not need much food; if, on the other hand, you are sitting indoors all day, much food makes you fat and sleepy, so that in either case you are better for taking a little; still, growing boys should not starve themselves, but, at the same time, they need not be like the boy at the school feast, who, when asked, " Can't you eat any more? " replied, " Yes, I could *eat* more, but I've no room to *swallow* it."

A great cause of illness nowadays is the amount of medicine which people dose themselves with when there is no reason for taking any medicine at all. The best medicine is open air and exercise, and a big cup of water in the early morning if you are constipated, and a pint of hot water on going to bed.

Clothing

A scout's clothing should be of flannel or wool as much as possible, because it dries easily. Cotton next the skin is not good unless you change it directly it gets wet — it is so likely to give you a chill, and a scout is no use if he gets laid up.

One great point that a scout should take care about, to insure his endurance and being able to go on the march for a long time, is his boots.

A scout who gets sore feet with much walking becomes useless.

You should, therefore, take great care to have good, well-fitting, roomy boots, and fairly stout ones, and as like the natural shape of your bare feet as possible, with a straighter edge on the inside than bootmakers usually give to the fashionable boot. Scouts have no use for fashionable boots.

The feet should be kept as dry as possible; if they are allowed to get wet, the skin is softened, and very soon gets blistered and rubbed raw where there is a little pressure of the boot.

Of course they get wet from perspiration as well as from outside wet. Therefore, to dry this it is necessary to wear good woollen socks. I like shoes better than boots, because they let more air in for the feet.

If a man wears thin cotton or silk socks, you can tell at once that he is no walker. A man who goes out to a new country for the first time is called a " Tenderfoot," because he generally gets sore feet until by experience he learns how to keep his feet in good order. It is a good thing to soap or grease your feet and the inside of your socks before putting them on.

If your feet always perspire a good deal, it is a useful thing to powder them with powder made of boric acid, starch, and oxide of zinc in equal parts. This powder should be rubbed in between the toes, so as to prevent soft corns forming there. Your feet can be hardened to some extent by soaking them in alum and water, or salt and water.

Keep your boots soft with lots of grease, mutton fat, dubbin, or castor oil — especially when they have got wet from rain, etc. Wash the feet every day.

Practices

DRILL

In giving a simple system of drill for the Boy Scouts, I wish it to be understood that it is merely in order to enable scoutmasters to move their troops and patrols in good order for parade purposes, and not as an exercise for frequent practice with the boys when other occupations are possible.

When I see a troop drill well but fail to follow a trail or cook its own food, I recognize that 'he scoutmaster is no good as such. The indifferent or unimaginative officer always falls back upon drill as his one resource.

Scouts have to drill to enable them to be moved quickly from one point to another in good order. Drill also sets them up, and makes them smart and quick.

It strengthens the muscles which support the body, and by keeping the body upright the lungs and heart get plenty of room to work, and the inside organs are kept in the proper position for proper digestion of food and so on.

A slouching position, on the other hand, depresses all the other organs, and prevents them doing their work properly, so that a man in that position is generally weak and often ill.

Growing boys are very apt to slouch, and should therefore do all they can to get out of the habit by plenty of physical exercises and drill.

Stand upright when you are standing, and when you are sitting down sit upright, with your back well into the back part of the chair. Alertness of the body, whether you are moving, standing, or sitting, means alertness of mind, and it is a paying thing to have, because many an employer will select an alert-looking boy for work and pass over a sloucher. When you have to stoop over writing at a table, or even tying a boot-lace, do not round your back, but tuck in the small of your back, which thus helps to strengthen your body.

On the word " Alert " the scout stands upright with both feet together, hands hanging naturally at the sides, fingers straight, and looking straight to his front.

On the word " Easy " he carries the right foot away six inches to the right, and clasps his hands behind his back, and can turn his head about. At the word " Sit easy " he squats down on

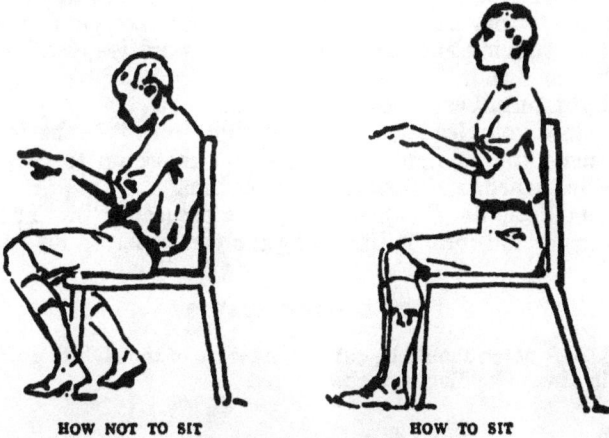

HOW NOT TO SIT   HOW TO SIT

the ground in any position he likes. " Sit easy " should usually be given whenever you don't want the boys to be at the " Alert," provided that the ground is dry.

On the command " Quick march," boys move off with the left foot leading at a smart pace, swinging the arms freely, as this gives good exercise to the body and muscles and inside organs.

WALKING FOR EXERCISE

1. — The right way.   2. — A common way.
3. — A usual and very bad way.   *Direction of Eyes.*

At the command " Double " boys run at a jog trot with short, easy steps, hands swinging loosely, not tucked up at the side.

On the command " Scout pace " the boys march at the quick march for twenty paces, then double twenty paces, and so on alternately running and walking, until the word is given " Quick march " or " Halt."

" Right turn," each boy turns to the right.

" Follow your leader," " Leader right turn " — the leading man turns to his right, the remainder move up to the place where he turned, and then follow after him.

" Front form line " (when " following the leader "). Those in rear run up and form in line alongside the leader on his left.

DRILL WITH STAVES

N.B. —A notch should be cut at the centre of the staff to guide the hand in always holding it in the centre.

Alert, or Order Staves.   At Ease.   Sit at Ease.

Trail Staves.   Slope Staves. Present Staves. Shoulder Staves. Support Staves.
*(Hand in line   (For parade   (For greater
with elbow, elbow   salute.)   ease when
touching side.)*   marching in
                                                               close order.)

SCOUTS' RALLY

Scouts do not parade, as a rule, like soldiers, in lines, etc., but they lie hidden away till their chief wants them, then they rush from all sides, each patrol following its leader, cheering and making their patrol calls, and form in a circle round the chief, at about twenty yards from him. All then sing " Be Prepared," and at once " Sit at ease," in silence, to hear his orders. If there are a large number of scouts, the patrols remain in single file; if a small number, they line up to form the circle. If the chief orders a " Figure of eight " or " Circle " or " Spiral," the scoutmaster in command orders " Alert," " Follow your leader." Then he, or any scoutmaster whom he orders, moves off through the circle, followed by the nearest patrol leader, whose patrol follow him in single file, and the next patrol follow them, and so on, till the whole parade is following in single file at a slow jog trot, staves at the trail. The scoutmaster leads at a slow pace, describing a big figure of eight or a big circle over the parade ground, or a spiral circle which gradually closes in round the chief, and then unwinds itself the reverse way. After this the scoutmaster orders " Reform rally," leads them round, and they reform on the original circle. When formed the scoutmaster orders "Sit at ease." The chief then addresses them, or gives the signal or order to disperse, when all turn about and run quietly away, each patrol sticking to its leader, every scout whistling a long drawn-out whistle till off the ground. They then squat down in their original hiding-place.

PARADE FIRE LIGHTING

The corporal of each patrol must carry his billy, and in it kindling paper, a box of matches, and a loop and hook.

The loop is for tying the heads of three staves together to form a tripod, and a cord with bent wire hook hangs from this, on which the billy can be suspended over the fire.

Nos. 3 and 4 carry brown paper to make an imitation camp fire.

On the command "Light fires, double," alternate patrols run out twenty paces (which they must count for themselves) to the front, and halt, in line with each other.

On the whistle or bugle sounding one note, the corporal in every patrol lays down his staff and gets the loop out of his billy. Scouts 3 and 4 lay their staves down on each side of the corporal's staff in this way : —

so that the heads just overlap.

The corporal then slips the loop over the three heads, and, assisted by the other two scouts, he twists his staff over two or three times to tighten up the loop, and then stands the three staves up as a tripod. All the tripods should be exactly in line with each other.

Directly the tripod is up, the patrol falls in at the " Alert " in a circle round the tripod, facing outwards.

On the bugle or whistle sounding two notes, all turn inwards.

The corporal takes paper and matches out of his billy, which he hangs on the hook; Nos. 3 and 4 make a little pile of the paper to represent the fire (or where real fires are to be made they produce the wood, every scout bringing a small bundle on the flap of his haversack).

Directly this is done all stand at " Alert " in a circle, the corporal to have his matches ready to light. The bugle or whistle then sounds three notes. *On the last note* the corporal strikes his match and lights the fire; and all the scouts sit down smartly.

The patrol leader's duty is to see that all this is done smartly and correctly. No talking.

On the command " Fires out," and one note of the bugle, all spring to their feet. The corporal takes off the billy. Nos. 3 and 4 throw down the tripod and pull it to bits, corporal puts the loop back into his billy. Other scouts stamp out the fire and collect all loose paper.

All stand to " Alert " in a circle, facing inwards.

On bugle sounding two notes, each patrol falls in line at the " Alert," ready to move off.

Both the " Rally " and "Lighting Fires " should be practised for inspection reviews, instead of marching past, which is only an imitation of a military parade.

NOTE. — These formations are inserted here only for use on special parades, such as guards of honor, reviews, and church parades, not for daily drill purposes. We want to avoid military drill in our training; the scouts are young backwoodsmen, not imitation soldiers.

Secure Staves.
(For close order or at funerals.)

Rest on Staves.
(At funerals.)

TROOP FORMATIONS

"Line" (means parties side by side). Each patrol has its scouts in line; corporal on right, bugler or drummer on left, leader three paces in front of centre.

Troop in Line

♀ = Scoutmasters.
✖ = Patrol Leader.
▨ = Bugler.
☐ = Scout.
◼ = Corporal.

"Column" means parties one behind the other.

Troop in Column of Patrols

Command "Patrols right wheel" (from line). "Halt" (when exactly behind each other at their proper distance (such as will enable them to wheel either to right or left into line). This is called "open column."

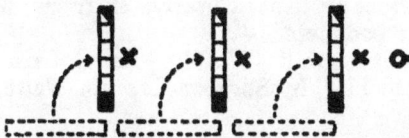

Close Column = Rear patrols moved up to leading patrols, for taking up less room on parade, or for being addressed by an inspecting officer.

Line can be formed from "open column," to the right or left by wheeling the patrols to that hand; or to the front by the leading patrol standing fast (or advancing), the second patrol inclining and moving up on its right, the third patrol moving up into line on its left, and so on with other patrols in rear, even numbers going up on the right, odd numbers on the left of the leading patrol. The patrols which move up always do so at the "double."

Line can be formed to the rear from "open column" by "about turn" for everybody (always turn about to the right hand), and then proceeding to form line as above.

NOTE. — A pamphlet on Fire, Ambulance Drills, etc., is being prepared at headquarters.

Games

"Ju-Jitsu" — contains numerous interesting games to teach grips and holds, and development of muscles.

"Doctoring" — each scout in turn acts as an explorer or missionary, with a few simple remedies. Three patients are brought to him in succession to be treated, each having a different disease or injury. He has to advise or show what treatment should be carried out.

All ordinary boys' games, where all are players and none lookers-on, are good for health and cheerfulness — "Leap-frog," "Rounders," "Squash football," "Tip-and-run."

BOOKS TO READ

"Japanese Physical Training," by Irving Hancock. 5s. nett. (Putnam.)

"How to be Well and Strong," by W. Edwards. 4d. (Melrose.)

"Walking," by C. Lang Neil. 1s. Useful hints on walking, training, mountain-climbing, food, etc.

"Modern Physical Culture," by C. Lang Neil. 1s. Gives summary of various systems: Curative exercises; hints on food, on organs of the body, etc.

"Health and Strength." Weekly Journal. 1d.

"How to Keep Fit," by Surgeon-Captain Waite. 3d. (Gale & Polden.)

CHAPTER VII

CHIVALRY OF THE KNIGHTS

HINTS TO INSTRUCTORS

One aim of the Boy Scouts scheme is to revive amongst us, if possible, some of the rules of the knights of old, which did so much for the moral tone of our race, just as the Bush do of the ancient Samurai Knights has done, and is still doing, for Japan. Unfortunately, chivalry with us has, to a large extent, been allowed to die out, whereas in Japan it is taught to the children, so that it becomes with them a practice of their life, and it is also taught to children in Germany and Switzerland with the best results. Our effort is not so much to discipline the boys as to teach them to discipline themselves.

It is impossible in so short a space as I have at my disposal to do more than touch upon subjects which the instructor may elaborate for himself. The different qualities which the Knight's Code demanded are grouped under the three heads:—

1. *— Chivalry to Others.*
2. *— Discipline of Self.*
3. *— Self-improvement.*

CAMP FIRE YARN. No. 20

CHIVALRY TO OTHERS

Knights Errant — Helpfulness to Others — Courtesy to Women

" IN days of old, when knights were bold," it must have been a fine sight to see one of these steel-clad horsemen come riding through the dark green woods in his shining armor, with shield and lance and waving plumes, bestriding his gallant war-horse, strong to bear its load, and full of fire to charge upon an enemy. And near him rode his squire, a young man, his assistant and companion, who would some day become a knight.

Behind him rode his group, or patrol of men-at-arms — stout, hearty warriors, ready to follow their knight to the gates of death if need be. They were the tough yeomen of the old days, who won so many of her fine fights for England through their pluck and loyal devotion to their knights.

In peace time, when there was no fighting to be done, the knight would daily ride about looking for a chance of doing a good turn to any needing help, especially a woman or child who might be in distress. When engaged in thus doing good turns, he was called a " Knight Errant." His patrol naturally acted in the same way as their leader, and a man-at-arms was always equally ready to help the distressed with his strong right arm. The knights of old were the patrol leaders of the nation, and the men-at-arms were the scouts.

You patrol leaders and scouts are therefore very like the knights and their retainers, especially if you keep your honor ever before you in the first place, and do your best to help other people who are in trouble or who need assistance. Your motto is, " Be Prepared " to do this, and the motto of the knights was a similar one, "Be always Ready."

Chivalry — that is, the order of the knights — was started in England some 1500 years ago by King Arthur.

On the death of his father, King Uther Pendragon, he was living with his uncle, and nobody knew who was to be King. He did not himself know that he was son of the late King.

Then a great stone was found in the churchyard, into which a sword was sticking, and on the stone was written:

" Whosoever pulleth this sword out of this stone is the rightwise King born of all England."

All the chief lords attempted to pull the sword out, but none could move it.

That day there was a tournament at which Arthur's cousin was to fight, but when he got to the ground he found he had left his sword at home, and he sent Arthur to fetch it. Arthur could not find it, but remembering the sword in the churchyard he went there and pulled at it, and it came out of the stone at once; and he took it to his cousin. After the sports he put it back again into the stone; and they all tried to pull it out, but could not move it, but when he tried he drew it out quite easily. So he was proclaimed King.

He afterwards got together a number of knights, and used to sit with them at a great round table, and so they were called the "Knights of the Round Table." The table at which the knights are said to have sat is still to be seen at Winchester.

They had as their patron saint St. George, because he was the only one of all the saints who was a horseman. He is the special saint of England. The battle-cry of the knights used to be, "For Saint George and Merrie England!"

The Knights' Code

The laws of the knights were these: —

"*Be Always Ready*, with your armor on, except when you are taking your rest at night.

"Defend the poor, and help them that cannot defend themselves.

"Do nothing to hurt or offend any one else.

"Be prepared to fight in the defence of England.

"At whatever you are working try and win honor and a name for honesty.

"Never break your promise.

"Maintain the honor of your country with your life.

"Rather die honest than live shamelessly.

"Chivalry requireth that youth should be trained to perform the most laborious and humble offices with *cheerfulness* and grace; and to do good unto others."

These are the first rules with which the old knights started, and from which the scout laws of to-day come.

A knight (or scout) is at all times a gentleman. So many people seem to think that a gentleman must have lots of money. That does not make a gentleman. A gentleman is any one who carries out the rules of chivalry of the knights.

A London policeman, for instance, is a gentleman, because he is well disciplined, loyal, polite, brave, good-tempered, and helpful to women and children.

Unselfishness

Captain John Smith, the old English adventurer of three hundred years ago, was a dangerous man to oppose, as he had fought in every part of the world and had been wounded over and over again; but he also had a good, kind heart within him. He was as good a type of scout as you could find anywhere. One of his favorite expressions was, "We were born, not for ourselves, but to do good to others," and he carried this out very much in his life, for he was the most unselfish of men.

Self-sacrifice

King Richard I, who was one of the first of the Scouts of the Empire, left his kingdom, his family, and everything to go and fight against the enemies of the Christian religion, and very nearly lost his kingdom by doing so, for he was absent for some years, and in the meantime his brother tried to usurp his place. On his way home from the wars in Palestine he was caught by the Emperor of Austria, and was put by him in prison, where he lingered for twelve months. He was discovered by his minstrel, Blondel, who, knowing that he must have been captured somewhere, went about Europe singing his favorite songs outside the prisons until he was answered from inside; and so he found him and procured his release. (See "The Talisman," by Sir Walter Scott.)

But self-sacrifice is also to be found among us to-day. Last year a lad of eighteen named Currie saw a little girl playing on the railway line at Clydebank in front of an approaching train. He tried to rescue her, but he was lame from an injury he had got at football, and it delayed him in getting her clear. The train knocked both of them over, and both were killed.

But Currie's gallant attempt is an example of chivalry for scouts to follow. It was sacrifice of himself in the attempt to save a child. Over one hundred cases of gallantry in saving life by scouts have occurred. And only a short time ago another brave scout, Donald Smith, 4th Ealing Troop, dived into a canal to rescue a drowning boy without stopping to think of the risk to himself. He was drowned, but by his heroic act he gave a splendid example to his comrades of pluck and self-sacrifice.

Kindness

" Kindness and gentleness are great virtues," says an old Spanish proverb; and another says, " Oblige without regarding whom you oblige," which means be kind to any one, great or small, rich or poor.

The great point about a knight was that he was always doing kindnesses or good turns to people. His idea was that every one must die, but you should make up your mind that before your time comes you will do something good. Therefore do it at once, for you never know when you may be taken away.

So, with the scouts, it has been made one of our laws that we do a good turn to somebody every day. It does not matter how small that good turn may be, if it were only to help an old woman lift her bundle, or to guide a child across a crowded street, or to put a cent in the poor-box. Something good ought to be done each day of your life, and you should begin to-day to carry out this rule, and never forget it during the remaining days of your life. Remember the knot in your necktie and on your scout's badge — they are reminders to you to do a good turn. And do your good turn not only to your friends, but also to strangers and even to your enemies.

When the Russians were besieged in Port Arthur by the Japanese in 1905, the Japs got close up to their forts by digging long, deep trenches, into which the Russians were not able to shoot. On one occasion they were so close that a Russian soldier was able to throw a letter into the Japanese trench. In this letter he said that he wanted to send a message to his mother in Russia, as she was very anxious about him; but as Port Arthur was now cut off from all communication he begged that the Japs would send the message for him; and he inclosed a note for his mother and a gold coin to pay the cost.

The Japanese soldier who found the note, instead of tearing up the letter and keeping the money, did what every scout would do, took it to his officer, and the officer telegraphed the Russian's message to his mother, and threw a note back into the enemy's fort to tell him that he had done so.

This, with other instances of chivalry on both sides, is described in Mr. Richmond Smith's book, " The Siege and Fall of Port Arthur."

Generosity

Some people are fond of hoarding up their money and never spending it. It is well to be thrifty, but it is also well to give away money where it is needed; in fact, that is part of the object of saving up your money. In being charitable, be careful that you do not fall into the mistake of false charity. That is to say, it is very easy and comforting to you to give five or ten cents to a poor beggar in the street, but you ought not to do it. That poor beggar is ninety-nine times out of a hundred a fraud, and by giving your money, you are encouraging him and others to go on with that trade. There may be, probably are, hundreds of really poor and miserable people hiding away, whom you never see and to whom that money would be a godsend. Any charitable organization knows where they are, and who they are, and if you give your money to them they will put it into the right hands for you.

You need not be rich in order to be charitable. Many of the knights were poor men. At one time some of them wore as their crest two knights riding on one horse, which meant they were too poor to afford a horse apiece.

Tips

Then " tips " are a very bad thing.

Wherever you go, people want to be " tipped " for doing the slightest thing which they ought to do out of common good feeling. A scout will never accept a " tip," even if it is offered him, unless it is pay for work done. It is often difficult to refuse, but for a scout it is easy. He has only to say, " Thank you very much, but I am a scout, and our rules don't allow us to accept anything for doing a good turn."

" Tips " put you on a wrong footing with every one.

You cannot work in a friendly way with a man if you are thinking how much " tip " you are going to get out of him, or he is thinking how much he'll have to " tip " you. And all scouts' work for another ought to be done in a friendly way.

I have had a number of letters of admiration for the scouts in many parts of the country on account of their doing good acts and then declining to be tipped for it. I am very glad to hear it, scouts.

Of course, proper pay that is earned by your work is another thing, and you will be right to accept it.

"Hump your own Pack"

When you are on the trail in the woods, you will find that it is the way with backwoodsmen that each man takes his share equally in the rough and dirty work, and in carrying the loads. A man who shirked his share would be so despised by the rest that he could not remain with them. It ought to be the same everywhere, whether you are in the woods or not; be a worker and not a shirker. Carry your own load, and, if possible, a part of the other boy's as well. A boy scout should, like Kim, be a "friend of all the world."

Politeness

An instance of politeness in war occurred at the Battle of Fontenoy, when the British were fighting against the French.

The Coldstream Guards, coming up over a hill, suddenly found themselves close up to the French Guards. Both parties were surprised, and neither fired a shot for a minute or two.

In those days when gallant men quarrelled they used to settle their differences by fighting duels with pistols. At a duel both combatants were supposed to fire at the same moment when the word was given, but it often happened that one man, in order to show how brave he was, would tell his adversary to fire first. And so in this case. When both parties were about to fire, the officer commanding the British Guards, to show his politeness and fearlessness, bowed to the French commander, and said, "You fire first, sir."

When the French Guards levelled their rifles to fire, one of the soldiers of the Coldstreams exclaimed, "For what we are going to receive may the Lord make us truly thankful." In the volley that followed, a great number of our men fell, but the survivors returned an equally deadly volley, and immediately charged in with the bayonet, and drove the French off the field.

One of the stories that the knights used to tell as an example of politeness was that Julius Cæsar, when he was entertained at supper by a poor peasant, was so polite that when the man gave him a dish of pickles to eat, thinking that they were the sort of vegetables that a high-born officer would like, Cæsar ate the whole dish, and pretended to like them, although they burnt his mouth and disagreed with him considerably.

In Spain you ask a man the way — he does not merely point it out, but takes off his hat, bows, and says that it will be a great pleasure to him to show it, and walks with you till he has set you properly upon it. He will take no reward.

A Frenchman will take off his hat when he addresses a stranger, as you may often see him do, wherever he may be, even when he asks a policeman the way.

The Dutch fishermen, big and brawny as they are, take up the whole street when walking down it; but when a stranger comes along they stand to one side, and smilingly take off their caps as he passes.

Courtesy to Women

The knights of old were particularly attentive in respect and courtesy to women.

Sir Nigel Loring in " The White Company " is a type of a chivalrous knight of the old times. Although very small, and half blind by reason of some lime which an enemy had thrown in his eyes early in his career, he was an exceedingly brave man, and at the same time very humble, and very helpful to others.

But above all things he reverenced women. He had a big, plain lady as his wife, but he always upheld her beauty and virtue, and was ready to fight anybody who doubted him.

Then with poor women, old or young, he was always courteous and helpful. And that is how a scout should act.

King Arthur, who made the rules of chivalry, was himself chivalrous to women of whatever class.

One day a girl rushed into his hall crying for help. Her hair was streaming and smeared with mud, her arms were torn with brambles, and she was dressed in rags. She had been ill-treated by a band of robbers who roved the country, doing all the harm they could. When he heard her tale King Arthur sprang on to his horse and rode off himself to the robbers' cave, and, even at the risk of his own life, he fought and defeated them, so that they could no more trouble his people.

When walking with a lady or a child a scout should always have her on his left side, so that his right is free to protect her.

This rule is altered when walking in the streets: then a man will walk on the side of her nearest to the traffic, to protect her against accident or mud-splashes, etc.

In meeting a woman or a child a man should, as a matter of course, always make way for her, even if he has to step off the pavement into the mud.

So also in riding in a crowded street car or railway train, no man worthy of the name will allow a woman or a child to stand up if he has a seat. He will at once give it up to the woman and stand himself. As a scout you should set an example in this by being the first man in the carriage to do it. And in doing so, do it cheerfully, with a smile, so that she may not think you are annoyed at having to do it.

When in the street always be on the lookout to help women and children. A good opportunity is when they want to cross a street, or to find the way, or to call a carriage. If you see them, go and help them at once — and don't accept any reward.

The other day I saw a boy help a lady out of a carriage, and as he shut the door after her she turned to give him some money, but he touched his cap and smilingly said, " No, thank you, Marm; it's my duty," and walked off. So I shook hands with him, for I felt that although he had not been taught, he was a scout by nature.

This is the kind of courtesy one would like to see more amongst boys of to-day. Only the other day in London a girl who had been robbed ran after a thief and pursued him, till he dashed down into a narrow alley, where she could not follow; but she waited for him — so did the crowd. And when he came out again, she collared him and struggled to prevent him escaping; but not one of the crowd would help her, although there were men and boys present there. They must have been a poor lot not to help a girl !

Of course, in accidents men and boys will always see that the women and children are safely got out of danger before they think of going themselves. In two wrecks which occurred in 1907 on the south coast of England, viz. the *Jebba* and the *Suevic*, it was very noticeable how carefully arrangements were made for saving the women and children and old people, before any idea was given as to how the men were to be rescued. You should carry your courtesy on with ladies at all times. If you are sitting down and a lady comes into the room, stand up, and see if you can help her in any way before you sit down.

Don't go about with a girl whom you would not like your mother or sister to see you with.

Don't make love to any girl unless you mean to marry her.

Don't marry a girl unless you are in a position to support her and to support some children.

Practices

Other ways of doing good turns are such small things as these: sprinkle sand on a frozen road where horses are likely to slip; remove orange or banana skins from the pavement, as they are apt to throw people down; don't leave gates open, and don't injure fences or walk over crops in the country; help old people in drawing water or carrying fuel, etc., to their homes; help to keep the streets clean by removing scraps of paper; provide meals for poor children.

HINTS TO INSTRUCTORS

HOW TO PRACTISE CHIVALRY

Make each scout tie a knot in his necktie every morning as a reminder to carry out his idea of doing a good turn every day, till it becomes a habit with him.

Make a scout bring in a boy, who is a total stranger, as his guest for the evening to play in club games, and hear camp yarns, etc.

Games

" KNIGHT ERRANTRY." — Scouts go out singly, or in pairs, or as a patrol. If in a town, to find women or children in need of help, and to return and report, on their honor, what they have done. If in the country, call at any farms or cottages and ask to do odd jobs — for nothing. The same can be made into a race called a " Good Turn " race.

Play

" King Arthur and the Round Table."
Also other stories of chivalry, as in " Stories of King Arthur."

BOOKS TO READ

" Ivanhoe," by Sir Walter Scott. 1s.
" Stories of King Arthur," by Cutler. 1s. 6d. nett.
" The White Company," by Sir Conan Doyle. 6d.
" The Broad Stone of Honor," by Kenelm Digby.
" Puck of Pook's Hill," by Rudyard Kipling. 6s.

CAMP FIRE YARN.   No. 21

SELF-DISCIPLINE

Honor — Obedience — Courage — Cheeriness.

TO INSTRUCTORS

The self-disciplined man is described by Browning as: —

" One who never turned his back, but marched breast forward;
    Never doubted clouds would break;
    Never dreamed, though right were worsted, wrong would triumph;
    Held, we fall to rise, are baffled to fight better,
        Sleep — to wake."

Lycurgus said that the wealth of a state lay not so much in money as in men who were sound in body and mind, with a body fit for toil and endurance, and with a mind well disciplined, and seeing things in their proper proportions.

Honor

The true knight placed his honor before all things; it was sacred. A man who is honorable is always to be trusted; he will never do a dishonorable action, such as telling an untruth or deceiving his superiors or employers, and always commands the respect of his fellow-men. His honor guides him in everything that he does. A captain sticks to the ship till the last, in every wreck that was ever heard of. Why? She is only a lump of iron and wood; his life is as valuable as that of any of the women and children on board, but he makes everybody get away safely before he attempts to save his more valuable life. Why? Because the ship is his ship, and he has been taught that it is his duty to stick to it, and he considers it would be dishonorable in him to do otherwise; so he puts honor before safety. So also a scout should value his honor most of anything.

Fair Play

Britons, above all other people, insist on fair play.
If you see a big bully going for a small or weak boy, you stop him because it is not " fair play."
And if a man, in fighting another, knocks him down, he must

not hit or kick him while he is down; everybody would think him a brute if he did. Yet there is no law about it; you could not get him imprisoned for it. The truth is that "fair play" is an old idea of chivalry that has come down to us from the knights of old, and we must always keep up that idea.

Other nations are not all so good.

Often we hear of wounded men being again shot, and killed in battle when they are lying helpless on the ground. In the South African War, when Major MacLaren, lately our Manager in the Boy Scouts, was lying helpless, with his thigh broken by a bullet and his horse shot on top of him, a Boer came up, and finding him alive, fired two more shots into him. Luckily he recovered, and is alive to-day. But that Boer had no chivalry in him.

Honesty

Honesty is a form of honor. An honorable man can be trusted with any amount of money or other valuables with the certainty that he will not steal it.

Cheating at any time is a sneaking, underhand thing to do.

When you feel inclined to cheat in order to win a game, or feel very distressed when a game in which you are playing is going against you, just say to yourself: " After all, it is only a game. It won't kill me if I do lose. One can't win always, though I will stick to it in case of a chance coming."

If you keep your head in this way, you will very often find that you win after all from not being over-anxious or despairing.

And don't forget, whenever you *do* lose a game, if you are a true scout, you will at once cheer the winning team or shake hands with and congratulate the fellow who has beaten you.

This rule will be carried out in *all* games and competitions among Boy Scouts.

Loyalty

Loyalty was, above all, one of the distinguishing points about the knights. They were always devotedly loyal to their King and to their country, and were always ready and eager to die in their defence. In the same way a follower of the knights should be loyal, not only to the King, but also to every one who is above him, whether his officers or employers, and he should stick to them through thick and thin as part of his duty. If he does not intend to be loyal, he will, if he has any honor in him, resign his place.

He should also be equally loyal to his own friends and should support them in evil times as well as in good times.

Loyalty to duty was shown by the Roman soldier of old who stuck to his post when the city of Pompeii was overwhelmed with ashes and lava from the volcano Vesuvius. His remains are still there, with his hand covering his mouth and nose to prevent the suffocation which in the end overcame him.

His example was followed at some manœuvres not long ago by a cadet of Reigate Grammar School, who, when posted as sentry, was accidentally left on his post when the field day was over. But though night came on, and it was very cold — in November — the lad stuck to his post till he was found in the middle of the night, half perished with cold, but alive and alert.

Obedience and Discipline

Discipline and obedience are as important as bravery for scouts and for soldiers.

The *Birkenhead* was a transport-ship carrying troops. She had on board 630 soldiers with their families, and 130 seamen. Near the Cape of Good Hope one night she ran on to some rocks, and began to break up. The soldiers were at once paraded on deck. Some were told off to get out the boats, and to put the women and children into them, and others were told off to get the horses up out of the hold, and to lower them overboard into the sea, in order that they might have a chance of swimming ashore. When this had all been done, it was found that there were not enough boats to take the men, and so the men were ordered to remain in their ranks. Then the ship broke in half and began to go down. The captain shouted to the men to jump over and save themselves, but the colonel, Colonel Seaton, said, "No, keep your ranks." For he saw that if they swam to the boats, and tried to get in, they would probably sink them, too. So the men kept their ranks, and as the ship rolled over and sank, they gave a cheer and went down with her. Out of the whole 760 on board, only 192 were saved, but even those would probably have been lost had it not been for the discipline and self-sacrifice of the others.

Recently a British training ship, the *Fort Jackson*, full of boy sailors, was run into by a steamer, but just as on the *Birkenhead*, there was no panic or crying out. The boys fell in quickly on parade, put on their life-belts, and faced the danger calmly and well. And not a life was lost.

Gibraltar is a great big fortified rock which belongs to Britain, down on the south coast of Spain. One hundred and twenty years ago it was besieged by the Spanish and French armies together.

The Spanish army attacked Gibraltar on the land side, while the French attacked it by sea; but though they fought hard and with greatest endurance for over three years, the British troops defending the place were a match for them, and held out successfully until they were relieved by the fleet from home.

General Elliot, who had been a cavalry officer in the 15th Hussars, commanded the troops at Gibraltar, and it was largely owing to his strict discipline that the garrison succeeded in holding out. Every man had learned to obey orders without any hesitation or question.

One day a man disobeyed an order, so General Elliot had him up before him and explained that for a man to be insubordinate at such a time showed that he could not be in his right senses; he must be mad. So he ordered that his head should be shaved, and that he should be blistered, bled, and put into a strait-waistcoat, and should be put in the cells, with bread and water, as a lunatic, and should also be prayed for in church !

Humility

Humility, or being humble, was one of the things which was practised by the knights; that is to say, that, although they were generally superior to other people in fighting or campaigning, they never allowed themselves to boast about it. So don't boast.

And don't imagine that you have any rights in this world except those that you earn for yourself. You've got the right to be believed if you earn it by always telling the truth, and you've got the right to go to prison if you earn it by thieving; but there are lots of men who go about talking about their rights who have never done anything to earn any rights. Do your duty first, and you will get your rights afterwards.

Courage

Very few men are born brave, but any man can make himself brave if he tries — and especially if he begins trying when he is a boy.

The brave man dashes into danger without any hesitation, when a less brave man is inclined to hang back. It is very like bathing. A lot of boys will come to a river to bathe, and will cower shivering on the bank, wondering how deep the water is, and whether it is very cold — but the brave one will run through them and take his header into the water, and will be swimming about happily a few seconds later.

The thing is, when there is danger before you, don't stop and look at it — the more you look at it the less you will like it — but take the plunge, go boldly in at it, and it won't be half so bad as it looked, when you are once in it.

In the late war between Japan and Russia some Japanese pioneers had been ordered to blow up the gate of a Russian fort, so that the attackers could get in. After nearly all of them had been shot down, a few of them managed to get to the gate with their charges of powder. These had to be "tamped" or jammed tight against the door somehow, and then fired. The Japs "tamped" them by pushing them against the door with their chests; they then lit their matches, fired the charge, and blew up the gates, but blew up themselves in doing so. But their plucky self-sacrifice enabled their comrades to get in and win the place for the Emperor.

Fortitude

The knights were men who never said "Die" till they were dead; they were always ready to stick it out till the last extremity, but it is a very common fault with men to give in to trouble or fear long before there is any necessity. They often give up working because they don't get success all at once, and probably if they stuck to it a little longer, success would come. A man must expect hard work and want of success at first.

In Japan, whenever a child is born, the parents hang up outside the house either a doll or a fish, according as the child is a girl or boy. It is a sign to the neighbors: the doll means it is a girl, who will some day have children to nurse; the fish means it is a boy, who, as he grows into manhood, will, like a fish, have to make his way against a stream of difficulties and dangers. A man who cannot face hard work or trouble is not worth calling a man.

Some of you have heard the story of the two frogs. If you have not, here it is: —

Two frogs were out for a walk one day, and they came to a big bowl of cream. In looking into it they both fell in.

One said: "This is a new kind of water to me. How can a

fellow swim in stuff like this? It is no use trying." So he sank to the bottom and was drowned through having no pluck.

But the other was a more manly frog, and he struggled to swim, using his arms and legs as hard as he could to keep himself afloat; and whenever he felt he was sinking he struggled harder than ever, and never gave up hope.

At last, just as he was getting so tired that he thought he *must* give it up, a curious thing happened. By his hard work with his

PERSEVERANCE : FROGS IN THE CREAM

arms and legs he had churned up the cream so much that he suddenly found himself standing all safe on a pat of butter!

So when things look bad just smile and sing to yourself, as the thrush sings: "Stick to it, stick to it, stick to it," and you will come through all right.

A very great step to success is to be able to stand disappointments.

Good Temper and Cheeriness

The knights laid great stress on being never out of temper. They thought it bad form to lose their temper and to show anger. Captain John Smith, of whom I spoke just now, was himself a type of a cheerful man. In fact, towards the end of his life two boys (and he was very fond of boys) to whom he told his adventures, wrote them down in a book, but they said that they found great difficulty in hearing all that he said, because he roared with laughter so over his own descriptions of his troubles. But it is very certain that had he not been a cheery man, he never could have got through half the dangers with which he was faced at different times in his career.

Over and over again he was made prisoner by his enemies — sometimes savage enemies — but he managed always to captivate them with his pleasant manner, and become friends with them, so that often they let him go, or did not trouble to catch him when he made his escape.

If you do your work cheerfully, your work becomes much more of a pleasure to you, and also if you are cheerful it makes other people cheerful as well, which is part of your duty as a scout. Mr. J. M. Barrie writes: " Those who bring sunshine to the lives of others cannot keep happiness from themselves," which means, if you make other people happy, you make yourself happy.

If you are in the habit of taking things cheerfully, you will very seldom find yourself in serious trouble, because if a difficulty or annoyance or danger seems very great, you will, if you are wise, force yourself to laugh at it, although I will allow it is very difficult to do so at first. Still, the moment you do laugh, most of the difficulty seems to disappear at once, and you can tackle it quite easily.

Good temper can be attained by a boy who wants to have it, and it will help him in every game under the sun, and more especially in difficulty and danger, and will often keep him in a situation where a short-tempered fellow gets turned out, or leaves in a huff.

Bad language and swearing are generally used, like smoking, by boys who want to try and show off how manly they are, but it only makes them look foolish. Generally, a man who swears is a man easily upset, who loses his head in a difficult situation, and he is not, therefore, to be depended upon. You should be quite undisturbed under the greatest difficulties; and so, when you find yourself particularly anxious or excited, or angry, don't swear; force yourself to smile, and it will set you right in a moment.

Captain John Smith, who neither smoked nor swore, had a way of dealing with swearers, which is also adopted by our scouts. He says in his diary that when his men were cutting down trees, the axes blistered their tender fingers, so that at about every third blow a loud oath would drown the echo of the axe. To remedy this, he devised a plan of having every man's oath noted down, and at night, for every oath, he had a can of water poured down the swearer's sleeve, "with which an offender was so washed that a man would scarce hear an oath for a week."

BOOKS TO READ

"Courage," by Charles Wagner. 1s. nett. (T. Fisher Unwin, London.)

"The Book of Golden Deeds," by Charlotte M. Yonge. 2s. 6d. nett. (Macmillan.)

"Parents and Children," by Charlotte Mason. 3s. 6d. nett. (Kegan Paul.)

"Duty," by Samuel Smiles. 2s. nett. (Murray.)

"The Soul of a People," by H. F. Hall. 7s. 6d. nett. (Macmillan.)

Practice in Self-discipline

Practise unselfishness by a picnic to which all contribute according to their means. No remarks to be allowed on the amounts given.

Games

Any games such as football, basketball, etc., where rules are strictly enforced, are good for teaching discipline and unselfishness.

Ju-Jitsu has many excellent points, too, in that direction.

"Longbowmanship," as practised by the archers of the Middle Ages. Scouts to make their own bows and arrows if possible. Read Aylward's doings in "The White Company."

"Quarter Staff Play" with scouts' staves, as played by the yeomen and apprentices in old days. See Scout Chart, No. 12. 2d., post free, 3d., from *The Scout* Office.

CAMP FIRE YARN. No. 22

SELF-IMPROVEMENT

Religion — Thrift — How to get On.

To Instructors

This camp fire yarn opens to instructors a wide field for the most important work of all in the scheme of Boy Scouts, and gives you an opportunity for doing really valuable work for the nation.

The prevailing lack of religion should be remedied by a practical working religion rather than a too spiritual one at first.

SUNDAY SCOUTING. — *In Christian countries Boy Scouts should, without fail, attend church, or a church parade of their own, on Sundays. The afternoon walk might then be devoted to quiet scouting practices, such as " Nature Study," by exploring for plants or insects, observing animals or birds; also "Knight Errantry," doing good turns by collecting flowers and taking them to patients in hospitals, reading newspapers to the patients, and so on. Sunday is a day of rest ; loafing is not rest. Change of occupation from the workshop to the fields is rest ; but the Sabbath is too often a day of loafing, and, morally, made the worst day in the whole week for our boys and girls. Combine with the instruction of your church the study of God in nature, and the practice of good turns on God's day.*

SELF-IMPROVEMENT. — *A great amount of poverty and unemployedness results from boys being allowed to run riot outside the school walls as loafers, or from being used early in life as small wage-earners, such as errand boys, etc., and then finding themselves at the commencement of manhood without any knowledge of a trade or business to go on with, and unable to turn their hand to any work out of their own immediate line. They are helpless and unemployable. It is here that as instructor you can do invaluable work for the boy, by getting each in turn to talk privately over his future, and to map out a line for himself, and to start preparing himself for it. Encourage him to believe in himself and to take up " hobbies " or handicrafts.*

The suggestions offered here are, owing to the want of space, very limited in number, but your own experience or imagination will probably provide many more.

Duty to God

An old English chieftain, some thirteen hundred years ago said: —

" Our life has always seemed to me like the flight of a sparrow through the great hall, when one is sitting at meals with the log-fire blazing on the hearth, while all is storm and darkness outside. He comes in, no one knows from where, and hovers for a short time in the warmth and light, and then flies forth again into the darkness. And so it is with the life of a man; he comes no one knows from where; he is here in the world for a short time, till he flies forth again, no one knows whither. But now you show us that if we do our duty during our life we shall not fly out into darkness again, when life is ended, since Christ has opened a door for us to enter a brighter room, a heaven where we can go and dwell in peace forever."

This old chief was speaking for all the chiefs of northern England when King Edwin had introduced to them a knowledge of the Christian religion; and they adopted it then and there as one more comforting to them than their old Pagan worship of heathen gods; and ever since those days the Christian religion has been the one to rule our country.

Religion seems a very simple thing:—

        1st.   To trust in God.

        2d.   To do good to other people..

The old knights, who were the scouts of the nation, were very religious. They were always careful to attend church or chapel, especially before going into battle or undertaking any serious difficulty. They considered it was the right thing always to be prepared for death. In the great church of Malta you can see to-day where the old knights used to pray, and they all stood up and drew their swords during the reading of the Creed, as a sign that they were prepared to defend the gospel with their swords and lives. Besides worshipping God in church, the knights always recognized His work in the things which He made, such as animals, plants, and scenery. And so it is with peace scouts to-day, that wherever they go they love the woodlands, the mountains, and the prairies, and they like to watch and know about the animals that inhabit them, and the wonders of the flowers and plants. No man is much good unless he believes in God and obeys His laws. So every scout should have a religion.

There are many kinds of religion, such as Roman Catholics, Protestants, Jews, Mohammedans, and so on, but the main point about them is that they all worship God, although in different ways. They are like an army which serves one king, though it is divided into different branches, such as cavalry, artillery, and infantry, and these wear different uniforms. So, when you meet a boy of a different religion to your own, you should not be hostile to him, but recognize that he is like a soldier in your own army, though in a different uniform, and still serving the same king as you.

In doing your duty to God always be grateful to Him. Whenever you enjoy a pleasure or a good game, or succeed in doing a good thing, thank Him for it, if only with a word or two, just as you say grace after a meal. And it is a good thing to bless other people. For instance, if you see a train starting off, just pray for God's blessing on all that are in the train.

In doing your duty towards man be helpful and generous, and also always be grateful for any kindness done to you, and be careful to show that you are grateful.

Remember that a present given to you is not yours until you have thanked for it. While you are the sparrow flying through the hall, that is to say, while you are living your life on this earth, try and do something good which may remain after you. One writer says: —

" I often think that when the sun goes down the world is hidden by a big blanket from the light of heaven, but the stars are little holes pierced in that blanket by those who have done good deeds in this world. The stars are not all the same size; some are big, some little, and some men have done great deeds and others have done small deeds, but they have made their hole in the blanket by doing good before they went to heaven."

Try and make your hole in the blanket by good work while you are on the earth.

It is something to *be* good, but it is far better to *do* good.

Duty before All

You have all heard of " Lynch-Law," by which is meant stern justice by hanging an evil-doer without the regular form of law.

The name came from Galway, in Ireland, where a memorial still commemorates the act of a chief magistrate of that city named Lynch, who in the year 1493 had his own son Walter Lynch executed for killing a young Spaniard.

The murderer had been properly tried and convicted. His mother begged the citizens to rescue her son when he was brought out from the jail to suffer punishment, but the father, foreseeing this, had the sentence carried out in the prison, and young Lynch was hanged from the prison window.

The elder Lynch's sense of duty must have been very strong indeed to enable him to make his feelings as a father give way to his conscience as a magistrate.

General Gordon sacrificed his life to his sense of duty. When he was besieged at Khartum, he could have got away himself had he liked, but he considered it his duty to remain with the Egyptians whom he had brought there, although he had no admiration for them. So he stuck to them, and when at last the place was captured by the enemy he was killed.

Sobriety

Remember that drink never yet cured a single trouble; it only makes trouble grow worse and worse the more you go on with it. It makes a man forget for a few hours what exactly his trouble is, but it also makes him forget everything else. If he has wife and children, it makes him forget that his duty is to work and help them out of their difficulties, instead of making himself all the more unfit to work.

A man who is drunken is generally a coward — and one used to see it very much among soldiers. Nowadays they are a better class and do not drink.

Some men drink because they like the feeling of getting half stupid, but they are very foolish, because once they take to drink no employer will trust them, and they soon lose their positions, and easily get ill, and finally come to a miserable end. There is nothing manly about getting drunk. Once a man gives way to drink, it ruins his health, his career, and his happiness, as well as that of his family. There is only one cure for this disease, and that is — never to get it.

Thrift

It is a peculiar thing that out of you boys who now read these words, some of you are certain to become rich men, and some of you may die in poverty and misery. And it just depends on your own selves which you are going to do.

And you can very soon tell which your future is going to be.

The man who begins making money as a boy will go on making it as a man. You may find it difficult to do at first, but it will come easier later on; but if you begin and if you go on, remember, you are pretty certain to succeed in the end — especially if you get your money by hard work.

If you try to make it only by easy means — that is by betting, say, on a football match or a horse-race — you are bound to lose after a time. Nobody who makes bets ever wins in the end; it is the bookmaker, the man who receives the bets, that scores over it. Yet there are thousands of men who go on betting because they won once or hope to win some day.

Any number of poor boys have become rich men — but in nearly every case it was because they meant to do so from the first; they worked for it, and put every cent they could make into the bank to begin with.

So each one of you has the chance, if you like to take it. The great owner of millions of dollars, J. Astor, began his career as a poor boy-pedler with seven German flutes as his stock-in-trade. He sold them for more than he gave, and went on increasing his business.

The knights of old were ordered by their rules to be thrifty; that is, to save money as much as possible, not to expend large sums on their own enjoyment, but to save it in order that they might keep themselves, and not be a burden to others, and also in order that they might have it to give away to charity; and if they had no money of their own. They were not allowed to beg for it, they must work and make it in one way or another. Thus money-making goes with manliness, hard work, and sobriety.

Boys are not too young to work for money.

Mr. Thomas Holmes, the policecourt missionary, tells us how hundreds of poor boys in London are working pluckily and well at making their living, even while doing their school work. They get up early, at half-past four in the morning, and go round with milk or bakers' barrows till about eight, and after that off to school; back in the afternoon to the shop to clean the pails and cans. They save up their money every day; those who have mothers hand it over to them; those who have not, store it up or bank it. They are regular men before they are twelve years of age, and good examples to other boys wherever they may be.

How to make Money

There are many ways by which a scout, or a patrol working together, can make money, such as: —

Making arm-chairs, re-covering old furniture, etc., is a very paying trade. Fretwork and carving, picture-frames, bird-cages, cabinets, carved pipe bowls can be sold through a shop.

Get permission to cut certain sticks in hedges or woods, and trim them into walking-sticks, after hanging them with weights attached to straighten and dry them. Breeding canaries, chickens, rabbits, or dogs pays well. Bee-keeping is profitable, if well looked after.

You can make novel sets of buttons out of bootlaces; a scout in England made $3.50 in a few days lately in this way. Collect old packing-cases and boxes, and chop them into bundles of firewood. Make nets, besoms, etc., for gardeners. Keeping goats and selling their milk will pay in some places. Basket-making, pottery, book-binding, etc., all bring money. Or a patrol work-

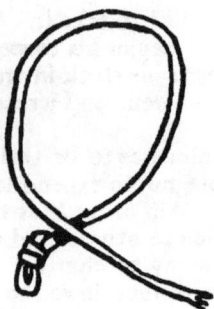

1

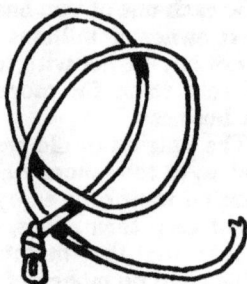

2

3

4

Continue till you have the whole
knot doubled or trebled.

5

The loop for attaching the button
is moved from its original position to hang from the centre of
the knot.

6

Pull all tight, cut off loose end, and
the button is complete.

HOW TO MAKE BUTTONS OUT OF BOOTLACES

ing together can form themselves into a corps of messenger boys in a country town, or they can get an allotment garden and work it for selling vegetables and flowers, or they can make themselves into a minstrel troop, or perform scouting displays or pageants, etc., like those shown in " Scouting Games," and take money at the doors. A scouts' " cake and candy sale " brought in $475 the other day in a small town.

These are only a few suggestions; there are loads of other ways of making money which you can think out for yourself, according to the place you are in.

But in order to get money you must expect to work The actor, Ted Payne, used to say in one of his plays, " I don't know what is wrong with me. I eat well, I drink well, and I sleep well; but somehow whenever anybody mentions the word ' work ' to me, I get a cold shudder all over me." That is what happens to a great many men, I am afraid. There are a good many chicken-hearted men, who, when any work faces them, " get a cold shudder all over them "; or, when trouble comes, they go and take to drink, instead of facing it and working it off.

Start a money-box, put any money you can make into that, and when you have got a fair amount in it, hand it over to a bank, and start an account for yourself. As a scout, you have to have a certain amount in the savings bank before you can become entitled to wear a badge. Save your cents, and you'll get dollars.

(*Scouts' money-boxes, price 1s. each, and patterns for fret-saw work can be obtained from Secretary, Boy Scouts, 116, Victoria Street, London, S.W.*)

How to get On

A few years ago Spain was at war with rebels in the island of Cuba. (*Point out on map.*)

William McKinley, who was at that time President of the United States, wanted to send a letter to Garcia, the chief of the rebels in Cuba, but did not know how to get it taken to him, as the rebels were a savage lot, inhabiting a wild and difficult country.

When he was talking it over with his advisers, some one said: " There's a young fellow called Rowan who seems to be able to get anything done that you ask him. Why not try him? "

So Rowan was sent for, and when he came in the President explained why he had sent for him, and, putting the letter in his hand, said, " Now, I want that letter delivered to Garcia."

The young man simply smiled and said, "I see," and walked out of the room, without saying another word.

Some weeks passed, and Rowan appeared again at the President's door, and said, "I gave your letter to Garcia, sir," and walked out again. Of course Mr. McKinley had him back and made him explain how he had done it.

It turned out that he had got a boat and sailed away in her for some days; had landed on the coast of Cuba, and disappeared into the jungle; in three weeks' time he reappeared on the other side of the island, having gone through the enemy, and found Garcia, and given him the letter.

He was a true scout, and that is the way a scout should carry out an order when he gets it. No matter how difficult it may seem, he should tackle it, with a smile; the more difficult it is the more interesting it will be to carry out.

Most men would have asked a lot of questions — first as to how they were to set about it, how they could get to the place, where they were to get food from, and so on; but not so Rowan; he merely learned what duty was required of him, and *he* did the rest without a word; any man who acts like that is certain to get on.

We have a lot of good scouts already enrolled among the District Messenger Boys in London. These lads, from having difficult jobs frequently given them and being *expected* to carry them out successfully, take them on with the greatest confidence in themselves; and, without asking a lot of silly questions, they start off in a businesslike way, and do them.

That is the way to deal with any difficulty in life. If you get a job or a trouble that seems to you to be too big for you, don't shirk it; smile, think out a way by which you might get successfully through with it, and then go at it.

Remember that "a difficulty is no longer a difficulty when once you laugh at it — and tackle it."

Don't be afraid of making a mistake. Napoleon said "Nobody ever made anything who never made a mistake."

MEMORY. — Then practise remembering things. A boy who has a good memory will get on because so many other people have bad memories from not practising them.

At the Olympic Theatre, Liverpool, the forgetfulness on the part of the people in the audience gradually made it necessary for the manager to keep a special room and ledgers for all lost articles left behind in the theatre after each performance. But the happy idea struck him of putting a notice on the curtain by means of a bioscope lantern a few minutes before the end of the performance, saying, "Please look under your seats before leaving."

This has made a great difference in the number of things left behind.

People used to leave every kind of thing, even medicine bottles and false teeth; and once a check for £50 was left.

A great coral island is built up of tiny sea insects blocking themselves together; so also great knowledge in a man is built up by his noticing all sorts of little details and blocking them together in his mind by *remembering* them.

LUCK. — If you want to catch a street car when it is not at a stopping post, you don't sit down and let it run past you, and then say, " How unlucky I am "; you run and jump on. It is just the same with what some people call " luck "; they complain that luck never comes to them. Well, luck is really the chance of getting something good or of doing something great; the thing is to look out for every chance and seize it — run at it and jump on — don't sit down and wait for it to pass. Opportunity is a street car which has very few stopping places.

CHOOSE A CAREER. — " Be prepared " for what is going to happen to you in the future. If you are in a situation where you are earning money as a boy, what are you going to do when you finish that job? You ought to be learning some proper business or trade to take up; and save your pay in the meantime, to keep you going till you get employment in your new occupation.

And try to learn something of a second business, in case the first one fails you at any time, as so very often happens.

An employer told me once that he never engaged a boy who had yellow finger-tips (from smoking), or who carried his mouth open (boys who breathe through the mouth are generally stupid). Any man is sure of employment who has money in the bank, is a teetotaler, and is cheery.

Canada is a land of great opportunities, and no boy who keeps his eyes open and is not afraid of work can help but succeed.

If you find yourself in difficulty about choosing a profession, business, or trade, talk to your scoutmaster ; he will advise you and will tell you where to get the best information.

Practices in Self-improvement

MARKET GARDENING. — The patrol or troop can work an allotment or other garden and sell the produce for their fund.

FOR A TROOP OR A NUMBER OF TROOPS. — Offer a good prize for the best article made by a scout with materials which have not cost more than 50 cents. Entrance fee to competition, 5 cents.

Have an exhibition of these, coupled with displays and scenes, etc., by the scouts, and take money at the doors.

At the end sell the articles by auction; the articles which fetch the highest prices win the prizes.

EACH SCOUT TO KEEP A MONEY-BOX, in which to save every spare cent, and deposit his savings every now and then in the bank.

INSTRUCTION CLASSES in Esperanto, Bookkeeping, Mechanics, Electricity, and especially Shorthand.

MEMORIZING. — Read something to the boys, a line or two at a time, to see who can repeat it best. To concentrate the mind and develop memory.

Mr. G. L. Boundy of Exeter, England, has had great success in developing intelligence amongst his boys by taking parties of them round to see the different factories in Exeter. They all take notes and rough drawings as they go along, and reproduce them the following meeting, and report on what they have seen.

BOOKS TO READ

" Thrift," by Samuel Smiles. 2s. nett. (John Murray.)

" One Hundred and One Ways of Making Money." 1s. (Sell and Olding, London.)

" Bradshaw's Railway Guide." To teach Scouts how to look out trains.

" Do it Now," by Peter Keary. 1s. nett. (C. A. Pearson Limited.)

" Get On or Get Out " (Success Library, No. 2), by Peter Keary. 1s. nett.

" The Secrets of Success," by Peter Keary. 1s. nett.

" Success after Failure: Some Men who Got Out and Got On." Edited by Peter Keary. Price 1s. nett.

" Rabbit Keeping," by Geo. Gardner. 1s. Postage 2d.

" Bees for Pleasure and Profit," by Samson. 1s.

" Esperanto for the Million," 1d. (Stead, 39, Whitefriars Street, London, E.C.)

" Cassell's Handbooks." 2s. nett. Joinery, Pottery, Painters' Work, etc.

" Work Handbook " series. 1s. nett. On Harness-making, Tinplate, Pumps, Bookbinding, Signwriting, Beehives, etc.

" Basket-making," by Mary White. 2s. 6d.

" Raffia Work," by M. Swannell. 2s. nett. (Geo. Philip and Son, Fleet Street.) [" Raffia " or " Bast " is the inner bark of a tree, and is used for making baskets, mats, hats, etc.]

" Self Help," by Samuel Smiles. 2s. nett. (John Murray.)

CHAPTER VIII

SAVING LIFE

or

How to Deal with Accidents

CAMP FIRE YARN. No. 23

BE PREPARED FOR ACCIDENTS

The Knights Hospitallers of St. John — Boy Heroes and Girl
Heroines — Life-saving Medals

HINTS TO INSTRUCTORS

*The subjects in this chapter should not only be explained to
the scouts, but should, also, wherever possible, be demonstrated
practically, and should be practised by each scout in turn.*

*Theoretical instruction in these points is nothing without prac-
tice.*

The Knights of St. John

THE knights of old days were called "Knights Hospitallers"
because they had hospitals for the treatment of the sick poor,
and those injured in accidents or in war. They used to save
up their money and keep these hospitals going, and although

they were brave fighting men they used also to act as nurses and doctors themselves.

The Knights of St. John of Jerusalem especially devoted themselves to this work eight hundred years ago, and the St. John's Ambulance Corps is to-day a branch which represents those knights. Their badge is an eight-pointed white cross on a black ground, and when worn as an Order it has a black ribbon.

Explorers and hunters and other scouts in out-of-the-way parts of the world have to know what to do in the case of accident or sickness, either to themselves or their followers, as they are often hundreds of miles away from any doctors. For these reasons Boy Scouts should, of course, learn all they can about looking after sick people and dealing with accidents.

My brother was once camping with a friend away in the bush in Australia. His friend was drawing a cork, holding the bottle between his knees to get a better purchase. The bottle burst, and the jagged edge of it ran deeply into his thigh, cutting an artery. My brother quickly got a stone, and wrapped it in a handkerchief to act as a pad, and he then tied the handkerchief round the limb above the wound, so that the stone pressed on the artery. He then got a stick, and, passing it through the loop of the handkerchief, twisted it round till the bandage was drawn so tight that it stopped the flow of blood. Had he not known what to do, the man would have bled to death in a few minutes. As it was he saved his life by knowing what to do and doing it at once.

[*Demonstrate how to bind up an artery and also the course taken by the arteries, viz. practically down the inside seam of sleeves and trousers.*]

Accidents are continually happening, and Boy Scouts will continually have a chance of giving assistance at first aid. In London alone during one year 212 people were killed and 14,000 injured in street accidents.

We all think a great deal of any man who, at the risk of his own life, saves some one else's.

He is a hero.

Boys especially think him so, because he seems to them to be a being altogether different from themselves. But he isn't; every boy has just as much a chance of being a life-saving hero if he chooses to prepare himself for it.

It is pretty certain that nearly every one of you scouts will some day or another be present at an accident where, if you know what to do, and do it promptly, you may win for yourself the life-long satisfaction of having rescued or helped a fellow creature.

Remember your motto, " BE PREPARED." Be prepared for accidents by learning beforehand what you ought to do in the different kinds that are likely to occur.

Be prepared to do that thing the moment the accident does occur.

I will explain to you what ought to be done in the different kinds of accidents, and you must practise them as far as possible. But the great thing for you scouts to bear in mind is that wherever you are, and whatever you are doing, you should think to yourself, " What accident is likely to occur here?" and, " What is my duty if it occurs?"

You are then prepared to act.

And when an accident does occur remember always that as a scout it is your business to be the first man to go to the rescue; don't let an outsider be beforehand with you.

Suppose, for instance, that you are standing on a crowded platform at a station, waiting for the train.

You think to yourself, " Now, supposing some one falls off this platform on to the rails just as the train is coming in, what shall I do? I must jump down and jerk him off the track on to the far side into the six-foot way — there would be no time to get him up on the platform again. Or if the train were very close, the only way would be to lie flat and make him lie flat too, between the rails, and let the train go over us both."

Then, if this accident happened, you would at once jump down and carry out your idea, while everybody else would be running about screaming and excited and doing nothing, not knowing what to do.

Such a case actually happened recently. A lady fell off the platform at Finsbury Park Station just as the train was coming in; a man named Albert Hardwick jumped down and lay flat, and held her down, too, between the rails, while the train passed over both of them without touching them. The King gave him the Albert Medal for it.

When there is a panic among those around you, you get a momentary inclination to do as the others are doing. Perhaps it is to run away, perhaps it is to stand still and cry out " Oh! " Well, you should check yourself when you have this feeling. Don't catch the panic, as you see others do; keep your head and think what is the right thing to do, and do it at once.

Then there was that disgraceful scene which occurred at Hampstead, where a woman drowned herself before a whole lot of people in a shallow pond, and took half an hour doing it, while not one of them had the pluck to go in and bring her out. One would not have thought it possible with Englishmen that a lot of men could stand on the bank and chatter only, but so it was — to their eternal disgrace.

It was again a case of panic. The first man to arrive on the scene did not like going in, and merely called another. More came up, but finding that those already there did not go in, they got a sort of fear of something uncanny, and would not go in themselves, and so let the poor woman drown before their eyes.

Had one Boy Scout been there, there would, I hope, have been a very different tale to tell. It was just the opportunity for a Boy Scout to distinguish himself. He would have remembered his training.

Do your duty.

Help your fellow-creature, especially if it be a woman.

Don't mind if other people are holding back.

Plunge in boldly and look to the object you are trying to attain, and don't bother about your own safety.

Boys have an idea that they are too young and too small to take any but an outside part in saving life. But this is a great mistake.

Since I wrote "Scouting for Boys" two years ago, four different cases have occurred of Boy Scouts plunging in to save drowning people where the crowd were afraid to help, and several more of scouts helping the police or stopping runaway horses when other people drew back. Boy Scouts have in that time won four Bronze Medals, fifty-three Silver, and fifty-four Badges of Merit for saving life.

Scout Douglas Smith, of the 4th Ealing Troop, lost his life in attempting to save another boy from drowning.

Four boys were bathing together when one of them, Harold Upton, got out of his depth, and was swept away by the current. Scout Smith, who was undressing on the bank, did not do as the men had done in the other case; he did not stand and look on. Like a true scout, he sprang to the rescue without stopping to think of the risk himself.

He could not swim well, but this did not stop him from having a try; he leaped into the water, saying, "I'll have a try to get him," and tried to grasp the drowning boy, but he, too, was carried off by the current into deep water — and soon sank, fighting manfully, never to rise again.

But he had died gloriously, doing his duty, putting to greater shame the men who had not such pluck, and showing an example to all, whether brother scouts or not, of Being Prepared to do your duty at every moment, no matter what may be the risk.

Had Scout Smith survived his brave attempt, he would have received our highest award, the Bronze Cross for Gallantry. As it is, the cross was awarded to him, though dead.

In addition to this a boy named Albert Abraham was recommended for the highest honor that any man can get for saving life, and that is the Albert Medal.

Three boys were climbing up some cliffs from the seashore when one of them fell to the bottom and was very badly hurt. Another climbed up the rest of the cliff and ran away home, but told nobody for fear of getting into trouble. The third one, Albert Abraham, climbed down again to the assistance of the boy who had fallen, and he found him lying head downwards between two rocks, with his scalp nearly torn off and his leg broken.

Abraham dragged him up out of reach of the tide, for where he had fallen he was in danger of being drowned, and then replaced his scalp and bound it on, and also set his leg as well as he could, and bound it up in splints, having learned the " First Aid " duties of the St. John's Ambulance Society. Then he climbed up the cliff and gathered some ferns and made a bed for the injured boy.

He stayed with him all that day, and when night came on he still remained with him, nor did he desert him even when a great seal climbed on to the rocks close to him and appeared to be rather aggressive. He drove it off with stones.

Parties went out and eventually rescued both boys, but the injured one died soon after, in spite of the efforts that Albert Abraham had made to save him.

Life-saving Medals

In war, as you know, the Victoria Cross is awarded to soldiers for performing acts of valor.

So, in peace, a decoration is given to anybody who distinguishes himself by bravery in saving life at the risk of his own.

The Albert Medal is the highest of these rewards.

The Royal Humane Society also give medals or certificates.

The Edward Medal is granted for gallantry in accidents which so frequently happen in mines.

The Stanhope is also a medal for special gallantry.

In the Boy Scouts we have three medals for gallantry, which are granted for similar acts.

But of all these the Albert Medal and the Edward Medal are the most valued, being given by the King himself, and only in very special cases.

So let every Boy Scout prepare himself to win one of these. Some day, most probably, an accident will happen before you to give you your chance. If you have learned beforehand what to do, you can step forward at once and do the right thing; you may find yourself decorated with the medal. In any case, you will have what is far greater than a mere medal — you will have the satisfaction of having helped a fellow-creature at the risk of your own life.

Practice for Life-saving

FLINGING THE SQUALER

The squaler is a piece of cane, 19 inches long, loaded at the butt with 1¾ pound of lead, and having attached to it at the other end a life-saving line of six-thread Italian hemp. The target is a crossbar and head, life size, representing the head and arms of a drowning man, planted in the ground twenty yards away. Each competitor throws in turn from behind a line drawn on the ground; he may stand or run to make the throw. Whoever throws the farthest wins, provided that the line falls on some part of the dummy, so that it could be caught by the drowning man.

Or have heats to find out who is the worst thrower.

Practise throwing a life-belt the same way.

Practise making two lines of bucket men, for full and empty buckets. Each line to relieve the other frequently by exchanging duties.

Practise carrying, unrolling, and rolling up hose; joining up lengths; affixing to hydrants; throwing on water, and directing its fall.

Practise use of ladders, poles, ropes, lowering people from window by ropes or bedclothes, jumping sheet, and shoot escape; how to rig, hold, and use carpets or double blankets, but not flimsy ones or sheets.

CAMP FIRE YARN. No. 24

ACCIDENTS AND HOW TO DEAL WITH THEM

Panic — Fire — Drowning — Runaway Horse —
Mad Dog — Miscellaneous.

Panics

EVERY year numbers of lives are lost by panics, which very
often are due to the smallest causes, and which might be stopped
if only one or two men would keep their heads. One evening
a short time ago, on board a ferry-boat in New York, a man who
had been catching some crabs thought it would be a good joke
to let one of them loose on board the boat. This crab caught
hold of the ship's cat and made it squeal, and it jumped into the
middle of a crowd of school-girls, who at once scattered, screaming. This started a panic among the hundreds of passengers
on board; they rushed in every direction, and in a moment
the railings broke and eight people fell overboard, and before
anything could be done they were swept away by the tide and
drowned.

In Germany, a girl who was bathing suddenly pretended to
be drowning, just for fun. Three men sprang into the river to
rescue her, but one began to sink, and another went to his
help, and both were drowned. Not very long ago a tobacconist
in a town in Russia, on opening his shop in the morning, saw a
big black bomb lying on the counter. He rushed out into the
street to get away from it, and a policeman seeing him running
mistook him for a thief, and when he would not stop he fired at
him. The bullet missed him, but hit another man, who was a
Jew; the remainder of the Jews immediately collected and made
a riot, and many lives were lost. After it was over the tobacconist went back to his shop and found the bomb still on his
counter — but it was not a bomb, it was only a black water-
melon !

Last year occurred a case of panic among children in a theatre
at Barnsley, where a crush and panic occurred from no cause
at all except overcrowding, and eight children were crushed
to death. More lives would certainly have been lost had not
two men kept their heads and done the right thing. One man,
named Gray, called to a number of the children in a cheery
voice to come another way, while the man who was working

a lantern-slide show threw a picture on the screen and so diverted the attention of the rest, and prevented them catching the panic. That is the great point in a panic. If only one or two men keep their heads and do the right thing on the spur of the moment they can often calm hundreds of people, and thus save many lives.

This is a great opportunity for a boy scout. Force yourself to keep calm and not to lose your head. Think what is the right thing to do, and do it at once.

Rescue from Fire

Instances of gallant rescues of people from burning houses are frequent. One sees them every day in the newspapers, and scouts should study each of these cases as they occur, and imagine to themselves what they would have done under the circumstances, and in this way you begin to learn how to deal with the different accidents. An instance occurred only the other day where a young sailor, named George Obeney, stationed at Chatham in H.M.S. *Andromeda*, was walking along the Kingsland Road, when he suddenly saw a house on fire, and a woman on the second story was screaming that she had some children there who could not get out. The sailor rushed from his friends and somehow scrambled up the face of the wall till he reached the window on the first story, and broke in that window so that he could obtain room to stand. The woman at the window above was then able to lower a child so that he could catch it, and he again passed it down to the ground. Child after child was thus handed down till he passed six of them to the ground, and finally two women; and then he, overcome by smoke himself, fell insensible, but was caught by the people below. His act was an example to you how to do your duty AT ONCE, without thinking of dangers or difficulties.

A house caught fire at Shoreham Beach the other day, and the 1st Latimer Troop of Boy Scouts were quickly on the scene under Scoutmaster Cummings. They did their work as true scouts, not only in acting as firemen and getting the fire under control, but also as life-savers in rescuing two ladies and a child, and then in rendering first aid to them and dressing their injuries.

There are now several efficient Fire Brigade patrols of Boy Scouts.

Directions

These are some of their directions:

If you discover a house on fire you should —
1st. — Alarm the people inside.
2d. — Warn the nearest policeman or fire brigade station.
3d. — Rouse neighbors to bring ladders, mattresses, carpets, to catch people jumping.

After arrival of fire engines, the best thing boys can do is to help the police in keeping back the crowd out of the way of the firemen, hose, etc.

The Boys' Life Brigade are taught a certain drill called " Scrum " for keeping back the crowd. They form a line, or

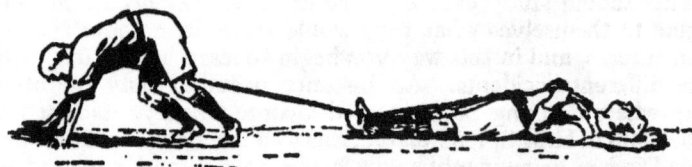

DRAGGING INSENSIBLE MAN: BOTH HEADS NEAR THE FLOOR

double line, and pass their arms round each other's waists, and shove, head down, into the crowd, and so drive it back.

If it is necessary to go into a house to search for feeble or insensible people, the thing is to place a wet handkerchief or worsted stocking over your nose and mouth and walk in a stooping position or crawl along on your hands and knees quite near the floor, as it is here that there is least smoke or gas. Also, for passing through fire and sparks, if you can, get hold of a blanket and wet it, and cut a hole in the middle through which to put your head; it forms a kind of fireproof mantle, with which you can push through flames and sparks. [*Practise this.*]

When a fire occurs anywhere near, the Boy Scouts should assemble their patrols as quickly as possible and go off at scouts' pace to the fire, guided by the glare or the smoke. Then the patrol leader should report to the police or firemen, and offer the help of his patrol either to form a fence to keep the crowd back, or to run messages, or guard property, or to help in any way.

If you find a person with his clothes on fire, you should throw him flat on the floor, because flames burn upwards only, then roll him up in the hearthrug or carpet, coat or blanket, and take care in doing so that you don't catch fire yourself. The reason for doing this is that fire cannot continue to burn where it has no air. Then pour water over the patient to put out all sparks.

When you find an insensible person (and very often in their fright they will have hidden themselves under beds and tables, etc.), you should either carry him out on your shoulder, or, what is often more practicable in the case of heavy smoke, gas fumes, etc., harness yourself onto him with sheets or cords and drag him out of the room along the floor, crawling on all fours yourself.

[*Practise this by tying a bowline round the patient's waist, another round his ankles, and another round your own neck. Turn your back to him, go on all fours, with the rope underneath you, and thus drag him out. Also practise the " Fireman's Lift " for getting an insensible person on to your shoulders (see page 275).*]

Rescue from Drowning

The list of Boy Scouts heroes shows you what a large proportion of accidents is due to not knowing how to swim. It is therefore most important that everybody should learn to swim, and, having done so, to learn how to save others from being drowned.

Mr. Holbein, the great Channel swimmer, writing in *The Boys' Own Paper*, points out that a boy, when learning to swim, should learn first how to get in and out of a boat, *i.e.*, by climbing in over the stern. Secondly, how to support himself on an oar or plank, *i.e.*, by riding astride on it, or by catching hold of one end and pushing it before him and swimming with his legs. Thirdly, how to get into a floating lifebuoy, *i.e.*, by shoving the nearest side of it down under water and capsizing it over his head and shoulders, so that he is inside it when it floats. Fourthly, how to save life.

[*Practise these at swimming baths or parade bathing.*]

A moderate swimmer can save a drowning man if he knows how, and has practised it a few times with his friends. The popular idea that a drowning person rises three times before he finally sinks is all nonsense. He often drowns at once, unless some one is quick to help him. The important point is not to let the drowning person catch hold of you, or he will probably drown you too. Keep behind him always. If you find yourself clutched by the wrist, turn your wrist against his thumb and force yourself free. Your best way in helping a drowning man is to keep behind and hold him up by the hair, or by the back of the neck, or by putting your arms under his armpits, and telling him to keep quiet and not to struggle. If he obeys, you can easily keep him afloat; but otherwise be careful that in his terror he does not turn over and catch hold of you. If he should seize you by the neck, Holbein says, " Scrag him, and scrag him quickly. Place your arm round his waist, and the other hand, palm upwards, under his chin, with your finger-tips under his nose. Pull and push with all your might, and he must perforce let go." But you will never remember this unless you practise it frequently with other boys first, each taking it in turns to be the drowning man or rescuer.

[*Practise this.*]

No scout can be of real use till he can swim, and to learn swimming is no more difficult than to learn bicycling.

All you have to do is at first try to swim like a dog, as if trying to crawl slowly along in the water; don't try all at once to swim with the ordinary breast stroke that swimmers use, because this only lets your mouth go under water every time. When paddling along like a dog, get a friend to support you at first with a pole or his hand under your belly.

Scout Archibald Reginald Cox, fifteen years, of the 9th Ipswich Troop, received the Bronze Medal for gallantry in saving life for the following act: —

A man, who afterwards proved to be temporarily insane, threw himself into the River Orwell, with the intention of drowning himself. Scout Cox at once plunged in to his rescue, but as soon as he reached him the lunatic fought him, and tried to grab him. The scout, however, kept behind his man, and grasped him in such a way that every time he attempted to fight he ducked him under water. This struggle continued for ten minutes, until the lunatic, after continual ducking, became insensible, and Cox then brought him ashore, and applied artificial breathing, and so brought him to.

In addition to our medal, Scout Cox was also awarded a medal by the Royal Humane Society for his plucky act.

A Canadian scout has also won the Bronze Cross, our highest honor, for saving life at risk of his own. Patrol Leader George Jackson was with some other boys bathing in the river. One of them, Harry Forrester, got into difficulties owing to the water-wings with which he was swimming coming off. His brother Asa, seeing his danger, went to his assistance, although he, too, was only a poor swimmer. They got hold of each other, but both lost their heads in fear of drowning and clutched each other to the extent that they both went under. Patrol Leader Jackson at once went in to their assistance, and though he got to them and succeeded in getting them apart, he in his turn, was grappled by Asa, and it was only with the greatest difficulty that he managed to fight himself free of his grip and, taking him from behind, he then succeeded in bringing him ashore. He was pretty well done himself, and had narrowly escaped being drowned, but like a true scout who never says die till he's dead, he plunged in again and went to the assistance of the second boy, Harry, who was now in the greatest possible danger. Jackson succeeded in reaching him, but Harry did as his brother had done and in what was practically his death-grip he grappled Jackson with a tight hold. The scout struggled and fought against it, but was himself weakened by his efforts and was very nearly dragged down; and when at length he succeeded in breaking away, he was rescued only with some difficulty, while the other poor lad was drowned. His pluck in returning to make the second attempt entitled him to the highest scout honor that could be awarded.

Fifty-five out of the one hundred and seven medals won by scouts for saving life were awarded for saving life from drowning.

Any of you who cannot swim as yet, and who fall into the water out of your depth, remember that you need not sink if you take care to do the following things. First, keep your mouth upwards by throwing the head well back. Secondly, keep your lungs full of air by taking in long breaths, but breathe out very little. Thirdly, keep your arms under water. To do this you should not begin to shout, which will only empty your lungs, and you should not throw your arms about or beckon for help, else you will sink.

If you see a person fall into the water and begin to drown, and you yourself are unable to swim, you must throw a rope, or an oar, or plank right over him, so that when he comes up again he may clutch at it and hold it. If a person falls through ice, and is unable to get out again because of the edges breaking, throw him a rope and tell him not to struggle. This may give him confidence until you can get a long ladder or pole across the hole, which will enable him to crawl out, or will allow you to crawl out to catch hold of him.

Rescue from Runaway Horses

Accidents are continually occurring from runaway horses running over people. In fact, on an average, the number of runaway horses that are stopped by policemen during the year is very large, and it is well that everybody should know how to stop a runaway horse, and thus to save numerous accidents and injuries.

Private Davies, of the 16th Lancers, was awarded the Albert Medal, at Aldershot, for stopping the horses of an artillery wagon, which had become unmanageable and run away. The driver, who was riding one of them, had been thrown off, and the horses were careering down hill towards the married quarters of the cavalry barracks, where a number of children were at play, when Private Davies, seeing the danger to the children, ran to the horses, and, seizing the off horse with his right hand, held on to the shaft with his left, and endeavored to stop the wagon. He was dragged in that position for some yards, when the chain fastening the shafts to the wagon gave way and let the shafts fall, bringing Davies also to the ground.

The wagon passed over his legs, and very severely injured him, and though he did not actually succeed in stopping the horses, he so diverted them from their course that time was given for the children to be saved from being run over.

Our Commissioner for Hertford, Mr. P. W. Everett, stopped a runaway horse and trap the other day and rescued a boy who was entangled in the reins.

And eighteen cases of runaway horses being stopped by Boy Scouts have been rewarded.

Scout Albert Stevenson, aged fifteen, 1st Rotherhithe Troop, was walking along High Street, Deptford, when he heard people shouting to others to get out of the way of a pair of horses which were running away with an empty van. He dodged aside just in time to escape the wheels. As he did so he thought to himself, "If I, who am a scout and always on the lookout, was so near being run over, how about an ordinary boy? He is sure to be knocked down." Se he ran as hard as he could with the van, and managed to climb on to it behind. When he got to the driver's seat, he found that the reins were dangling about the horses' heads and could not be got at. So he clambered along the pole between the galloping horses till he reached their heads, and, squatting down on the pole with his feet against the pole chains, he got hold of the bridles in each hand and tried to bang the two horses' heads together. In this way he gradually got them to pull up, and prevented them from doing any further damage to life or property.

This is a lesson to every one to BE PREPARED, even at most ordinary moments of strolling along, talking to a friend, to spring at once to the assistance of a fellow-creature who is in danger.

The other day I myself found a horse and cab running away over Westminster Bridge, but I stopped it without any difficulty. The way to stop a runaway horse is not to run out in front of it and wave your arms, as so many people do, but to try and race alongside it. catch hold of the shaft to keep yourself from falling, and seize the reins with the other hand, and drag the horse's head round towards you, and so turn him until you can bring him up against a wall or house, or otherwise compel him to stop. But, of course, for a boy, with his light weight, this is a very difficult thing to do. The share he would have in such an accident would probably be to look after the people injured by the runaway horse.

Miscellaneous Accidents

One cannot go through the whole list of accidents that might come under your notice, but the point is that a scout should always remember to keep his head, and think what is the right thing to do at the moment, and be the man to do it, even under the most unexpected circumstances.

Scout L. Rudd, 2d Leigh Troop, saw a little girl playing about on the railway line at Shoebury when a train was approaching. He rushed forwards, got over the railway fence, crossed the line in front of the train, and just reached the child in time to pull her out of the way. He himself received a blow on the head, which left him in a dazed condition for some time. If it had not been for his promptness and pluck, the child must have been killed. Rudd received the Bronze Medal for gallantry.

Scout J. C. Davel, 1st Bloemfontein Troop (South Africa), saw a little girl entangled in some electric light wires on the roof of a house. Although he was warned not to go to her, as he would probably be killed too, he climbed up and got her down, receiving a shock himself in doing so. The child was dead.

Scout Gregory, 1st Ilbeston Troop, was working down a mine when he heard a roaring noise which made him guess that a train of trucks had broken loose and was rushing down into the mine.   He at once ran across the line in front of the train, and put in the safety blocks to stop it.   By his prompt and plucky act he probably saved a number of lives.   For this he received the Silver Medal for saving life.

Scout Lockley, 1st Atherstone Troop, was looking on at a roundabout at a fair which was being worked by electricity from a steam traction engine.   The driver of this in leaning over got his clothes caught in the machinery, and was being dragged into it when Lockley sprang on to the engine, and, knowing something of mechanics, pulled over the lever, and stopped it just in time to save the man's life.

There is an example of a boy Being Prepared, knowing what to do, and doing it without a moment's waiting.

Mad Dog

A dog that is mad runs along snapping at everybody in his path.   Every scout should know what to do when there is a mad dog about, and should be prepared to do it.

Sir Thomas Fowell Buxton was one day out for a ride when his dog, which was running with him, went mad, and started to run through the town.

Sir Thomas edged him off the road and drove him into a garden.   He then jumped off his horse, ran at the dog, and succeeded in grabbing him by the neck without getting bitten.   Then followed a tremendous struggle between man and dog.

At last the gardener came and brought a chain, which Sir Thomas then clipped on, and only when the other end had been securely fastened to a tree did he let go his hold of the dog.   The dog was then raving mad, and tore at his chain so badly that it was in danger of breaking, when Sir Thomas went at him again with a second and stronger chain, and, pinning him down by the neck with a pitchfork, he fastened it on to him.   When this was done and the pitchfork removed, the dog sprang at him with such force that it burst the old chain.   Luckily the new one held, and soon after the dog died.

The way to prevent a dog biting you is to hold a stick, or even a handkerchief, in your two hands across your front, and the dog will generally try to paw it down before he actually bites you, and you may thus get a chance of landing him a kick under the jaw.

Practices in Life-saving

Practise "scrum"; also forming a fence with staves for keeping back a crowd at a fire.

Practise holding and wrestling with drowning men.

How to prevent a man shooting another with a pistol.

Make ladders out of poles, twine, and cross sticks.

Instruct scouts to know the position of neighboring fire plugs and hydrants, police points, fire alarms, fire stations, ambulances, hospitals, etc.

Books to Read

"Manual of Boys' Life Brigade ": Life-saving drill. Price 2d. (56 Old Bailey, London.)

"Manual of Fire Drill " of London County Council. 1s. (P. S. King and Son, 9 Bridge Street, Westminster.)

"Swimming," by Prof. Holbein. 1s. (C. A. Pearson, Limited.)

CAMP FIRE YARN. No. 25

HELPING OTHERS

Rendering First Aid — How to Revive a Drowned Man — Suicides — How to Carry a Patient.

Rendering First Aid

[NOTE TO INSTRUCTOR. — *It is impossible in the short space at one's disposal to give all the details of First Aid. These can be found in any of the books mentioned at the end of this Camp Fire Yarn, and in " Scout Charts," price 2d.*]

IN an accident, when you are alone with the injured person, if he is unconscious lay him on his back with his head a little raised and on one side so that he does not choke, and so that any vomit or water, etc., can run out of his mouth. Loosen the clothing about his neck and chest. See where he is injured, and treat him according to what you are taught in learning " First Aid."

If you have found the man lying insensible, you should carefully examine the ground round him for any " sign," and take note of it and of his position, etc., in case it should afterwards appear that he had been attacked by others.

[*Practise above, one boy as patient, the other to find him. Make " sign " round the patient.*]

If you are out with a patrol and an accident happens, or you find an injured man, the patrol leader should direct one scout to go for a doctor; he himself will attend to the patient with one scout to help him. The corporal will use the other scouts in assisting by getting water or blankets, or making a stretcher, or keeping the crowd back by forming a fence with their staves.

As a rule it is best to keep the patient quite quiet at first ; unless it is necessary, do not try to move him; and don't bother him with questions until he recovers a little.

[*Practise above.*]

ARTIFICIAL BREATHING. — To restore any one who is apparently drowned, it is necessary at once to clear the water out of his lungs, for which purpose therefore you should incline him face downwards and head downwards, so that the water may run out of his mouth, and to help it you should open his mouth and pull forwards his tongue. After running the water out of the patient, place him on his side with his body slightly hanging down, and keep the tongue hanging out. If he is breathing, let him rest; if he is not breathing, you must at once endeavor to restore breathing artificially.

How to Revive a Drowned Man

There are several methods, but the simplest is, I think, that called after its inventor the Schäfer system. It consists merely in laying the patient on his front, and then squeezing the air out of him and letting it run in again.

1. Immediately after the removal from the water, and before taking time to loosen clothing, etc., lay the patient face downwards, with arms extended and the face turned to the side. Kneel or squat alongside or astride of the patient, facing towards his head.

2. Place your hands on the small of the patient's back, one on each side, with thumbs parallel and nearly touching, and the fingers reaching only to the lowest ribs.

3. Bend forwards with the arms straight, so as to allow the weight of your body to fall on your wrists, and then make a firm, steady downward pressure on the loins of the patient, while you count slowly, one — two — three, to press the patient's stomach against the ground and to force the air from his chest.

4. Then swing your body backwards so as to relieve the

pressure, and without removing your hands, while you count slowly, one — two.

Continue this backwards and forwards movement, alternately relieving and pressing the patient's stomach against the ground in order to drive the air out of his chest and mouth, and allowing it to suck itself in again, until gradually the patient begins to do it for himself.

The proper pace for the movement should be about twelve pressures to the minute.

As soon as the patient is breathing you can leave off the pressure; but watch him, and if he fails you must start again till he can breathe for himself.

Then let him lie in a natural position, and set to work to get him warm by putting hot flannels or bottles of hot water between his thighs, and under the arms, and against the soles of his feet.

Wet clothing should be taken off, and hot blankets rolled round him. The patient should be disturbed as little as possible, and encouraged to sleep, while carefully watched for at least an hour afterwards.

Now just practise this with another scout a few times, so that you understand exactly how to do it, and so Be Prepared to do it to some poor fellow, maybe, really in need of it, one day.

This is called the Schäfer method, and can be used equally well for drowned people or for those overcome with smoke or gas fumes.

[*Make the scouts, in pairs, practise above.*]

SMOKE OR FUMES. — Accidents are continually occurring from escapes of gas in mines, sewers, and houses.

In endeavoring to rescue a person, keep your nose and mouth well covered with a wet handkerchief, and get your head as close to the floor as possible, and drag the insensible person out as I have suggested in case of fire. Drag your patient as quickly as possible into the fresh air (I say as quickly as possible, because if you delay about it you are very apt to be overcome by the noxious gas yourself); then loosen all his clothing about the neck and chest, dash cold water in his face, and apply burnt feathers under his nose. If you find that he is no longer breathing, then treat him as you would a drowned person, and try and work back the breath into his body.

BURNS. — In treating a man who has been burnt, remove his clothes, not by peeling them off, but by cutting them with a SHARP knife or scissors. If any part of the dress sticks to the skin from having been burnt there, do not tear it away, but cut the cloth round it, then as quickly as possible protect the burnt parts from the air, which causes intense pain.   The best way to protect them is by dusting them with powdered chalk or flour, or by laying strips of lint well soaked in sweet oil or linseed oil, and covering the whole with cotton wool, or by pouring on oil. Keep the patient warm, and give warm drinks, such as hot tea, hot milk, or spirits and water.

Major John Garroway, M.D., strongly recommends, instead of flour or oil to stop the pain of a burn, to put a piece of paper firmly over the wound, and the pain will be relieved in a few seconds.

BROKEN LIMBS. — How to tell when a limb is broken.

There is generally a swelling and pain about the place where the bone has broken, and sometimes the limb is bent in an unnatural way and the patient cannot use it.

The broken limb should not be moved about at all, but should be straightened and bound to something stiff that will keep it stiff and straight while the patient is being moved to hospital or home.

SPLINTS. — The stiff thing that you tie to the injured limb is called a splint.   This may be anything, such as a wooden batten, scout's staff, tightly rolled newspaper, etc.

Splints should be long enough to go beyond the joints above and below the break.   You should put a splint on each side of the limb if possible.

Then bind the splints firmly from end to end with handkerchiefs or strips of linen c⁻ ⁻loth, but not so tightly as to stop the blood circulating or to press into the swelling.

[*Practise this.*]

BANDAGE. — For binding a broken limb you need a good large three-cornered bandage.   Its two sides should be each about forty inches long.

To make a sling for broken arm or collarbone, hang the bandage round the patient's neck, tying the two ends together in a reefknot with the point of the bandage towards the damaged arm.   Rest the arm in this sling and bring the point round the back of the arm and pin it to hold the elbow in the sling.

BLEEDING. — When a man is bleeding badly from a wound, press the wound or the flesh just above it — that is, between the wound and the heart — press it hard with your thumb to try and stop the blood running in the artery. Then make a pad with something like a flat rounded pebble, and bind it over the wound. If bleeding violently, tie a handkerchief loosely round the limb above the wound, and twist it tight with a stick. [*Demonstrate this*.] Keep the wounded part raised above the rest of the body if possible. Apply cold water, or ice if possible, wet rags, etc.

Bleeding from the ears and insensibility after a fall means injury to the skull. The patient should not be moved at all if possible. It is best even to keep him lying on the spot, and put cold water or ice to his head and keep him quiet till a doctor comes.

Spitting or throwing up blood means internal injury or bursting of a small blood-vessel inside the patient. The case often looks more serious than it really is. If the blood is light red in color and mixed with froth, it means injury to the lungs. In either case keep the patient quiet and give ice to suck or cold water to sip.

Don't be alarmed at the amount of blood that flows from a patient. It used to be a common thing for the barber to bleed a man to the extent of five or six cupfuls of blood.

FISHHOOK IN THE SKIN. — I got a fishhook into my finger the other day. I got a knife and cut off all the fly which was on the hook, then pushed the hook farther into my finger till the point began to push against the skin from inside. With a sharp knife I cut a little slit in the skin so that the point came easily through, and I was then able to get hold of it and to pull the whole hook through. Of course you cannot get a hook out backwards, as the barb holds tight in the flesh all the time.·

FROST BITE. — In Arctic countries, or extreme cold, men are liable to get frost-bitten. That is, their ears, or nose, or fingers, or toes get killed by the cold. The patient does not feel any pain; the part becomes numb and turns very white and waxy, and afterwards purple.

Directly this is noticed the part should be rubbed with snow, or with the hand until the blood comes back to it. On no account should it be warmed by putting the patient in a warm room or near a fire; that would kill the part at once.

HYSTERICS. · – Nervous people, especially women, get hysterics when excited, crying, laughing, and screaming. The best treatment is to shut the patient into a room and leave him entirely alone till he gets over it. Don't try and soothe him; it only makes him worse.

ELECTRIC SHOCK. — Men frequently get knocked insensible by touching an electric cable or rail. The patient should be moved from the rail, but you have to be careful in doing this that you don't get the electric shock also. In the first place put glass, if possible, for yourself to stand upon, or dry wood if glass is not obtainable, or put on india-rubber boots. Also put on india-rubber gloves before touching the patient. If you have none, wrap your hands in several thicknesses of *dry* cloth, and pull the patient away with a stick.

A boy was hunting butterflies at St. Ouen, in France, the other day, when he fell on the " live " rail of the electric railway and was instantly killed by the shock. A passer-by, in trying to lift him off, fell dead beside him. A brickmaker ran up and tried to rescue them, and was himself struck dead in the same way. The two would-be rescuers were killed through not having learned beforehand what was the right thing to do.

FAINTING. — If your patient faints and is pale — fainting comes from too little blood in the head — let him lie flat down with head on the ground. If his face is flushed, raise the head — there is too much blood in it, as an apoplexy or sunstroke.

FITS. — A man cries out and falls, and twitches and jerks his limbs about, froths at the mouth: he is in a fit. It is no good to do anything to him but to put a bit of wood or cork between his jaws, so that he does not bite his tongue. Let him sleep well after a fit.

POISONING. — If a person suddenly falls very ill after taking food, or is known to have taken poison, the first thing to do is to make him swallow some milk or raw eggs. These seem to collect all the poison that is otherwise spread about inside him. Then, if the mouth is not stained or burnt by the poison, make him sick if possible by giving him salt and warm water, and try tickling the inside of his throat with a feather. Then more eggs and milk, and weak tea. If the poison is an acid that burns, the patient should not be made to vomit, but milk or salad oil should be given. The patient should be kept awake if he gets drowsy.

BLOOD-POISONING. — This results from dirt being allowed to get into a wound. Swelling, pain, red veins appear. Fomenting with hot water is the best relief.

CHOKING. — Loosen collar; hold the patient's nose with one hand and with the forefinger of the other, or with the handle of a spoon try and pull out whatever is stuck in his throat. By pressing down the root of the tongue you may make him sick and throw out the obstruction. For slight choking make patient bend head well back and swallow small pills made of bread, and sip water. Sometimes a good hard smack on the back will do him good.

Choking sometimes comes from a sudden swelling inside the throat. In this case put hot steaming flannel fomentations to the neck and give the patient ice to suck or cold water to sip.

QUINSY. — When I was in the Andes Mountains in South America recently, I heard of two Englishmen who had died there not long before from choking by quinsy, simply because there was no one by who knew what to do in such a case. Everybody ought to Be Prepared to deal with quinsy if away from the help of doctors.

Most people suffer from tonsilitis at one time or another in their lives — that is, a swelling of the tonsils — the round lumps of flesh on each side of the back of the throat. And sometimes, on rare occasions, the swelling becomes so great that the patient cannot breathe, the throat becomes completely blocked up. This is quinsy.

Three courses are open where no doctor is available, and in an obvious case of life and death:

1. If hot fomentation does no good, get a tube of some sort, such as that of a bicycle pump, or a pea-shooter, a pencil-case with the end opened, etc., and push it into the throat so as to keep a passage open for air to get into the lungs. Use the handle of a spoon to help you in keeping the tongue flat while you push in the tube.

2. If the tonsils close up too much for this, you must make a little cut in each to let out the matter which is causing the swelling.

Get a sharp lancet or penknife, wrap it round with rag until only just the tip of the blade is exposed. Hold the patient's tongue down with a spoon handle, and cut a small slit or two into each tonsil. This will generally give immediate relief.

In all cases while performing the operation block the patient's mouth open with a lump of india-rubber, or a cork, etc. It is also useful to get some one to hold a mirror to throw a light into the patient's mouth so that you can see what you are at.

ACID BURNING. — A case occurred only the other day of a woman throwing vitriol over a man's face. This is an awful acid, which burns and eats away the flesh wherever it touches. Fortunately a policeman happened to be on the spot at the time, and knew what to do. He at once applied half warm water to which some soda had been added to wash off the acid, and then applied flour or whitening to protect the wound from the air and ease the pain as you would do for a burn.

SNAKE BITE. — Fortunately poisonous snakes are very uncommon in Canada, but if you travel much you are sure to come across them, and you ought always to know how to deal with bites from them. The same treatment does also for wounds from poisoned arrows, mad dogs, etc. Remember the poison from a bite gets into your blood and goes all through your body in a very few beats of your pulse. Therefore, whatever you do must be done immediately. The great thing is to stop the poison rushing up the veins into the body. To do this, bind a cord or handkerchief immediately round the limb above the place where the patient has been bitten, so as to stop the blood flying ˙ack to the heart with the poison. Then try and suck the poison · ut of the wound, and, if possible, cut the wound still more, to make it bleed, and run the poison out. The poison, when sucked into the mouth, does no harm unless you have a wound in your mouth. The patient should also be given stimulants, such as coffee or spirits, to a very big extent, and not allowed to become drowsy, but should be walked about and pricked and smacked in order to keep his senses alive.

[*Practise this process in make-believe.*]

GRIT IN THE EYE. — Do not let your patient rub the eye; it will only cause inflammation and swelling, and so make the difficulty of removing the grit all the greater.

If the grit is in the lower eyelid, draw down the lid as far as you can, and gently brush it out with the corner of a moistened handkerchief, or with a paint brush, or feather.

If it is under the upper lid, pull the lid away from the eyeball and push the under lid up underneath the upper one. In this way the eyelashes of the lower lid will generally clean the inside of the upper one.

Another way, which every scout must practise, is to seat your patient and stand behind him yourself with the back of his head against your chest. Lay a card, match, or any flat substance under your own thumb on the upper part of the upper eyelid, and then catch hold of the edge of the eyelid and draw it upwards over the match so that it turns inside out; gently remove the grit with a feather or wet handkerchief, and roll the eyelid down again.

If the eye is much inflamed, bathe it with lukewarm weak tea.

If the grit is firmly embedded in the eye, drop a little oil (olive or castor oil) into the lower lid; close the eye, and bandage it with a soft wet pad and bandage, and get a doctor to see it.

[*Practise above.*]

How to make eye-tweezers for removing a piece of grit from eye. Fold a piece of paper in two. With a sharp knife cut it to a point at an angle of 30°, and slightly moisten the point. Then bring it straight down over the eyeball of the patient, so that it can nip the obstruction, which it generally removes at the first attempt.

Suicides

I was once travelling in the train in Algeria, a part of North Africa which belongs to the French, and there was with me only one other passenger in the carriage, a French farmer, with whom I got into conversation. He became very communicative, and told me that if I had not come into the carriage he would by this time have been a dead man, as he had got into the train with the intention of killing himself. So I asked him about his troubles, and, as he unfolded them to me, I was able to tell him various remedies which promised success for him in the future, for he was chiefly upset over his recent failures in farming. After we had been going on for some time he quite cheered up, and told me that he was going to get out at the next station, and go back and set to work in the way suggested.

You may have opportunities of saving people who are thinking of killing themselves. The newspapers give cases of suicides almost every day, and go into details of them, because they know that so many people have a foolish love of reading horrors.

Most people at one time or other of their lives get a feeling that they will kill themselves; as a rule they get over it in a day or two, and find that it comes from nothing worse than an attack of indigestion, liver, or influenza, or from disappointment or over-anxiety; but there are others with weaker minds, who read these newspaper accounts, and brood over them till they can think of nothing else. They hug the idea to themselves, although with horror, and get panic-stricken. They think too much of their own trouble, without thinking how the rest of the world is doing.

It needs only a sympathizing friend to come along and take command of the would-be suicide, and to give him something

else to think about and to do.   You can point out that suicide
does no good to anybody; that it generally comes from something wrong with the bodily health, which makes the patient
hysterical; that he has only got to command his own mind firmly,
and the attack will pass off again.   In this way you may be
able to save lives.

[*The Salvation Army in England have now a department which
gives advice to people who are feeling inclined to kill themselves.
This past year 1125 men and 90 women have applied to their
London office alone ; and of these probably three-quarters would
have killed themselves if it had not been for the sympathy and
advice of the officers, who reasoned with them, and found for them
ways out of their difficulties.   The official returns of suicides for
the past year show a much smaller number than usual.*]

Where a man has gone so far as to attempt suicide, a scout
should know what to do with him.   In the case of a man cutting
his throat, the great point is to stop the bleeding from the artery,
if it be cut.   The artery runs from where the collar-bone and
breast-bone join, up to the corner of the jaw, and the way to
stop bleeding is to press hard with the thumb on the side of the
wound nearest to the heart, and pressure should be kept up as
hard as possible until assistance arrives.   [*Demonstrate this.*]
In a case where the would-be suicide has taken poison, give
milk and make him vomit, which is done by tickling the inside
of the throat with the finger or a feather, or pouring down his
throat a tumbler of water mixed with a tablespoonful of mustard
or salt.

In the case of hanging, cut down the body at once, taking
care to support it with one arm while cutting the cord.   Cut
the noose, loosen all tight clothing about the neck and chest.
Let the patient have as much fresh air as possible, throw cold
water on the face and chest, or cold and hot water alternately.
Perform artificial breathing, as in the case of apparently drowned
people.

A tenderfoot is sometimes inclined to be timid about handling
an insensible man or a dead man, or even seeing blood.   Well,
he won't be much use till he gets over such nonsense; the poor
insensible fellow can't hurt him, and he must force himself
to catch hold of him; when once he has done this his fears will
pass off.   And if he visits a butcher's slaughter-house he will
soon get accustomed to the sight of blood.

At Reading, not long ago, two men were severely reprimanded
by the coroner for being afraid to go and cut down a man who

had hanged himself — they only ran and fetched some one else, and so he was killed.   What would you have done had you been one of the men?

How to Carry a Patient

(See National Health Society's Manual.)

To Carry Single-handed an Unconscious Person. — Turn patient on his face.   Raise him into a kneeling posture. Kneel, and place yourself across and under him, so that his stomach rests on your right shoulder. Pass your right arm between his legs and behind his right thigh.   With your left arm draw his right hand forwards under your left, and grasp the wrist with your right hand; then raise yourself to an erect position.

[*Make scouts practise this in pairs.*]

LIFTING INSENSIBLE MAN

With Two Helpers to Carry a Conscious Person.   (See Manual.)

Stretchers may be arranged in some of the following ways:

(a) A hurdle, shutter, door, gate, covered well with straw, hay, clothing, sacking.

(b) A piece of carpet, blanket, sacking, tarpaulin, spread out, and two stout poles rolled up in the sides.   Put clothes for a pillow.

(c) Two coats, with the sleeves turned inside out; pass two poles through the sleeves; button the coats over them.

(d) Two poles passed through a couple of sacks, through holes at the bottom corners of each.

In carrying a patient on a stretcher be careful that he is made quite comfortable before you start.   Let both bearers rise together; they must walk *out of step*, and take short paces.   It should be the duty of the hinder bearer to keep a careful watch on the patient.

If the poles are short, four bearers will be necessary, one at each corner of the stretcher.

[*Practise these different methods.*]

Ambulance Badge.   For tests see page 27.

How to Practise

In practising First Aid it is a great thing to bespatter the patient with blood and mud to accustom the rescuer to the sight of it, otherwise it will often unnerve him in a real accident. Sheep's blood can be got from the butcher's shop.

Prepare a heavy smoke fire in a neighboring room or building (if possible on the first floor), while you are lecturing in the club room. Secretly arrange with two or three boys that if an alarm of fire is given they should run about frightened and try and start a panic.

Have the alarm given either by getting some one to rush in and tell you of the fire, or by having some explosive bombs fired. Then let a patrol, or two patrols, tackle the fire under direction of their patrol leaders. They should shut windows and doors. Send scouts into different parts of the building to see if the fire is spreading, and to search for people in need of rescue.

These scouts should have wet handkerchiefs over their mouths and noses. "Insensible" people (or sack dummies) should be hidden under tables, etc.

Scouts rescue them by shouldering or dragging them out and getting them down to the ground. Use jumping sheet, chute, etc.

Other parties lay and connect the hose, or make lines for passing fire buckets.

Another party revive the rescued by restoring animation. Another party form " scrum " or " fence " to help the police and fire brigade by keeping the crowd back.

Game

" DRAGGING RACE." — A line of patients of one patrol are laid out at fifty yards distance from start. Another patrol, each carrying a rope, run out, tie ropes to the patients, and drag them in. Time taken of last in. Patrols change places. The one which completes in shortest time wins. Knots must be correctly tied, and patients' coats laid out under their heads.

Books to Read

" First Aid to the Injured." Price 1s. St. John's Ambulance, St. John's Gate, Clerkenwell, London.

" What to do in Emergencies." By Dr. Andrew Wilson. Pearson, 1s.

Handbook of Instruction, published by the Royal Life Saving Society. Price 1s.

"Ambulance Illustrated," 6d. Dr. Cullen. Published by Gowman & Grey.

"Aid to the Injured or Sick." H. W. Gell, M.B. 2d.

National Health Society's Booklets, one penny, on hygiene and sanitation. National Health Society, Berners Street, Oxford Street, W.

"R.E.P." Elliman's Handbook. Apart from its advertising, it contains a very complete *vade mecum* of First Aid and Sick Room Hints and Massage. (Apply to Messrs. Elliman, Slough.)

Displays

A few ideas for life-saving displays can be taken from programmes of the Boys' Life Brigade, as suggestions. These displays are very popular both with performers and with the spectators.

A BICYCLE ACCIDENT. — Boys returning from camp. A rash bicyclist. Misfortune. Injuries attended to and patients carried away to hospital on improvised stretchers.

A GAS EXPLOSION. — Mrs. Coddles and family take a walk. They witness a terrible railway accident. Mrs. Coddles on her way home meets a friend. Maria is sent on to light the gas-stove and prepare father's tea. Father gets back from work and finds the house full of gas. Ambulance squad to the rescue. "Fireman's lift" and artificial respiration. Constable arrives on the scene. How not to look for a gas escape. Sad end of a gallant but thoughtless policeman.

FIRE DISPLAY. — Evening at No. 5 Suburbi Villas. Fire alarm. Inmates aroused. Fence formed to keep back the crowd. Escape by the chute. Arrival of fire section with jumping-sheet. Life-lines and ladders. Rescue of remaining occupants.

SYNOPSIS. — The workmen are engaged in their daily occupation when an explosion occurs, causing a fire inside the building and an exterior wall to collapse, which injures a man who happens to be passing at the time. The uninjured workmen attend to their unfortunate comrades, while others rush off for help and return with the ambulance and fire apparatus. Some of the men are rescued from the burning building by jumping from the tower into the carpet.

CHAPTER IX

PATRIOTISM

Or, Our Duties as Citizens

CAMP FIRE YARN. NO. 26

OUR EMPIRE

How it Grew — How it must be Held.

HINTS TO INSTRUCTORS

The use of a large Map of the Empire is very desirable for illustrating this. The Arnold Forster, or the Navy League, or the League of the Empire Maps are very good.

A small globe can now be bought at five cents, and a globe gives, better than any map, a tangible idea of the relative sizes and distances of countries.

Look up the local history of your neighborhood, and give your scouts the more interesting and dramatic bits of it, on the actual scene of the events if possible.

The visits to museums and armories as suggested in this book are on the lines of what is regularly done in Germany as part of the training of boys, while at school, in the history of their fatherland.

278

To Canada belongs the honor of being the largest Dominion of the British Empire. Canada is about ten times the size of the parent country, Great Britain; it is larger than Australia; one and a half times the size of India and Burma put together, twice the size of South Africa, and twice the size of East Africa, Uganda and the Soudan together. So it is a pretty big country; and it contains about a quarter of the territory of the whole Empire. At the same time, Great Britain has eight times the number of people in it. But Canada, as, indeed, the whole of the Empire, is going ahead fast, and, as the boys grow up to increase the number of men, the British Empire will be a still mightier one than it is now. If the Canadian boys rise to be men worth their salt, Canada will have the place of honor in that Empire.

How our Empire Grew

All the vast overseas Dominions did not come to Great Britain of themselves. They were won by the hard work and the hard fighting of our forefathers.

In SOUTH AFRICA we had to fight the natives for our foothold, which once gained we never let go — and though it has cost us thousands of lives and millions of money, we have got it now.

AUSTRALIA was got by our sailor-adventurers, like Captain Cook, outstripping all other nations in their plucky navigation of immense, unknown oceans.

INDIA was practically in possession of the French when Clive and Wellesley drove them out, and then in turn had to fight the hordes of fighting natives of the interior, and gradually, foot by foot, by dint of hard fighting we have won that country for our Empire.

EAST AFRICA, UGANDA, and the SOUDAN beyond Egypt, and SOMALILAND have also been fought for and won in quite recent times.

Most of North America belonged to Great Britain at one time. Sir Walter Raleigh, Captain John Smith, and other pioneers founded colonies in the southern and eastern parts, coming across the ocean in little cockleshells of ships, some of them only thirty tons, in measurement no bigger than a barge. Think of the pluck of your forefathers in tackling a voyage like that, which took them some months to carry out, with only a limited supply of food and water. And then, when they got to land with their handful of men, they had to overcome the Indians, and in some cases other European adventurers, before they could call the land their own; and for years they could hold it only by continual fighting with Indians.

Eastern Canada was similarly discovered by Jacques Cartier and a gallant lot of sailor-explorers from France, who set up French colonies along the coast and the St. Lawrence, nearly four hundred years ago. The English were near them to the south, and in Newfoundland, which had been annexed for England by Sir Humphrey Gilbert — the half-brother of Sir Walter Raleigh — in Queen Elizabeth's time.

As Britain and France in Europe were continually at war, it was natural that their respective colonies in North America could not be on the best of terms, so that friction and fighting were frequent between them, and both were brave and seasoned fighters, for they both had continually to be fighting the Indians, and thus the struggle between them was a long and tough one. Sometimes the French won, and sometimes the British.

In the fight at Ticonderoga, 3600 French, after a gallant resistance, beat off the British attack which had been also carried out with the greatest bravery by the 42nd Black Watch Highlanders. Six times the attackers tried to carry the fort by storm, and even climbed the parapet, only to be pushed back again with heavy losses, until at last they were forced to retreat with the loss of 1944 officers and men. Of the Highlanders, nearly all the officers were killed or wounded, and three quarters of the men. For its gallantry on this occasion, the regiment received from the King the title which it bears to-day, "The Royal Highlanders."

However, the French were not helped by their people in France, and in the end Nova Scotia was annexed; and finally Wolfe captured Quebec after the famous battle on the Plains of Abraham, just outside the city, in which the generals on both sides — Wolfe on the British and Montcalm on the French — were killed. And thus Canada became a British possession.

But the French Canadians, deserted by their own countrymen, like the brave and manly fellows they were, accepted their defeat in the best spirit — just like a team which has got the worst of a football match — they did not bear any grudge against their late enemies, but set to work to join with them as true Canadians, in making their country great and prosperous.

The story should never be forgotten by any Canadian boy, how the young French-Canadian, Adam Dollard, with his sixteen brave companions, fought the Iroquois on the Ottawa River, whither they had gone to meet a threatened attack on Montreal.

For seven days they held their little fort against overwhelming numbers of the Redskins, fighting untiringly day and night, until, worn out, wounded, and helpless, they were rushed by superior numbers. They never yielded, they fought it out to the very last — never saying die till they were dead. But their sacrifice was worth it. The Iroquois, with their best men killed and their pride broken, dared go no farther against such plucky settlers, and gave up all idea of further attacks on them. They retired awa; back to their own villages, with a wholesome respect for the hite men. And it was not only the French men who were brave, but the women also took their share. Madeleine de Verchères, a girl of fifteen, with one old man, one soldier, and her two small brothers, defended her father's fortified farm for a week against hostile Iroquois — chiefly by dressing herself in a soldier's helmet and showing her head at different parts of the defences so that the Indians thought the place must be full of soldiers, and were afraid to make a real attack ; and on the eighth day a relief force came and drove off the besiegers.

Thus the French-speaking Canadians not only helped in defeating the Indians, but also took the field shoulder to shoulder, with the English-speaking Canadians, for the King, against the Americans. The British Colonies to the south of Canada had had orders given them by the government at home which were distasteful to them, and they broke out in revolt and refused to be under the home government any longer, and proclaimed their independence. They tried to get the Canadians to join in their revolt, but this the Canadians were too loyal to do ! So later the Americans tried to take Canada. Then it was that the British troops came to the assistance of Canada, and the French-Canadians also joined with zest in fighting loyally for their new King and country, against the American forces.

The French-Canadians did excellent service for Canada. On one occasion, during the war of 1812–14, about one thousand of them, assisted by a band of Indians, under Colonel de Salaberry, defeated a much superior force of Americans under General Hampton, by scouting round them, hidden in the woods, and sounding bugles and firing rifles from all points, so that the Americans believed themselves surrounded by a very strong force, and consequently they retreated in the greatest hurry, never stopping till they were some twenty-five miles away from the place.

The gallant General Brock was killed in leading a charge on Queenston Heights, near Niagara, in which battle the Americans were beaten, after a severe tussle. His body was laid for a time in the house of a man named Secord. This man's wife, Laura Secord, shortly afterwards became one of the heroines·of the war, for she overheard some American officers talking about their plan for attacking and surprising a British fort at Beaver Dam, twenty miles away. So, as her husband was lying wounded and unable to get away, she herself made her way through the American outpost line by driving her cow before her as if taking her out to graze; and then slipping into the woods, — in spite of the Indians being everywhere, — she cleverly made her way to the British post under command of Lieut. FitzGibbon, and gave him such timely warning that he was able to make an ambuscade with his forty-seven men and a band of Indians, and to catch the American force as it came along. He thus captured five hundred and forty of the enemy.

Finally, the battle of Lundy's Lane, fought near Niagara by about 3000 British and Canadian troops under Generals Riall and Drummond, defeated 4000 Americans under General Brown. It was a desperate fight of seven hours during the night, at the end of which the Americans, having lost over 1000 men, retreated, leaving the Canadians victorious with a loss of 84 killed and 559 wounded.

And that was the end of the war. Canada was served by the bravery of its men and by all working loyally together — French and English-speaking Canadians and British soldiers.

And since then there have been several occasions on which they have taken the field together, both in the Red River Expedition in Manitoba, 1870, in the Nile Expedition in Egypt, 1882, and in the late South African War, 1899, in which the Canadian troops particularly distinguished themselves.

In the wars of this country, with the great rivers and vast lakes leading far into the interior, it was only natural that a great deal of fighting went on on the water. Gun-boats and small cruisers did great work on both sides, and will do again if there should unfortunately be any fighting; and true patriots should also, therefore, fit themselves for sailors' as well as soldiers' work in case it should ever be needed for defence of their country.

Sea scouts in Canada have better chances than their brother scouts elsewhere of learning boat and canoe management, swimming, and other things that go to make good sailors, and you should practise these as much as possible — for the good of your country.

It only rests with you boys of Canada — for whether you have French names or English, you are all good Canadians — to Be Prepared to do as your forefathers did before you. Train yourselves so that if at any time your country or your Empire needs your help by land or by sea, you will not be cowards or shirk your duties, but will be ready to come forward and take your share in defending your home and liberty.

How the Empire must be Held

I do not want you to suppose from this that you should think that the only way to get on is by fighting. Quite the opposite. All countries ought to try to be the best of friends, and with the scouts we can do a good deal in this way. Our law says that " a Scout is a brother to every other Scout — wherever he may be, — and a friend to everybody." Try and carry out that idea. Write to your brother scouts in Britain, in Australia, New Zealand, South Africa, and in the United States, — for the boys of the United States also are of British blood and speak the English language, — get in touch with them and make friends among them.

At the same time remember that the Roman Empire, two thousand years ago, was comparatively just as great as the British Empire of to-day. And though it had defeated any number of attempts against it, it fell at last, chiefly because the young Romans gave up soldiering and manliness altogether; they paid men to play their games for them, so that they themselves could look on without the fag of playing, just as we are doing in some of our games now. They paid soldiers to fight their battles for them, instead of learning the use of arms themselves; they had no patriotism or love for their grand old country, nor any wish to help the rest of the world to be peaceful and prosperous, and they went under with a run when a stronger nation attacked them. We must see that the same fate does not befall our Empire. And it will largely depend upon you, the younger generation of Britons that are now growing up to be the men of the Empire. Don't be disgraced like the young Romans, who lost the Empire of their forefathers by being wishy-washy slackers without any go or patriotism in them.

Play up! Each man in his place, and play the game! Your

forefathers worked hard, fought hard, and died hard, to make this Empire for you. Don't let them look down from heaven and see you loafing about with your hands in your pockets, doing nothing to keep it up.

HINTS TO INSTRUCTORS

Teach the words and choruses of —

" *The Maple Leaf.*"
" *A Patrol Song.*" (Page 303.)
" *Rule Britannia.*"
" *There's a King in the Land To-day*" ("*King of Cadonia*").
" *Hearts of Oak.*"
" *The Flag of Britain.*"
" *God Save the King.*" (Page 302.)

BOOKS TO READ

" St. Paul's Cathedral " and " Westminster Abbey," both by Mrs. Frewen Lord. 1s. each. (Clowes and Son, Charing Cross.) Excellent short histories of our famous men and their deeds.

" Travels of Captain John Smith," by Dr. Rouse. 6d. (Blackie.)

" The Story of Captain Cook," edited by John Lang. 1s. 6d. nett. (T. C. & E. C. Jack.)

" Deeds that Won the Empire," by Fitchett. 6s. (Smith, Elder and Co.)

" Heroes of Pioneering " (in America, India, Africa), by Sanderson. 5s. (Seeley.)

" Heroic Deeds Simply Told; " " Heroes and Heroines of Everyday Life as well as those of War," by Ernest Protheroe. 2s. 6d. (Newmann.)

Tableau of the Storming of Delhi

[*Scene, ruined drawbridge at Kashmir Gate. Group of officers and soldiers about to blow in the gate. Description to be read during the picture.*]

Lord Roberts, in " Forty-one Years in India," describes how the Kashmir Gate of Delhi was captured by the British troops during the Mutiny. Lieutenants Home and Salkeld, with eight sappers and a bugler of the 52nd Regiment, went forward to blow the gate open for the column to get into Delhi.

The enemy were apparently so astounded at the audacity of this proceeding that for a minute or two they offered but slight resistance.

They soon, however, discovered how small the party was and the object for which it had come, and forthwith opened a deadly fire upon the gallant little band from the top of the gateway, om the city wall, and through the open wicket.

The bridge over the ditch in front of the gateway had been destroyed, and it was with some difficulty that the single beam which remained could be crossed. Home, with the men carrying the powder bags, got over first. As the bags were being attached to the gate Sergeant Carmichael was killed, and Hav' 'ar (native Sergeant) Madhoo wounded. The rest then slipped into the ditch to allow the firing party, which had come up under Salkeld, to carry out its share of the duty.

While endeavoring to fire the charge Salkeld was shot through the leg and arm, and handed the slow match to Corporal Burgess. Burgess succeeded in his task, but fell mortally wounded as he did so.

As soon as the explosion took place, Bugler Hawthorne sounded the regimental call of the 52nd as a signal to the attacking column to advance. In this way the troops got in through the Kashmir Gate, and Delhi was taken.

Lieutenant Home was unfortunately killed within a few weeks by an accidental explosion of a mine he was firing, otherwise he would have received the Victoria Cross.

CAMP FIRE YARN. NO. 27

CITIZENSHIP

Duties of Scouts as Citizens — Duties as Citizen-soldiers — Marksmanship — Helping the Police.

Scout's Duty as a Citizen

Sir Wilfrid Laurier, the Premier of Canada, advocates the development among the rising generation of unity of spirit, and of energetic and progressive citizenship.

THERE are two ways by which every good Briton ought to be prepared to keep up our Empire.

The first is by peaceful means as a citizen.

If every citizen of the Empire were to make himself a really good, useful man, our nation would be such a blessing to the civilized world, as it has been in the past, that nobody would wish to see it broken up by any other nation.   No other nation would want to do it.   But to hold that position we must be good citizens and firm friends all round among ourselves in our great Empire.   A house divided against itself cannot stand.

Try and prepare yourself for your duties as a citizen by seriously taking up the subjects you are taught at school, not because it amuses you, but because it is your duty to your country to improve yourself.   Take up your mathematics, your history, and your language-learning in that spirit, and you'll get on.

Don't think of yourself, but think of your country and your employers.   Self-sacrifice pays all round.

Duties as Citizen-Soldier

A cuttlefish is an animal with a small, round body, and several enormously long arms, which reach out in every direction to hold on to rocks to enable it to keep its position and to get food.

Great Britain has been compared to a cuttlefish, the British Isles being the body, and the distant overseas Dominions the arms spread all over the world.

CUTTLEFISH

When any one wants to kill a cuttlefish he does not go and lop off one of its arms; the other arms would probably tackle him and hold him for the cuttlefish to eat.   No, the way to kill a cuttlefish is to suddenly stab him to the heart, and then his arms fall helpless and dead.

Well, we have powerful enemies round about us in Europe who want very much to get hold of the trade in our great manufacturing towns, and of the vast farm-lands in our Dominions and colonies. If they tried to lop off one of our Dominions, it would be like trying to lop off one of the arms of the cuttlefish. All the rest would tackle him at once, as happened in the last war in South Africa.

Their only way — and they know it — is to stab suddenly at the heart of the Empire, that is, to attack Britain. If they succeed, the whole of the Empire must fall at once, because the different parts of it cannot yet defend themselves without help from home.

For this reason every Briton who has any grit in him will Be Prepared to help in defending his country.

When Mafeking was attacked by the Boers the boys of the town made themselves into a Cadet Corps, and did very useful work in the defence. It is quite likely that Britain will some day be attacked just as Mafeking was, unexpectedly, by a large number of enemies.

If this happens, every boy in the country should be prepared to take his place and help in the defence, as those Mafeking boys did.

We don't think much of a fellow who is no good at cricket or football, and who only loafs about trying (without success) to look like a man by smoking cheap cigarettes. But we ought really not to think too much of any boy, even though a cricketer and a footballer, unless he can scout and can shoot and drill.

That is the fellow who is going to be useful if we are attacked.

I hope that before long every eleven, whether football or cricket, will also make itself a good eleven for shooting and scouting, and therefore useful for defence of our King and country when needed.

Theodore Roosevelt, late President of the United States of America, writes: —

" The qualities that make a good scout are, in large part, the qualities that make a good hunter. Most important of all is the ability to shift for one's self — the mixture of hardihood and resourcefulness which enables a man to tramp all day in the right direction, and, when night comes, to make the best of whatever opportunities for shelter and warmth may be at hand. Skill in the use of the rifle is another trait; quickness in seeing game, another; ability to take advantage of cover, yet another; while patience, endurance, keenness of observation, resolution, good nerves, and instant readiness in an emergency, are all indispensable to a really good hunter."

Roosevelt is not, like certain men I know of, a man who pays others to do his fighting for him, but, when the United States went to war with Spain about Cuba, he went to the front as a soldier — as many good Britons did in South Africa — and was of greatest value to his side because he had begun life as a scout.

So make yourselves good scouts and good rifle shots in order to protect the women and children of your country if it should ever become necessary.

Marksmanship

Lord Roberts, who has seen more of war than almost anybody alive, knows how terrible a thing it would be if war came into England, and he urges everybody to join in preventing it by

BOER BOYS SHOOTING WITH CROSSBOWS

becoming a good marksman with the rifle. Thanks to him, all those who have patriotism in them are taking it up everywhere.

The value of non-smoking again comes in, in rifle shooting. I used to smoke myself as a youngster, but I had to do some rifle shooting, and when in training I found my eyesight was better when I did not smoke. So I gave up smoking altogether, and am very glad I did.

I heard another reason given the other day for not smoking, and that was that St. Paul did not smoke. I don't suppose he did. Tobacco wasn't invented in his time.

The Boers are all good shots, and so are the Swiss. In both countries the boys begin learning marksmanship at an early age by using crossbows. They have much the same action for the firer as the rifle, since they are aimed from the shoulder and fired by pulling a trigger when the aim is taken. Boys trained with the crossbow have no difficulty in shooting accurately with a rifle directly it is put in their hands.

To be able to shoot well, a great secret is to hold your rifle properly; if it leans over a little bit to one side or the other, the bullet will fly low over to that side. Keep your left arm well underneath the rifle to support it, and hold it well into the shoulder with your left hand. The right hand should have the thumb on the top of the stock, and the forefinger as far round the trigger as you can get it; then in firing don't give a pull with your forefinger, or you will pull the aim off the target just as you fire; you should squeeze the woodwork and the trigger of the rifle between your thumb and forefinger, and that will fire it with steadiness.

Then, when your rifle has gone off, don't throw up the muzzle in a hurry, but do like all old scouts, continue to look along your sights after firing to see how much you have jumped off your aim in firing, and try and correct it next time.

Shooting at a fixed target is only a step towards shooting at a moving one, like a man. Firing at moving objects is, of course, more difficult, but more real, because you will not find a deer or an enemy as a rule kind enough to stand still while you shoot at him; he will be running and dodging behind cover, so you have to get your aim quick and to shoot quick.

The very best practice for this is always to be aiming at moving objects with your staff, using it as if it were a rifle.

Aim first at the man, then, moving the muzzle a little faster than he is moving, and fire while moving it when it is pointing where he will be a second or two later, and the bullet will just get there at the same time that he does and will hit him.

Helping the Police

Boy Scouts can be of special use in assisting the police in towns. In the first place, every Boy Scout ought to know where the fixed police points are — that is, where a constable is always stationed, apart from the policemen on their beats. He ought to know where to find the fire alarm; where is the nearest fire brigade station, and the nearest hospital or ambulance station and drug store.

On seeing an accident, if you cannot help at it you should run and inform the nearest policeman, and ask him how you can help him, whether you can call a doctor, a cab, and so on. If you hear a policeman's whistle sounding, run and offer to help him; it is your duty, as he is the King's servant. If you happen to see a door or window left open and unguarded at night, it is as well to

THE BOYS OF BULUWAYO
From "Sketches in Mafeking and East Africa."
By permission of Messrs. Smith, Elder & Co.

inform a policeman on that beat; but you should on no account attempt to do detective work by watching people or playing the spy.

If you find a lost child or lost dog, or any lost property, you should take them at once to the police station.

Of the ten cases of scouts being rewarded for helping the police the following are examples: —

Scoutmaster Crowther, of the 1st Huddersfield Troop, went to the assistance of a constable who was being attacked by a drunken couple armed with a bottle and a crutch. A crowd was looking on, but doing nothing to help the policeman.

Scoutmaster Harold Ware, 2nd Streatham, did much the same, and was thanked by the magistrate for his plucky assistance.

Patrol Leader G. Brown, 4th Southampton, saw a policeman struggling with four men, with a crowd looking on. He got in through the crowd, and managed to get the policeman's whistle and blew it for him, and so brought more police to the rescue. He himself got a kick on the knee, but he did his duty for the King right well.

Fire Brigade Scouts

The Boy Scouts can do really useful work as firemen, and have in many cases already gained great honor in that line; but, of course, it needs a bit of training and practice first: how to use a hose, turn on water, pump a manual engine, use extinguishers, put up fire ladders, pass buckets, pull down neighboring buildings, carry or drag out injured people and give them first aid, form fence to keep back the crowd.

In a battle a mob of untrained volunteers are no use compared with a small lot of well-trained soldiers obeying the orders of their leader and each knowing his duty; and it is just the same in fighting a fire. There are always crowds of people willing to help, but no one knowing exactly what to do, and in small towns where there is no fire brigade, and with no trained officer in command they are all hustling about, very busy, but getting very little real work done. But with a well-trained troop of scouts on the scene it is a very different matter. The scoutmaster takes command: one or two patrols form a fence to keep the crowd back and give room to the workers: and the patrol works the hose; another the pumping, or ladders; another the first-aid work, and so on. Or if it is evident that the burning house cannot be saved, the scoutmaster may put the troop on to water or pull down neighboring buildings in order to prevent the conflagration from spreading.

A great many troops provide themselves with a handcart, which they pull with drag ropes, and which carries chemical extinguishers, fire ladders, canvas buckets and stretchers, and when emptied of these can be used as an ambulance for fire duty.

Then in the case of forest and prairie fires Boy Scout troops can be of great service in helping the rangers, by watching and reporting outbreaks and beating them out before they become serious, or by helping inhabitants to save their homes or to get away before a fire.

The Vancouver Boy Scouts lately distinguished themselves and were thanked by the inhabitants of the district of Ocean View because they posted sentries by night and day, and succeeded in putting out two forest fires which threatened to come on to the houses there. They thus saved property valued at several thousands of dollars. Also recently at a fire in a flour mill near Toronto the Boy Scouts appeared and saved four hundred bags of flour.

Forest Fires. — When on the trail lately through the woods in Canada, I noticed that my guide, though a great devil-may-care sort of a man, was, nevertheless, most careful, on leaving a camp-ground, not only to tread out the fire, but also to get water and pour it over every bit of the firewood and surrounding ground, so that there could be no chance of its setting light to the under-brush around. This he did even if we were leaving the camp only for an hour or two. He knew the danger of carelessness in this respect, and he did merely what every true backwoods-man or scout does. A tenderfoot would probably merely kick the logs apart and leave the fire to die out of itself. That is how many a destructive forest fire is started. Sparks from locomotives or from matches thrown down by careless smokers are also other frequent causes of fires.

Boy Scouts can be of greatest use in helping the fire rangers in their work.

The Forest Commissioners of the State of Maine say that one good lookout man is worth eighty of the best patrol men. Look-out stations are established on the highest mountains in Maine; they are connected by telephone and are provided with range-finders, compass, and telescope, etc. So that the moment that the lookout man see signs of a fire, he locates it by the map and calls up the nearest forest warden.

Besides being able to keep a lookout, Boy Scout troops who are provided, as so many are, with wireless telegraph, or field telegraph, or telephone, or with flag signallers, can do most valuable work in making known the danger and in selecting men to put it out; then they can make their way through the woods, especially when they know the trails and logging roads, etc., and tackle a fire before it grows too big to deal with.

If water is scarce, good work can frequently be done by shovel-ling sand or earth on to the advancing fire, thus smothering it, gradually driving it back. But digging in the woods is often difficult work; men with shovels ought, therefore, to be accom-panied by men with picks or grub-hoes to help them.

Water, when it is not plentiful, can be made to go much further by dipping a wisp of branches in it and spraying the leaves, or beating down the fire with it.

In fighting a fire, keep to leeward of it with two or three men still farther to leeward of the working party to put out sparks, etc., flying over. Where the fire is running along the ground through grass and fallen wood, it can often be beaten back with a sack or blanket steeped in water, or with green branches. This is called a ground or " surface fire "; where the fire has a hold on the trees, it is called a " crown fire." To check a forest fire, the only way, in many cases, is to make a firebreak — that is, to clear away all timber and inflammable rubbish in a line to leeward and where the fire must presently come, and on a downhill slope if possible. An old logging trail or roadway often makes a useful firebreak. A firebreak may be made directly across the track of the fire, or diagonally across it, so as gradually to remove it down to a point where it can be easily dealt with.

[See also " Treatise on the Protection of Forests from Fire," by W. C. J. Hall, and B. L. O'Hara, published under authority of the Department of Lands and Forests, Quebec.]

HINTS TO INSTRUCTORS

Marksmanship can be taught indoors with the Blanchette Air Gun Tube. Price four guineas with Air Rifle. Targets 10d. per 100.

Crossbow. — Scouts can make their own crossbows and learn marksmanship with them.

Get leave to use or join a Miniature Rifle Club Range.

Games

" SHOOT OUT." — Two patrols compete. Targets: bottles or bricks set up on end to represent the opposing patrol. Both patrols are drawn up in line at about 20 to 25 yards from the targets. At the word " fire " they throw stones at the targets. Directly a target falls the umpire directs the corresponding man of the other patrol to sit down — killed. The game goes on, if there are plenty of stones, till the whole of one patrol is killed. Or a certain number of stones can be given to each patrol, or a certain time limit, say one minute.

" FRENCH AND ENGLISH," or " TUG OF WAR." — One patrol against another.

THE STORMING OF BADAJOZ. — One patrol (French) mounts on a very strong kitchen table or bank, and holds it against all comers. The British attack, and try to gain possession of the fortress by pulling the defenders off. Defenders may have half their number on the ground behind the "rampart." If the defenders pull a Briton over the rampart on to the ground behind, he is dead. No hitting or kicking allowed.

[Badajoz was a Spanish fortress held by 5000 French and Spaniards. It was attacked and stormed and taken by the British, who lost 3500 in the assault, on March 17, 1812.]

BOOKS TO READ

"Rules for Miniature Rifle Clubs." Secretary National Rifle Association, Bisley, Surrey.

"The Union Jack and How it was Made," by F. Wintour. 1d. (St. Dustan's Road, West Kensington, London, W.)

"A History of England," by Arnold-Forster. 5s. (Cassell.)

Play the Game!

POEM BY HENRY NEWBOLT

Scene I. — Tableau of boys playing cricket.

RECITATION

There's a breathless hush in the close to-night —
    Ten to make and the match to win —
A bumping pitch and a blinding light,
    An hour to play, and the last man in.
And it's not for the sake of a ribboned coat,
    Or the selfish hope of a season's fame,
But his captain's hand on his shoulder smote —

[*Action: The Captain steps up to the batsman, puts his hand on his shoulder, and says to him urgently —*]

"Play up! Play up! And play the game!"

Scene II. — Tableau. Soldiers in a hard-fought fight retreating — a young officer among them.

RECITATION

The sand of the desert is sodden red —
    Red with the wreck of the square that broke;
The gatling's jammed and the colonel dead,
    And the regiment blind with dust and smoke.
The river of death has brimmed its banks,
    And England's far and Honor a name,
But the voice of a schoolboy rallies the ranks —

[*Action: The young officer stands forward, pointing his sword to the enemy, and the retreating soldiers turn ready to charge with him as he cries —*]

"Play up! Play up! And play the game!"

Scene III. — A procession of all kinds of men, old ones at the head, middle-aged in centre, young ones behind — soldiers, sailors, lawyers, workmen, footballers, etc., etc. — Scotch, Irish, English, Canadian, Australian, South African — all linked hand in hand.

RECITATION

This is the word that year by year,
　　While in her place the school is set,
Every one of her sons must hear,
　　And none that hears it dare forget.
This they all with joyful mind
　　Bear through life like a torch in flame,
And falling fling to the host behind —

[*Action: The leader flings out a Union Jack and calls to the rest —*]

"Play up! Play up! And play the game!"

[*One in the centre then calls back to the juniors: "Play up! Play up! And play the game!" The smallest of the juniors steps forward and cries to the audience —*]

"PLAY UP! PLAY UP! AND PLAY THE GAME!"

CAMP FIRE YARN. NO. 28

UNITED WE STAND
DIVIDED WE FALL

Our Fleet and Army — Our Union Jack — Our Government
— Our King.

HINTS TO INSTRUCTORS

Hoist the flag and salute it every morning when in camp, and on special days get up a show, or sports, or competitions, etc., on such as King's Birthday, Empire Day, May 24th, an-

nually, or on the day of the Patron Saint of your Country. St. George, April 23rd; St. Patrick, March 17th; St. David, March 1st; St. Andrew, November 30th.

Get up tableaux, or small pageants by the scouts to illustrate scenes from history of your town, or of Britain, or of the Empire.

These interest the boys, and impress the incident upon them, and they educate spectators, and bring in money for your funds.

Take scouts to see meeting of town council and how business is carried out.

Take your scouts round and explain each statue in your town. Hold debates on questions of the day.

The British Army and Navy

THE British Navy and Army have made our Empire for us, and if it had not been for their help the Empire would have been broken up by our enemies long ago.

So we must be careful to keep those services supplied with good men, who, like the scouts, must Be Prepared to give their lives for their country at any time.

There are always members of Parliament in Great Britain who try to make the Navy and Army smaller, so as to save money. They want only to be popular with the voters, so that they and the party to which they belong may get into power. These men are called " politicians." They do not look to the good of the country. Most of them know and care very little about the Empire as a whole. If they had had their way before, the people in Great Britain should by this time have been talking French; and if they are allowed to have their way in the future, we may as well learn German or Japanese, for we shall be conquered by these.

But fortunately there are other better men in Parliament, who are called " statesmen "; these are men who look out for the welfare of the country, and do not mind about being popular or not, so long as they keep the country safe.

THE BRITISH NAVY. — Every British boy should study the Navy as much as possible, and learn the history of the different ships, and their power and guns, etc. A collection of post cards photographs of all His Majesty's ships is a very interesting one to make.

You should know the badges of rank of the officers, because it is the duty of a scout to salute officers of His Majesty's service.

Badges of rank on the sleeve or shoulder strap are these.

ADMIRAL   CAPTAIN   LIEUTENANT   SUB-LIEUTENANT

Perhaps you may like to know some facts about the dress of the sailors.

The reason they wear that flap collar on their back is a relic of the time when they wore their hair in pig-tails. The grease used to come off and spoil their jackets, so they wore big linen flaps, which could be easily taken off and washed.

They wear a black silk tie round their neck as a mark of mourning for the death of Nelson at the battle of Trafalgar.

They wear three lines of white braid to commemorate Nelson's naval victories, The Nile, Copenhagen, and Trafalgar.

They wear baggy trousers so that they can easily roll them up above their knees when they want to wade.

Soldiers and sailors tattoo their arms, with the idea that when they are killed in battle they can be identified the more easily.

THE BRITISH ARMY. — The Army is made up of —

The Regulars or Active Army, which includes infantry, cavalry, artillery, engineers, and many other branches of both white and native soldiers.

The Militia in Great Britain are to help the Regulars in time of war. The Militia exist also in most of the overseas Dominions and the colonies for their own defence. The militia of Canada is made up of volunteers who serve a certain length of time and are liable to be called upon at any time for the defence of the country.

In the army, field-marshals and generals (including major-generals and lieutenant-generals) wear cocked hats, with long white cock's feather plumes, and red tunics or black frock coats. Their swords are curved scimitars, with ivory handles. Colonels wear the uniform of their regiment with crown and star on the shoulder strap, or, in khaki, on the cuff; majors, one crown, captains, three stars; lieutenants, two stars.

You can tell what wars soldiers or sailors have been in by the colors of their medal ribbons. Here are the badges of rank of officers in the army.

FIELD-MARSHAL   GENERAL   LIEUT.-GENERAL   MAJOR-GENERAL   BRIG.-GENERAL

COLONEL   LIEUT.-COL.   MAJOR   CAPTAIN   LIEUT.   2ND LIEUT.

THE ROYAL NORTH-WEST MOUNTED POLICE

The best thing among many good things which I have seen in Canada was the Royal North-West Mounted Police.

These splendid fellows are the best type of the true scout that can be found in the world.

Each one of them has to be partly soldier, partly policeman. Sent out to distant frontier posts, either alone or with one other, he has to be able to look after himself either in the Arctic winter or in the blazing summer; he has to be a good horseman, and at the same time able to manage a canoe, or a dog-sleigh. And as he has to tackle rough customers in mining-camps, or to keep order among Indians, or to arrest horse-thieves and other bad characters, he has to be plucky, strong, and determined— equal in fact to three or four ordinary men, and intent on doing his duty however difficult or dangerous, simply because it *is* his duty. But the Mounted Police have, in so very many cases, proved this, that every criminal knows it is useless to resist or to try to escape when the constable appears upon the scene; he feels he is a " gone coon."

Our Flag

Scouts will always salute the colors (or standard) of a regiment when they pass. There are generally two such standards, one the " King's Color," the other the " Regimental Color."

Men-of-war carry a pennant, *i.e.*, a long thin flag like a whi lash. You may remember that the Dutch fleet under Va. Tromp, after defeating ours, carried a broom at their mastheads, to show that they had swept us off the seas. But when we shortly after defeated them we put up a whip at the masthead to show that we had whipped the enemy, and this whip has been carried ever since by men-of-war.

The Royal Navy flies the White Ensign; no one else is allowed to except yachts belonging to the Royal Yacht Squadron. The White Ensign is a white flag with the Red Cross of St. George on it and a Union Jack in the corner. It is flown at the stern of the ship, a small Union Jack at the bow.

The mercantile navy flies the Red Ensign; or if the captain of the ship belongs to the Royal Reserve, the ship flies a Blue Ensign.

The Army and Government buildings fly the Union Jack. Private houses and individuals should fly only the Red Ensign.

The Royal Standard, which shows the Lions of England, the Harp of Ireland, and the Lion of Scotland, is flown only when the King or Queen is present.

The Union Jack is the national flag of the British Empire, and is made up of the flag of St. George, a red cross on a white ground. In 1606 King James I added to it the banner of Scotland, which was a blue flag with a white St. Andrew's Cross diagonal, that is, from corner to corner. In 1801, the banner of St. Patrick of Ireland was added to the flag; St. Patrick's Cross was a red diagonal cross on a white ground, so that the flag now means the union of England, Ireland, and Scotland.

But there is a right way and a wrong way of putting it up, which all of you ought to know and understand, because so very frequently one sees it hoisted the wrong way up, which literally means that you are in distress; but people put it that way by mistake or from ignorance. You will notice that the red diagonal arms of the flag have a narrow white band on one side of them and a broad one on the other. Well, the broad one should be to the top of the flag on the side nearest to the flag-post, that is, the "hoist" of the flag, and towards the bottom of the flag in the loose end, or, as it is called, the "fly" of the flag (see picture, page 19).

It was called a "Jack," either from "Jacques," the nickname of King James I, who first started it, or, more probably, from the "jack" or "jacket" which the knights used to wear over their armor to show which nation they belonged to. The English knights wore a white Jack with the red cross of St. George upon it. This was also their flag.

If the flag is flown upside down, it is a signal of distress. If it is half-mast, it is a sign of mourning.

On going on board a man-of-war, when you reach the quarter-deck — that is, the upper stern deck — always salute the ensign.

In the Navy flags are hoisted at eight o'clock and saluted. With the Boy Scouts when in camp the same practice will be observed.

Of course you will always rise and salute or take off your hat on hearing the National Anthem played.

The 24th of May, the birthday of the great Queen Victoria, is "Empire Day," and we all hoist the flag and salute in special honor of the Empire on that occasion.

Remember, it is going to be the business of every one of you to keep the old flag flying, even if you have to bleed for it — just as your forefathers did before you.

We have all got to die some day; a few years more or less of our own lives don't make much matter in the history of the world, but it is a very great matter, if by dying a year or two sooner than we should otherwise do from disease, we can help to save the flag of our country from going under.

Therefore think it over — Be Prepared to die for your country if need be; so that when the moment arrives you may charge home with confidence, not caring whether you are going to be killed or not.

If your enemy sees that you are bent on either killing or being killed, the probability is that he won't wait to oblige you.

Don't merely talk, as some gas-bags do, about shedding the last drop of your blood for your country — the difficulty with them, when the time comes, is to get them to shed the first drop of their blood.

The Union Jack stands for something more than only the union of England, Ireland, and Scotland — it means the union of Great Britain with all the Dominions and colonies across the seas; and also it means closer comradeship with our brothers in those distant lands, and between ourselves at home. We must all be bricks in the wall of that great edifice, — the British Empire, — and we must be careful that we do not let our differences of opinion on politics or other questions grow so strong as to divide us. We must still stick shoulder to shoulder as Britons if we want to keep our present leading position among the nations; and we must make ourselves the best men in the world for honor and goodness to others so that we may DESERVE to keep that position.

> " Unite the Empire; make it stand compact,
> Shoulder to shoulder let its members feel
> The touch of British Brotherhood, and act
> As one great nation — strong and true as steel."

Our Government

Of all the different kinds of government in the world the government of Great Britain and that of the great Dominions is the easiest and fairest for everybody.

Some countries have kings who make their laws for them, whether the people like the laws or not; other countries make their own laws and have as their head one elected by themselves at certain intervals for a term of years. But a government like our own, under a good King, is far better for all.

In Great Britain the House of Commons is made up of men chosen by the people to make known their wants and to suggest remedies, and the House of Lords sees whether these are equally good for all and for the future of the country; and what they recommend the King makes into law.

In Canada the King is represented by the Governor-General, who holds office usually for five years. The House of Commons is elected by and represents the whole people, while the Senate is appointed by the Governor-General, on the advice of his cabinet. You will have learned from your study of history in school just how your country is governed; the more you know about the making of our system of government, the better citizen you will be when you grow up.

And you will, many of you, be inclined, when you become voters, to belong to one or other of the great political parties, whichever your father or friends belong to. I should not, if I were you. I should hear what each party has to say. If you listen to one party you will certainly agree that that is the only right one, the rest must all be wrong. But if you go and listen to another, you will find that after all that one is quite right, and the first one wrong.

The thing is to listen to them all, and don't be persuaded by any particular one. And then be a man, make up your mind and decide for yourself which you think is best for the country and the future of the Empire — not for some two-for-a-cent little local question — and vote for that one so long as it works the right way, namely, for the good of the country.

Many people get led away by some new politician with some new extreme idea. Never believe in one man's idea till it has been well considered from all points of view. Extreme ideas are seldom much good; if you look them up in history you will see almost always that they have been tried before somewhere.

More thrift rather than a change of government will bring money to all. And a strong united Empire, where all are helpful and patriotic, will bring us power, peace, and prosperity such as no visionary politician's remedies could do.

Our King

The word "Empire" comes from an old Roman word "Imperium," which means "well-ordered rule."

And the title "Emperor," or ruler of the Empire, comes from the Roman word "Imperator." The King signs himself "R.I.," which means "Rex," or King of Great Britain and of the British Dominions beyond the Seas, and "Imperator," or Emperor of India.

"Imperator" comes from two Roman words, "Im" and "Parere," which together mean "To prepare for" — that is, to BE PREPARED. An Emperor is one who has to be prepared to face any difficulty or danger that may threaten the country.

Scouts have in the same way to BE PREPARED to *help* their country in any difficulty or danger; and we are therefore all working in the same direction as our King, for the good of our country.

God Save the King

God save our lord, the King,
Long live our noble King,
  God save the King!
Send him victorious,
Happy and glorious,
Long to reign over us,
  God save the King!

Thy choicest gifts in store
On him be pleas'd to pour,
 Long may he reign.
May he defend our laws,
And ever give us cause
To sing with heart and voice,
 God save the King!

The Song of Canada

"THE MAPLE LEAF FOR EVER"

ALEXANDER MUIR

In days of yore, from Britain's shore,
 Wolfe, the dauntless hero, came
And planted firm Britannia's flag
 On Canada's fair domain;
Here may it wave, our boast and pride,
 And join in love together,
The Lily, Thistle, Shamrock, Rose entwine
 The Maple Leaf for ever.

The Maple Leaf, our Emblem dear,
 The Maple Leaf for ever,
 God save our King, and Heaven bless
 The Maple Leaf for ever.

On Merry England's far-famed land
 May kind Heaven sweetly smile;
God bless Old Scotland evermore,
 And Ireland's Emerald Isle;
Then swell the song both loud and long
 Till rocks and forest quiver.
God save our King, and Heaven bless
 The Maple Leaf for ever.

The Maple Leaf, our Emblem dear.

A Patrol Song

BY RUDYARD KIPLING

These are *our* regulations —
There's just one law for the Scout,
And the first and the last, and the present and the past,
And the future and the perfect is " Look out!"
 I, thou, and he, look out!
 We, ye, and they, look out!

Though you didn't or you wouldn't,
Or you hadn't or you couldn't;
You jolly well *must* look out !

Look out when you start for the day
    That your kit is packed to your mind,
There's no use going away
    With half of it left behind.
Look out that your laces are tight,
    And your boots are easy and stout,
Or you'll end with a blister by night.
    (*Chorus*) *All* patrols look out !

Look out for the birds of the air,
    Look out for the beasts of the field ;
They'll tell you how and where
    The other side's concealed.
When the blackbird bolts from the copse,
    And the cattle are staring about,
The wise commander stops
    And (*Chorus*) All patrols look out !

Look out when your front is clear,
    And you feel you are bound to win ;
Look out for your flank and your rear —
    For that's where surprises begin.
For the rustle that isn't a rat,
    For the splash that isn't a trout,
For the boulder that may be a hat,
    (*Chorus*) All patrols look out !

Look out when your temper goes
    At the end of a losing game ;
And your boots are too tight for your toes,
    And you answer and argue and blame.
It's the hardest part of the law,
    But it has to be learnt by the Scout —
For whining and shirking and " jaw,"
    (*Chorus*) All patrols look out !

Otherwise : —
    We've no regulations —
    There's just one law for the Scout,
    And the first and the last, and the present and the past,
    And the future and the perfect is " Look out ! "
                    etc., etc.,

Note. — *Music can be obtained from Headquarters' Office.*

INSTRUCTION OF BOY SCOUTS

"The Boyhood of Raleigh," after Sir J. Millais.
From such instruction is character formed.

CHAPTER X

SCOUTING FOR BOYS

The Need — The Aim — The Method — The Organization
— Hints to Scoutmasters.

What is meant by " Scouting "

SCOUTING does not, as some people seem to think, necessarily mean soldiering and fighting; there is the form of peace-scouting which includes the work and attributes of pioneers of civilization. Those men who are working in the farthest corners of the earth reclaiming it for their race, whether as explorers, missionaries. hunters, or police — these men are the scouts of the nation. To carry out their work they have to be resourceful and self-reliant, to be able to endure climate, dangers, and difficulties with cheerfulness, to be helpful to each other as well as self-helpful; to be loyal to their employer or government; to do their work far from applause or reward simply because it is their work — in a word, they have to be *men* in the best sense of the word, that is, citizens of character, if they are going to do any good.

Character-Training for Nation Needed

The success of a nation does not depend so much upon her fighting powers as upon her " character," upon her commercial worth and integrity. If she can make herself indispensable on these lines to other nations, she will be great and prosperous.

At the same time, it does not do for a nation to be unprepared to assert itself should any danger arise to threaten its liberty. A nation that is unprepared to defend itself is guilty of the crime of inviting aggression, and deserves to be wiped out.

Every people that ever rose to be a nation in history did so by force of arms, and every nation that in its prosperity lapsed into the luxury of cities, or into the whirl of money making, and forgot to retain its hardihood and to maintain its power of self-defence on an adequate standard, fell as such nations always will fall, under the attack of a stronger foe, or from the rising of traitors within. So that the " character " required for a nation is that of energetic industry and integrity coupled with a strong and practical patriotism.

But the character of a nation is that of the individuals who compose it. Similarly if an individual wishes to succeed in life, it is not by his physical power that he will gain his end, but by his " character." Take the case of any great man of the country — it was not his muscle nor merely a knowledge of the school arts of reading, writing, and arithmetic which got him on, but his own individual energy, intelligence, and self-discipline, and his practical help given to his country. Incidentally, the training of a scout or frontiersman is conducive to this. As instances which occur at the moment, take Samuel Champlain, George Washington, Abraham Lincoln, Theodore Roosevelt, Lord Strathcona, among many others; all of them were frontiersmen.

So if you want to make your nation great, or if you want only to make your boys great, the process is the same — train the future men in the development of "character." This is the most important step in their education, and yet in the schools, for one reason or another, it is at present rather neglected.

Again, in building a new nation, you have to take many ingredients, men of all countries, classes, and creeds, and unite them by a common tie and common spirit, by a patriotic loyalty, such as will bind them to sacrifice their own ends for the good of the whole in a national crisis.

Otherwise — well, a house divided against itself cannot stand.

What is the present process for instilling these two important principles into the nation?   Presumably it must be done through the boy: the old dog cannot be taught new tricks.   Theodore Roosevelt truly says: " If you are going to do anything permanent for the average man you have got to begin with him before he is a man.   The chance of success lies in working with the boy, not with the man."

John Wanamaker says: " Save a man and you save one person: save a boy and you save a whole multiplication table."

So the boy is the important medium for the process.

But what are we doing for the boy?   In the great cities, in the midst of a crowd, with his electric light, his ready water, his restaurants, his trolley-cars, his doctors, and nurses, a man has no need of resourcefulness or self-reliance, he can — and does — drift through life entirely supported by others.   Out in the West, it is true, there is the strenuous life to be lived, and here the boys become self-reliant and independent from their earliest years.   The only danger is of their becoming too much so in many cases — having no idea of discipline or unselfishness, patriotism or chivalry.   These are all matters of education.   Yet the schools do not do very much to meet them.   Instruction in the three R's and the waving of a flag on public holidays are not all that is needed.

Again in the larger cities is beginning that evil which is becoming a canker in the European centres, namely the horde of unemployed and unemployable.   This army of wasters is largely recruited by lads who have been employed as boys in what are termed " Blind Alley " occupations—that is, in occupations such as messenger, van, and newspaper boys, which while giving him a wage until he is about eighteen lead to nothing afterwards, and do not train him in any handicraft that will be useful to him as a man: consequently a very large percentage of these boys drift into the waste product of modern civilization and become unemployed and unemployable.

The boys of the nation are full of enthusiasm and spirit, and require only that their heads be turned the right way to become good, useful citizens.   This splendid material is being allowed to run to waste — nay, worse than that, it is allowed to become harmful to the nation, simply for want of education, for want of a hand to guide the boys at the crisis of their lives when they are at the crossroads where their futures branch off for good or for evil.

They in their turn are to become the fathers of more boys,

whom they are supposed to train up on right lines for good citizenship, when in reality they have not themselves the haziest idea of the meaning of the term. This is not entirely their fault.

The present authorized scheme of education in our schools includes plenty of bookwork, but not sufficient attention is paid to the development of the quality that counts, namely, *character*, which after all is of the first importance. Many hundreds of boys in our great cities, after an education in reading sufficient to enable them to devour the horrors of the latest sensational literature, and in arithmetic to help them to make their bets, are being left to drift into the ranks of the " hooligans " and "wasters" with little attempt to stay them. They receive no teaching in resourcefulness, chivalry, thrift, citizenship, or patriotism.

(*a*) How is it possible to apply a remedy for this?
(*b*) What form can the remedy take?
(*c*) How can a private individual help?

It is useless to attempt much with the present adult wasters.

(*a*) The remedy must be applied to the rising generation.
(*b*) Its aim should be to instill "character" into the men of the future. By " character " is meant a spirit of manly self-reliance and of unselfishness — something of the *practical* Christianity which (although they are Buddhists in theory) distinguishes the Burmese in their daily life.
(*c*) Where the individual citizen can help in this great national work is shown by what has already been accomplished in this direction by the Boys' Brigade, Young Men's Christian Association, Church Lads' Brigade, and other numerous societies of the same kind. Yet good as their work has been, with all their effort they till only a portion of the field. They hold some 270,000 boys; but what is that out of the several millions who need their help?

That they do not influence a greater number is due to: —
Want of amalgamation of effort or mutual co-operation among the different societies.
Difficulty in getting enough young men to take up the work of training the boys.
Difficulty of attracting the boys and of maintaining their interest after they have got them.

One Remedy and its Application

These difficulties seemed to be remediable in some particulars, and induced me to suggest the scheme of "Scouting for Boys" as a step to meeting them, since being applicable to all these societies it might, by its common adoption, form a bond between them; by reason of its practical and sporting tendency and absence of red tape it might appeal to a wider field of possible instructors; and, above all, by its variety of attractions it would appeal directly to the boys themselves — even to the worst, the "hooligans."

Scoutcraft includes the qualities of the frontiersman, such as resourcefulness, endurance, pluck, trustworthiness, etc., plus the chivalry of the knights: these attributes, both moral and physical, are held up before the boys, in a practicable form, for imitation and daily practice.

We look at the training from the boys' point of view and shape it accordingly: and the organization is framed to meet the instructor's wants as far as possible by decentralizing authority, and giving local support without irritating supervision, red tape, or expense.

Training. — The key to successful education is not so much to *teach* the pupil as to get him to *learn* for himself. The subject to be instilled must be made to appeal, and you must lure your fish with a succulent worm, not with a bit of hard, dry biscuit.

Our system of instruction is first to get the boy to develop his own resourcefulness, self-reliance and individuality by means of scoutcraft ; then to pass tests in various qualifications, handicrafts, etc., such as are likely to be of value to him in his future career. Thus we have badges for electricians, horsemen, farmers, gardeners, musicians, carpenters, and so on (see page 26), in addition to the actual scouts' badges of first and second class, testifying to their capabilities in swimming, pioneering, cooking, woodmanship, boat management, and other points of manliness and handiness. We encourage personal responsibility in the boy for his own physical development and health; and we trust in his honor and expect him to do a good turn to some one every day. Further we teach the scouts personal self-sacrifice for others in saving life; also collective public duty to their country in working their troops as fire brigades, forest rangers, ambulance corps, police signal corps, seamen, etc.

Our training is non-military, even the ordinary drill employed by so many boys' leagues being reduced to the lowest necessary limits, since drill tends to destroy individuality, and one of our main aims is to develop the personal individual character.

As regards religion we are *inter-denominational;* we do not assume or interfere with the prerogative of parents or pastors by giving religious *instruction*, but we insist on the observance and practice of whatever form of religion the boy professes, and the main duty impressed upon him is the daily practice of chivalry and of helpfulness to others.

We are also non-political.

Organization

On page ii will be seen a diagram of our organization, which shows that the movement is regulated by a representative governing Council, under the highest patronage, to which a Headquarters Committee is responsible for the general administration. Responsibility for local administration is delegated to each country or Dominion, with a strong and representative council in each province or county, and with local associations in each town or centre.

Local Associations. — If it is desired to raise Boy Scouts in any centre of population where nothing has been previously done, the first step to be taken is the formation of a " Boy Scout Association," and a meeting should be arranged at which some leading citizen should be invited to take the chair. Any scoutmasters already appointed and representatives from the different boys' organizations working in the district should be invited to attend, as well as the school-teachers, clergy of the different denominations, and other gentlemen who are interested in work among boys. Particulars should be sent to the Secretary at Headquarters before the date is fixed, in order that one of the Headquarter Staff may attend, if possible.

The Association when formed should be constituted as follows: —

(*a*) A President, Vice-Presidents, Hon. Secretary and Hon. Treasurer, elected annually in October. (Where necessary the Association may appoint an Executive Committee, to whom its duties may be delegated, but a paid Secretary is the best means to success.)

Members

(*b*) Scoutmasters, representatives from existing boys' organizations, and gentlemen interested in the Movement who are willing to serve, on invitation.

The Duties of the Association will be: (*a*) To nominate suitable persons to act as scoutmasters, and recommend them to the District or Provincial Commissioner for the Chief Scout's Warrant.

(*b*) To register all scoutmasters, troops, and patrols in the district. No scoutmaster, troop, or patrol shall be recognized which is not so registered.

(*c*) Generally to supervise and encourage the movement in the district with the least possible amount of interference with the independence and initiative of the troops and patrols.

(*d*) To work in cordial co-operation with other boys' organizations in the district.

(*e*) To be responsible for the granting of all scout badges and awards in its district. Applications for these should be made to the Hon. Secretary, to whom alone they will be issued by Headquarters.

(*f*) To suspend any scoutmaster or assistant scoutmaster, or to withhold recognition from any troop, patrol, or scout within its area for grave dereliction of duty, unsuitability, or for disloyalty to the rules of the scout movement. Any case of suspension should be reported to the Secretary at Headquarters without delay.

(*g*) To hold periodical meetings. (A suitable quorum should be arranged, according to local conditions.)

(*h*) If local by-laws are adopted, to forward two copies to Headquarters, the one for filing, the other for approval and return.

A warrant giving the Association authority over its district is issued by Headquarters.

The Boy Scout scheme is for boys of every denomination and creed, and in order to enlist the sympathy of persons of all shades of opinion, the Association should be one which is representative of all parties and denominations, but at the same time troops may be raised and managed by any recognized existing organizations, and the membership may, if desired, be confined to boys connected with that organization. Such troops are affiliated to the Local Scout Association, and agree to conform generally to the principles laid down in the handbook, including the tests for badges, and the scoutmasters require only to have their appointment confirmed by the Local Scout Association, who are not empowered to interfere with the internal working of these troops, provided that they conform to the general principles of the movement.

Finance. — The spirit of the movement is that on the part of the boys themselves money should be earned and not solicited.

Local Associations will not be required to contribute towards the Central or Headquarters Funds, but they should be self-supporting, the small sums necessary for working expenses and for obtaining camp and equipment being raised by work of the boys and by local subscriptions.

All subscriptions and donations should be paid in to the Treasurer of the Local Association, and not to any individual scoutmaster. There is no objection to troops paying a small registration fee to their Local Association, if so desired.

A Scout Council is appointed for each province, partly nominated by the Headquarter's Executive and completed by representatives from Local Associations.

The Duties of the Provincial Scout Council will be: —

(a) To promote generally the welfare of the Boy Scout movement in the Province, and to arrange for harmonious coöperation with all the existing organizations for boys.

(b) To coördinate the policy of the Local Associations so as to secure uniformity on broad lines throughout the area as regards methods and ideals, without interference with the independence and initiative of such Associations and the troops under them. (Where necessary the Provincial Scout Council may appoint an Executive Committee from amongst its members, to whom the above duties may generally be delegated.)

Commissioners. — In each Province a Commissioner will be appointed by the Executive Committee of the Headquarters Council as its representative and, where necessary, District Commissioners, under the Provincial Commissioner. All Provincial and District Commissioners will be ex-officio members of the Scout Council of the Province to which they are appointed.

Warrants to Provincial and District Commissioners over the signature of the Chief Scout will be issued on application.

The Duties of a Scout Commissioner are : —

(a) To inspect troops and patrols, and advise how to conduct them on the lines laid down in " The Canadian Boy Scout."

(b) To test badge-wearers in their knowledge of their subjects.

(c) To secure the harmonious coöperation of all Associations and scoutmasters in the district.

(d) To be the concurring authority for the recommendation of Local Associations for the issue and withdrawal of scoutmasters' warrants before transmission to Headquarters.

(e) To foster and encourage the movement generally through the district.

Scoutmasters. — All scoutmasters receive warrants signed by the Chief Scout, for which they have to be recommended by the Local Association and by the Commissioner, after serving three months' probation in the rank. These warrants are the property of the Chief Scout, and are to be returned at his request.

The Qualifications for Scoutmasters are as follows : —

(a) A general knowledge of the Handbook " The Canadian Boy Scout," especially the " Scout Law."

(b) A full appreciation of the religious and moral aim underlying the practical instruction all through the scheme of Scouting.

(c) Personal standing and character such as will ensure a good moral influence over boys, and sufficient steadfastness of purpose to carry out the work with energy and perseverance.

(d) Age not less than twenty.

(e) Ability to obtain the use of some sort of club-room for Scout meetings.

Scoutmasters must have at least one assistant scoutmaster to work with them, to ensure continuity, and must have trained their troops for at least three months before warrants will be issued to them.

These qualifications apply equally to assistant scoutmasters, except that the age may be from eighteen years.

Issue of Badges. — Tenderfoot, Second Class, and Cyclist Badges are granted by the Association on the recommendation of scoutmasters. Tests for other badges must be passed before two qualified and, if possible, independent examiners approved by the Association.

Applications for badges will be made by Secretaries of Associations direct to the Secretary at Headquarters.

Badges may be withdrawn from the holder at any time by the Association on recommendation of the scoutmaster or Commissioner for neglect to maintain his efficiency, half the cost of the same being refunded to him.

Reports. — Secretaries of Associations are requested to send in to the Commissioner on the 1st of November very brief reports made up to the 30th September of the number of Scouts and the progress made generally in the district, and these reports will be forwarded to Headquarters on or before the 30th of November.

Titles. — The use of titles and terms denoting naval or military rank, such as Captain, Lieutenant, Sergeant, etc., etc., are not authorized, and should not be used.

RESULTS

The Boy Scout movement has grown up of itself out of the suggestion given by the book " Scouting for Boys," and has spread to almost every corner of the British Isles and in the chief centres in the British Oversea Dominions, as well as to most foreign countries.

Its principles appear to appeal to boys of every class and to be adaptable to every country, and this promises a closer bond of sympathy and comradeship between Great Britain and the other portions of the Empire (as well as locally between Boers and British in South Africa, and between French and English-speaking Canadians in Canada); and also between the British Empire and other nations in the near future, such as cannot but be conducive to peace in the world.

The good work of the Scouts at the Stoats Nest Railway disaster, and at the fatal accident to Mr. Tomkinson, M.P., recently, etc., are instances of many similar cases of their public utility. The gratuitous work done by them on the occasion of the funeral of King Edward in putting up the street decorations and taking them down again afterwards, and as ambulance detachments in tending distressed people in the crowd that day, tend to illustrate the fact that they realize that it is their duty to do something for their country or fellow-subjects when occasion offers — without looking for reward. The cases of saving life by Boy Scouts which have been rewarded in two and a half years amount to about one hundred and twenty, half of which were for rescuing people from drowning.

From a chief constable, who states that the Boy Scouts in one town are worth twenty extra constables to him, down to an old woman who has had her fuel brought to her daily by scouts, letters of appreciation come in from all parts.

A very encouraging testimony comes from those in touch with Boy Scouts, such as parents, school-teachers, etc., as to the good and immediate effect of the training upon boys who come within its influence. The Education Committee of Southport, in their annual report, state: —

" Of the boys leaving the school this year 5.2 per cent belonged to that valuable organization, the Boys' Brigade.

" The Boy Scouts included 44 boys leaving the school (i.e., 11 per cent) and 19 boys aged 10 (6.4 per cent). Membership of this institution confers very great physical and disciplinary benefits upon the boys, and every possible encouragement to join it should be given by those who can influence them."

The credit for this rapid attainment of results is undoubtedly due in the first instance to the scoutmasters, *i.e.*, men who have taken up the work and who have carried it out with the great difficulties incidental to first organization of training the boys. And credit is also due to those who have more recently taken up the duties of Commissioners and Local Presidents, among whom appear many of the best-known names in the country.

His late Majesty King Edward took the greatest interest in the aims and methods of the movement, and showed his appreciation of it both by honoring the founder, and by commanding a parade of the Boy Scouts before him during the summer, and also by throwing open to their particular use certain of the royal parks. The removal by death of his kindly encouragement has been a severe blow to the movement.

But His Majesty King George has graciously shown his similar interest, and has confirmed this by becoming our Patron.

Hints to Scoutmasters

The suggestion has been made that, since scouting has "caught on" with the boys themselves, it might with proper organization form an instrument for education   every boy in the Empire.

Whether it does so or not depends entirely on our getting men to come forward to act as scoutmasters in every district, with that aim constantly before them, namely, of roping in everything in the shape of a boy that is not already under some influence for good.

The Duties of a Scoutmaster

By our rules a scoutmaster has to serve three months on probation before he is recommended for his warrant. The object of this is mainly to give him the opportunity of seeing whether he finds scouting work is after all what he expected.

It so often happens in similar organizations that a man comes in full of high hopes and ideals, and then finds that he cannot fall in with the views of those in authority, or that after all he has not the gift of dealing with boys, and so on.

The attitude of the scoutmaster is of greatest importance, since his boys take their character very much from him; it is

incumbent upon him, therefore, to take this wider view of his
position than a merely personal one, and to be prepared to sink
his own feelings very much for the good of the whole.   That is
true discipline.

This is just the difficult problem of the age — the main danger
to our nation is that we are not sufficiently self-disciplined, we
put our personal views on a higher plane than the good of the
state; this failing is one which we want to reform when training
the rising generation.   Our training is largely by example.

A would-be scoutmaster, therefore, who finds himself unable
to get on with his boys, or unable to discipline himself to work
in harmony with his local committee or other authority, will do
the right thing by resigning his post before his attitude does
harm to the boys.

How to catch Our Boys

I do not in these " Hints " propose to teach those who perhaps know more than I do ; and, therefore, I address them only
to those who have had no previous practice in teaching boys, or
who wish for explanations with which to meet criticisms or inquiries into our scheme.   They are merely a few notes from
my own small experience in that line, and tend to explain some
of the arrangements of details in the Handbook.

When you are trying to get boys to come under good influence
I have likened you to a fisherman wishful to catch fish.

If you bait your hook with the kind of food that you like
yourself, it is probable that you will not catch many—certainly
not the shy, game kind of fish.   You therefore use as bait the
food that the fish likes.

So with boys; if you try to preach to them what you consider
elevating matter, you won't catch them.   Any obvious " goody-
goody" will scare away the more spirited among them, and those
are the ones you want to get hold of.   The only way is to hold
out something that really attracts and interests them.   And I
think you will find that scouting does this.

You can afterwards season it with what you want them to have.

To get a hold on your boys you must be their *friend;* but
don't be in too great a hurry at first to gain this footing until
they have got over their shyness of you.   Mr. F. D. How, in
his " Book of the Child," sums up the right course in the following story : —

" A man whose daily walk led him down a certain dingy street

saw a tiny boy with grimy face and badly developed limbs
playing with a banana-skin in the gutter. The man nodded to
him — the boy shrank away in terror. Next day the man
nodded again. The boy had decided there was nothing to be
afraid of, and spat at the man. Next day the little fellow only
stared. The day after he shouted " Hi ! " as the man went on.
In time the little fellow smiled back at the greeting which he now
began to expect. Finally, the triumph was complete when the
boy — a tiny chap — was waiting at the corner and seized the
man's fingers in his dirty little fist. It was a dismal street, but
it became one of the very brightest spots in all that man's life."

" Be Prepared "

The first essential for carrying out this training is to put yourself in the boy's place, look at it from his point of view — present
your subject to him as he would like to have it, and so get him *to
teach himself* without your having to hammer it into him.

Then remember that your own character soon reflects itself in
your boys. If you are impatient, they too become impatient,
and all goes awry.

But as you come to teach these things, you will very soon find
(unless you are a ready-made angel) that you are acquiring them
yourself all the time.

You must Be Prepared for disappointments at first, though
you will as often as not find them outweighed by unexpected
successes.

You must from the first Be Prepared for the prevailing want
of concentration of mind on the part of boys, and if you then
frame your teaching accordingly, I think you will have very few
disappointments. Do not expect boys to pay great attention
to any one subject for very long, until you have educated them
to do so. You must meet them half-way, and not give them
too long a dose of one drink. A short, pleasing sip of one
kind, and then off to another, gradually lengthening the sips till
they become steady draughts.

Thus a formal lecture on the subject which you want to
practise very soon palls on them, their thoughts begin to wander,
and they get bored because they have not learned the art of
switching their mind where they want it to be, and *holding it
there*.

This making the mind amenable to the will is one of the
important inner points in our training.

For this reason it is well to think out beforehand each day what you want to say on your subject, and then bring it out a bit at a time as opportunity offers — at the camp fire, or in intervals of play and practice, not in one long set address.

You will find the lectures in the Handbook broken up into sections for this purpose.

Frequent practical demonstrations and practices should be sandwiched in between the sections of the lectures to hold the attention of the boys and to drive home your theory.

A scoutmaster has a free hand given him to train his boys in his own way. The efficiency badges give scope and variety for useful training, and though many a scoutmaster may feel diffident about his power personally to give such varied instruction, he can generally obtain the temporary service of a friend or expert to help.

Many scoutmasters also specialize the work of their troops or patrols: thus one may have a Fire Brigade, Sailor, or Cadet troop, or patrols respectively of Signallers, Missioners, Telegraphists, Ambulance men, and so on.

Badges of Efficiency

These are established with a view to developing in each boy the taste for hobbies or handicrafts, one of which may ultimately give him a career and not leave him hopeless and helpless on going out into the world.

It is not with any idea of puffing them that I want to point out to scoutmasters that the *Boy Scouts' Headquarters Gazette* (monthly) and *The Scout* (weekly) are my only means of addressing myself directly to scoutmasters and to the boys in detailed continuation of what I have said in this book, but which space precludes me from inserting between its covers.

The Importance of a Clubroom

Half the battle is to get a room lent for certain nights in the week, or hired as a club for the scouts, even if they consist only of a patrol in the village.

It must be well lit and well ventilated, to prevent depression and boredom. Pictures of incidents (not landscapes or old portraits) help to make attraction.

A *bright* fire in winter.

Interesting illustrated books and magazines.

These can generally be got, furniture, games, etc., being given in the first instance by well-wishers.

A coffee-bar, commencing on the smallest lines, will generally succeed, and if carefully managed may develop a regular income for the upkeep of the clubroom.

The scouts themselves must do the cleaning and decorating, and making furniture.

Discipline and good order should be kept inside the room and neatness insisted on, patrol leaders being made responsible, patrols taking it in turn to be responsible for cleanliness and good order of the room for a week at a time.

If a bit of ground, even waste ground or a backyard, is available as club ground, so much the better. You want some place where the scouts can make huts, light fires, play basketball, cultivate gardens, make tracks, etc.

Make the boys themselves manage the club affairs as far as possible. Sit back yourselves and let them make their mistakes at first, till they learn sense and responsibility.

In some parts of the United States small self-managed boys' clubs are becoming exceedingly numerous and popular in towns and villages. And the educational authorities help them by allowing them the use of class-rooms in the school-buildings in the evenings.

At the same time, when you can get your own clubroom, no matter how small, it gives the boys more of a sense of proprietorship and responsibility, especially if they have taken a hand themselves in making the furniture, putting up pictures, etc.

The clubroom must not be made cosy like a lady's boudoir, as the boys must be able to romp in it occasionally, or play handball, or " Bang the bear," etc. So you want furniture that will pack away into a corner, such as folding wooden chairs, small tables, and a cupboard in which to put away book, games, etc., when the romp comes on.

The ideal club is one of two rooms — one for quiet games, reading, and talking; the other for romping, gymnastics, etc.

The boys must, of course, pay a subscription towards rent, lighting, furnishing, etc., and the major expenses must be provided for by means of some joint work by them, such as garden produce, toys, displays, or a bazaar. Two cents weekly, paid strictly in advance, is usually sufficient as membership subscription.

A Savings Bank should be started to enable boys to put by money wherewith to pay for outings, and eventually to start them in the practice of thrift.

Half the use of our uniform lies in its being an incentive to boys to find work and earn funds with which to buy it. This is a great step in teaching them how to earn a living later on.

Plays

Boys are full of romance, and they love " make-believe " to a greater extent than they like to show.

All you have to do is to play up to this, and to give rein to your imagination to meet their requirements. But you have to treat with all seriousness the many tickling incidents that will arise; the moment you laugh at a situation the boys are quick to feel that it is all a farce and to lose faith in it forthwith and forever.

For instance, in instructing a patrol to make the call of its tutelary animal, the situation borders on the ridiculous, but if the instructor remains perfectly serious the boys work at it with the idea that it is " business " — and, once accomplished, the call becomes a fetish for *esprit de corps* among the members of the patrol.

To stand on the right footing for getting the best out of your boys you must see things with their eyes. To you the orchard must, as it is with them, be Sherwood Forest with Robin Hood and his Merry Men in the background; the fishing harbor must be the Spanish Main with its pirates and privateers; even the town common may be a prairie teeming with buffaloes and Red Indians, or the narrow slum a mountain gorge where live the bandits or the bears.

(Read the " Golden Age," by Kenneth Graham. 1s.)

Once you take this line you see how deadly dreary and how wasteful seems the dull routine of drill upon which the unimaginative scoutmaster falls back for his medium of instruction.

Think out the points you want your boys to learn, and then make up games to bring them into practice.

Bacon said that play-acting is one of the best means of educating children, and one can quite believe him.

It develops the natural power in them of imitation, and of wit and imagination, all of which help in the development of character; and at the same time lessons of history and morality can be impressed on their minds far better by their assuming the characters and acting the incidents themselves than by any amount of preaching of the same on the part of the teacher.

The recent craze for historical pageants is in reality an excellent idea educationally. In places where pageants have been held, both old and young have learned — and learned for the rest of their lives — something of the history of their forefathers and their town; and have learned to sink differences, and to do something for their public without expecting payment for it.

Instructors will find it a genuinely useful practice to make their scouts act scenes from history or of incidents with which they desire to impress them. Such, for instance, as "The Wreck of the Birkenhead," "The Sentry at Pompeii."

When the performances attain a certain degree of merit, they might be used as a means of obtaining funds.

Responsibility to Juniors

The great thing in this scheme is to delegate responsibility — mainly through the patrol leaders.

Have, if possible, a good second in command to yourself to ensure continuity of instruction should you be unable on occasions to be present yourself, and to relieve you of many minor details of administration.

Give full responsibility and show full confidence in your patrol leaders. Expect a great deal from them, and you will get it.

This is the key to success in scout training.

Foster the patrol spirit and friendly rivalry between patrols, and you will get immediate good results in an improved standard of the whole. Don't try and do everything yourself, or the boys will merely look on, and the scheme will flag.

Discipline

Insist on discipline, and strict, quick obedience in small details; let them run riot only when you give leave for it, which is a good thing to do every now and then.

A nation to be powerful and prosperous must be well disciplined, and you get discipline in the mass only by discipline in the individual. By discipline I mean patient obedience to authority and to other dictates of duty.

This cannot be got by repressive measures, but by encouragement and by educating the boy first in self-discipline and in sacrificing of self and selfish pleasures for the benefit of others. This teaching is largely effected by means of example, and by expecting it of him. There lies our work.

Sir Henry Knyvett, in 1596, warned Queen Elizabeth that

the state which neglects to train and discipline its youth produces not merely rotten soldiers or sailors, but the far greater evil of equally rotten citizens for civil life; or, as he words it, "For want of true discipline the honor and wealth both of Prince and countrie is desperatlie and frivolouslie ruinated."

Discipline is not gained by punishing a child for a bad habit, but by substituting a better occupation, that will absorb his attention, and gradually lead him to forget and abandon the old one.

Continence

In this Handbook I have touched upon many important items of a boy's education, but there is scarcely one more important than that of continence.

The training of the boy would be very incomplete did it not contain some clear explanation and plain-spoken instruction on this head.

The prudish mystery with which we have come to veil this important question among the youth of both sexes is doing incalculable harm. The very secrecy with which we withhold all knowledge from the boy prompts him the more to take his own line equally secretly, and, therefore, injuriously.

I have never known a boy who was not the better for having the matter put to him frankly and fully. For an instructor to let his boys walk on this exceedingly thin ice without giving them a warning word, owing to some prudish sentimentality, would be little short of a crime.

Dr. J. B. Paton, M.A., has written very suggestively in his pamphlet, "Continuation School from a Higher Point of View." Price 6d. J. Clark, 13 Fleet Street.

Sea Scouting

Sea scouting has been introduced into this training because it may be of great value to the country. Now that the Canadian Navy has been established it should appeal strongly to large numbers of boys.

In many places it is possible to get the use of boats, barges, or hulks, instead of going into camp, where seamanship can be taught with all its good points of handiness, resourcefulness, activity, and health.

In this connection it would be well to read "Sea Scouting for Boys," by W. Baden-Powell, K.C., F.R.G.S., late Royal Reserve. Price 1s.

Thrift

A very large proportion of the distress and unemployedness in all countries is directly due to the want of thrift on the part of the people themselves. Our social reformers, before seeking for new remedies, would do well to set this part of the problem right in the first place. They would then probably find very little more left for them to do. There is money enough in Britain to go round if it were properly made use of by all working men. In some places, where thrift is practised, the men save their pay, buy their own houses, and become prosperous and contented citizens in happy homes. This might be very widely extended.

Mr. Will Crooks, one of the Labor Members of Parliament in Great Britain, has himself pointed out that there is little hope of genuine relief to the working man until he helps himself by realizing his duties as a citizen and as the head of his home, by seeing the folly of paying over his earnings to the gambler and the saloon keeper instead of to his wife and the bank.

If the rising generation could be started on a career of saving and thrift a great difference would result in the character and prosperity of the nation in the near future. In Toronto, Winnipeg, and many other Canadian cities School Savings Banks have been established, and with excellent results.

For this reason we have instituted money-boxes for Boy Scouts.

Objections to Scouting

In your work of spreading our scheme you will, of course, meet with critics who will object to various points in it, such as: militarism, want of religious training, abuse of Sunday, want of drill, the absurdity of plays and war-dances.

Most of these objections I have already dealt with, but I should like to say a few words on

Militarism

There is no military meaning attached to scouting. Peace scouting comprises the attributes of frontiersmen in the way of resourcefulness and self-reliance and the many other qualities which make them men among men. There is no intention of making the boys into soldiers or of teaching them blood-thirstiness. At the same time under "patriotism" they are taught that a citizen must be prepared to take his fair share among his fellows in the defence of the homeland against aggression in return for the safety and freedom enjoyed by him as an inhabitant. He who shirks and leaves this duty to others to do for him is neither playing a plucky nor a fair part.

I have never met a man who has seen war in a civilized country who remained a so-called anti-militarist. He knows too well the awful and cruel results of war, and until nations have agreed to disarm he will not invite aggression or leave his country at the mercy of an enemy by neglecting its defence. You might just as well abolish the police in order to do away with crime before you have educated the masses not to steal.

Drill

I am continually being asked by officers — not by the boys — to introduce more drill into the training of Boy Scouts; but although, after an experience of thirty-four years of it, I recognize the disciplinary value of drill, I also see very clearly its evils. Briefly they are these: —

(1) Military drill gives a feeble, unimaginative officer a something with which to occupy his boys. He does not consider whether it appeals to them or really does them good. It saves *him* a world of trouble.

(2) Military drill tends to destroy individuality, whereas we want, in the Boy Scouts, to develop individual character; and when once it has been learned it bores a boy who is longing to be tearing about on some enterprise or other; it blunts his keenness. Of boys drilled in Cadet Corps under 10 per cent go into the Army afterwards. Our aim is to make young backwoodsmen of them, not imitation soldiers.

Cadets

Until I visited America I had a feeling that, with the admirable Cadet Corps existing in Canada and the United States, there would be no need for Boy Scouts there, but I now see that there is plenty of room for Scouts and that they can materially help the Cadets.

For instance the Cadet establishment can include only a limited proportion of all the boys in the country, and this again is confined to those boys who can afford the expense of uniform, camping, etc.

Also in outlying districts where the sparseness of the population does not justify the establishment of a Cadet company, the smaller unit of the Scouts — viz. a troop of 32 or a patrol of 8 — can be formed to train the boys in patriotic duty.

Then there is a very divided number of parents who conscientiously object to their boys being imbued with ideas of fighting and bloodshed before they are of age to judge for themselves and who therefore are averse to their becoming Cadets. These have, however, no objection to their joining the Scouts, since our training is one for peaceful citizenship.

As regards the attractiveness of scouting luring boys from joining the Cadets, it is not found in practice that it does so : and on the other hand it can be — and indeed has already in many cases been — adopted by Cadet Corps for making their instruction more attractive and more practical, while its discipline of loyalty is of a more lasting kind than the mere veneer of military obedience to orders.

Religion

An organization of this kind would fail in its object if it did not bring its members to a knowledge of religion — but the usual fault in such cases is the manner in which this is done. If it were treated more as a necessary matter of every-day life, it would not lose its dignity and it would gain a hold. The definition of religious observance is purposely left elastic in this book in order to give a free hand to organizations and units making use of it, so that they can give their own instructions in the matter. In our association, dealing as we do with those of every faith, we cannot lay down strict rules — if we would.

Charles Stelzle, in his " Boys of the Streets and How to Win Them," says : —

" Sometimes we are so much concerned about there being enough religion in our plans for the boy, that we forget to leave enough boy in the plans."

Religion can and ought to be taught to the boy, but not in a milk-and-watery way, or in a mysterious and lugubrious manner; he is very ready to receive it if it is shown in its heroic side and as a natural, every-day quality in every proper man, and it can be well introduced to boys through the study of nature. The study of God's work is a fit subject for Sunday instruction, and is an antidote to that Sunday loafing which at present ruins a very large proportion of young men — and girls. A number of Sunday-schools have now taken up " Scouting " in this way as part of their training, and with best results.   There is no need for religious instruction to be dismal.   Arthur Benson, writing in *The Cornhill Magazine*, says there are four Christian virtues, not three.   They are Faith, Hope, Charity — and Humor. So also in the morning prayer of Robert Louis Stevenson: —

" The day returns and brings us the petty round of irritating concerns and duties.   Help us to play the man — help us to perform them with laughter and kind faces.   Let cheerfulness abound with industry.   Give us to go blithely on our business all this day.   Bring us to our resting beds weary and content and undishonored, and grant us in the end the gift of sleep."

The following pronouncement by the Governing Council on the subject of religious observances sums up the policy which has guided the Scout movement from its inception.

(1) It is expected that every Scout should belong to some religious denomination and attend its services.

(2) Where a troop is composed of members of one particular form of religion, it is hoped that the Scoutmaster will arrange such religious observances and instructions as he, in consultation with its Chaplain or other religious authority, may consider best.

(3) Where a troop consists of Scouts belonging to various religious bodies, they should be encouraged to attend the Service of their own denomination.   When in camp any form of daily prayer and of weekly Divine Service in such troop should be of the simplest character — attendance being entirely voluntary, and any boys whose parents object should be exempt from attendance.

Camps

The camp is what the boy looks forward to, and is the scoutmaster's great opportunity.

Large camps are bad from a scout training point of view. Several small camps are preferable to one large one, and each patrol should be camped as a separate unit from its neighbor.

Night operations should never be allowed to go on all night. They should definitely cease at 11.30, so that the boys are not kept unduly on the alert.   Tenderfoots should, when on night work, be posted in pairs till used to the darkness.

Raiding a camp, that is, taking away things belonging to an opposing force, should never be allowed; it produces only bad feeling.

Long marches (*i.e.*, over six miles) are bad for the boys.

There is a mistaken idea that they teach endurance; it is much more important to feed the boy and develop his strength as a *foundation* for endurance later on.

For every day of training the scoutmaster should prepare beforehand a programme of what he proposes to do. Nothing is worse for the keenness and efficiency of the boys than being taken out and then hanging about thinking what to do next.

To sum Up

The whole object of our scheme is to seize the boy's character in its red-hot stage of enthusiasm, and to weld it into the right shape and to encourage and develop its individuality — so that the boy may become a good man and a valuable citizen for our country in the immediate future, instead of being a waste of God's material.

The nation is showing signs of illness. We can diagnose it as " bad citizenship." We know the kind of remedy to apply, namely, education of the rising generation in " character."

" Scouting " offers one such remedy — if only as a " First Aid " pending the application of a better one. Meantime, every minute is precious.

The remedy needs widespread application. This can be got if every scout is made to bring in a recruit before he receives his badge; and especially if every scout officer and **every man or woman who reads this** will make an earnest effort to obtain a worker to take up the training, and in his turn to obtain the services of yet another.

It is by such a " snowball " movement that we may hope to take a really useful part in bringing strength, both moral and physical, to our Empire.

BOOKS ON THE SUBJECT

" Boys of the Street and How to Win Them," by Charles Stelzle. 1s. 6d. nett. (F. H. Revell.)

" The Boy Problem," by W. B. Forbush. A study of boys and how to train them. (Progress Press, Boston, U.S.A.)

" The Children of the Nation," by Sir John Gorst. 7s. 6d. nett.

" The Citizen of To-morrow," by Samuel Keeble. 2s. nett.

" The Canker at the Heart," by L. Cope Cornford. 3s. 6d. nett.

" The Abandoned Child," by Bramwell Booth.

INDEX

Index